In the ⸺ ⸺ ⸺ ⸺ more should be more to say, wanting to find the words, Craig heard the faint whine that he knew so well, "Hit the deck!" He yelled and fell to the floor beside Brewster.

"Quite a welcome home," Brewster said, hoping it sounded wry or sarcastic instead of fearful. He thought of his wife, his promise that this would be the last trip. Ever.

"Let's move to the bunker."

Outside, flares flashing like strobes, the two of them ran for the bunker, flak jackets on, helmets on their heads, each holding an M16.

The night grew quiet except for some distant artillery, but flames crackled from the spaces they had vacated. A direct hit. Craig and John Brewster stood in the doorway of the bunker and watched.

"We were going to move to the new Air Force spaces in a couple of weeks anyway," Craig said.

Brewster smiled, said, "Just like urban renewal."

But too close.

Much too close.

VIETNAM SPOOK SHOW

Wayne Care

IVY BOOKS • NEW YORK

To the crew of PR-21, murdered unceremoniously by the North Koreans in April of 1969, while on a routine mission in the Sea of Japan. I miss you still.

Ivy Books
Published by Ballantine Books
Copyright © 1989 by Wayne Care

All rights reserved under International and Pan-American Copyright Conventions. Published in the United States by Ballantine Books, a division of Random House, Inc., New York, and simultaneously in Canada by Random House of Canada Limited, Toronto.

Library of Congress Catalog Card Number: 89-91240

ISBN 0-8041-0372-0

Manufactured in the United States of America

First Edition: September 1989

Acknowledgements

So many, for so many varied reasons.

To my family: Dad, Mom (in our hearts you will always be with us), Buffy, Carla, Judy, Shirley and Wanda.

To Shell, for all the right reasons, you never let me give up.

To the men of Det Bravo, and other duty stations: wacky and wise, warm and challenging, you were as Steinbeck put it, "the beatitudes and the saints". You gave me hope, knowledge, a lot of fun, and sometimes more hope and help than I deserved.

To my good friends and comrades: Jeff and Durrie, Keith, Tom Weston, Martin Gaston, George Worell, Ed and Judi Crim (yes, Ed I still think I can talk to her sometimes, she was there in the beginning of it.), Tom and Dale, Rickie Rollo Roller, Brent, John and Kay Barg, Royce Taylor, Frenchy Poirier, Frank Azevedo, Willie Ayers, Steve Lewis (wherever you are), Stu Seigel, Daddy Wags, Chuck Dibble, Jim Lanigan, Rich Camp, SSgt Bruce Smith, Gunny Postma, Chief Henry Mashburn, LCDR's Strobel and Brown, Lt. Moffett, Danny Bayles, George Bergquist, Martin Todorovich, Chief Coty, Jay, Randy Taylor, Bob Erickson, Margaret Terrall, Lou Klug, Murray and Connie Miller, Bill Albert and Smith Goodrum (gosh was there really a mutiny in the bowling alley?), Rich Camp, Marty Mueller, Efram and Nitz, Joe Yurcovich, Paul Palmieri, John Mahoney, John Potts, John Singer, Tetsuko, Aaron Cook, Dan Ducey, Barry Weston, Scott and Charlene Knowlton, Alan Leidner, Tim Hall, so many I have probably lost the names in my memory, but not the feel in my heart. You helped to beat the insanities then, and some of you still do.

To Owen Lock, with the special thanks that without you, none of this could have come about, without your patience, encouragement, and a fine meal, I might have never believed it was happening at all. Thanks. You know as well as I do, how much you have done for me, and I do appreciate it.

And to you, the reader, I hope you like this book. It did not happen the way this book says—this is fiction—but sometimes it feels just like it did. Thank you for reading it.

Were you ever out in the wild alone?
and the moon was awfully clear,
and a muggy darkness hemmed you in,
with a silence you most could hear?

And only the sound of the Big Look plane
with its winging through the sky,
a half dead thing, in a stark dead world,
gone mad with the lust to fly.

WO1 Nelson E. Crim

Chapter 1

Reveille roused them from their sleep. Some rose cheerfully, others grumbled; but all grabbed towels and dop kits and moved herdlike toward the head.

Craig Nostrum groaned, slammed his hand against his locker and grabbed his favorite blue towel, draping it around his neck. "This is no way to wake up." He kicked the trash can out of his way and swore softly. "I need a shower."

"You ready for the quiz today?" Gerry Norton squeezed past Craig and two other men and stepped under a vacated shower head.

"Bite the blue-veined bag, turkey." Craig tied a towel around his waist, left the shower spray, and walked to the sinks and lathered up to shave. Around him men bitched and kibitzed; even the minutiae of their lives had assumed an importance to them: who had gotten drunk, who had gotten laid, who got what in their packages from home, who had been in the most trouble prior to joining the service.

Craig shaved slowly, and wondered idly how he had come to be in the navy at all. Everything that had happened to him since he joined the navy seemed capricious; and now two months after graduating boot camp he was in Monterey, California, at the Defense Language Institute studying the Vietnamese language. He finished shaving, washed his face and brushed his teeth, and walked back to his cubicle to dress in his summer white uniform. He ran a rag over his shoes, lit a cigarette, and settled to wait for Gerry before heading for the chow hall for coffee. He had met Gerry a week before their classes began, and they had begun a wary and tenuous friendship over the last three weeks. Gerry—tall, Nordic, and blond—had an easy affability that made him popular with most of the other men. Craig—dark-haired, shy, and insecure—worried as much over making friends as not making them.

The two young men, walking in a loose-gaited step, walked to the chow hall together, got cups of black coffee, and sat down at a table and talked.

Gerry rubbed a hand over his face and yawned. "How did you end up in the navy? I mean, you don't sound demented or anything."

"Accidentally, I guess," Craig answered. Craig thought that his reasons for enlisting seemed obscure now, as if they were bits of arcane lore. His decision had been little more than an accumulation of petty grievances that one day had outweighed his lethargy, and he had walked into a recruiting office and signed the documents. Despite his parents' objections he did not have second thoughts until boot camp when he found that even the simplest decision was out of his hands: he was now chattel. It occurred to him then that he was not making a decision as much as abdicating decisions for the next four years, but there was nothing he could do. The facts that he was being sued for a car accident, that he had no reason to think he would make college, that he was bored and scared of his drifting, seemed silly now. "How about you?" he asked.

"I was getting put on probation at college, and they said they needed to talk to my folks. I went out with some buddies and had some drinks and then, wow, there was a recruiting office and I walked in. My mom bawled her eyes out when I told her. Real stupid."

Craig nodded, ground out his cigarette in a butt can, and sipped his coffee. He crossed his legs to keep his right leg from jouncing like a metronome. "How'd you end up with Vietnamese?"

"I don't know. I picked Russian, Chinese, and Swahili, so what happens? I get Vietnamese. How about you?"

"Same story," Craig answered, wondering if a lie was easier believed when you said it quickly. The truth was too awkward to admit: he had asked for Vietnamese because he was not sure what else to do. He knew little about Vietnam, except that a chief petty officer had told him, "It might be a pissant little war, but it is the only one we got," and he had said yes, that's what I want—oh, yes. He looked at Gerry. "They told me that only one man in three hundred gets accepted to DLI. Ego trip, huh?"

"They told me only six in a thousand get in."

"Guess they didn't compare notes."

The two of them laughed together, stacked their cups in the dirty dishes, and walked up the hill, their schoolbooks under their arms.

Their classrooms were in World War Two–era wooden shanties built on stilts. Each building had a central balcony and two small porches on each end at the top of a wooden stairway. They settled on the steps with a cigarette and waited for homeroom to begin.

"You will have your quiz second period," Ba Thuy said, and gathered her papers on the desk. She was tiny, but her belly was distended with her pregnancy and she lumbered as she moved about the room. Finally settled into her chair, she called roll. Once done, she smiled. "Now repeat after me. *Cai nay nho, khong?*" (Is this small?)

The men repeated the phrase in unison, then individually. As each man spoke she offered either gentle criticism of his accent or encouragement. She scribbled notes in a cramped style in her roll book. "Now say, *Co, cai nay nho.*"

They repeated the phrase, just as they repeated each of the phrases or questions that she posed to them. It was a routine they had come to understand and appreciate: the repetition added order to the chaos of a new language. Ba Thuy smiled. "Very good. Ours is a language of tones and music and you are doing very well. The same word can mean six things depending on the tone. For instance, *ma: ma* can mean 'ghost,' but said with a down tone, *maaaaa*"—she swooped her hand into a slope as she spoke—"then it means 'but.'" She looked from one man to the other. "Each night you will have to memorize a dialogue and repeat it the next morning. Your partners will change, but I suggest you study with someone and learn both parts. You seem so very young to me, but soldiers are always the young, *n'est-ce pas?* It is this way everywhere, I think." She looked at Craig. "*Comment allez vous, monsieur?*"

Craig blushed. *"Je vais bien, merci, et vous?"*

"Toi manh khoai. Anh phai noi tieng Vietnam bay gioi."

"Co. Toi se noi tieng Vietnam, Ba Thuy."

"Cam on anh." Thuy shook her head in assent. "You must use Vietnamese every chance that you have. You must study. This is the only way to succeed. You may have your break now. Please be back in fifteen minutes."

Gerry walked to the geedunk truck that always parked in the lot at break times and bought cups of coffee for himself and Craig and Ted Trainer. "So that's a bitch, huh? I can't believe how much I have to learn."

Craig nodded assent. "I feel like a cabbage in there. I can't remember from one day to the next. Of course, I'll never be as bad as Ted."

Ted laughed raucously. "Give me virgins and not languages, and I'll show you what I can do." Ted ran a hand through his black curly hair, surprised suddenly at how short it was. He sipped his coffee. "I am the emperor of all that I survey."

Craig glanced down the steps at the yellowish dog turds that curled at the bottom of the steps. "Amen."

On the center balcony men gathered in small groups to talk: army, navy, air force, marines, two civilians—all of them students in one class of Vietnamese or another. Across the parking lot were other classrooms: Russian, Chinese, Swahili, Urdu, Arabic; the offering of languages seemed endless to them.

"Looks like break's over," Craig said, and stood up. He flipped his cigarette into the red butt can attached to the railing and led the way back to the room they were assigned.

"Vietnam has always been three countries: north, central, and south Vietnam. Bac Viet, Annam, and Cochin China, as they are sometimes called. Their periods of unification have been brief, and sometimes bloody. The north became more industrialized, the central and south were more agrarian, and the most beautiful cities in Asia were in the south. Saigon was called the pearl of the Orient." Ong Hieu spoke quietly, pointed to the map that hung over the blackboard. "Hue was built to be an imperial city, and even Da Nang, called Tourane by the French, was a wonderful city that sprawled on the bay. Some of the best beaches are in Da Nang and north of Saigon, and we have a wonderful resort called Da Lat. Outside Da Lat there is hunting that rivals any in Asia. This is the country that you are studying. We are not Annamites, or savages, or a people that need civilization: we are Vietnamese and we need your help to retain our independence."

Ong Hieu continued his lesson, his pointer held like an épée: he slashed the air with his comments, pointed to dots on the map, pointed to those who he thought were not listening.

Craig sat on a vinyl-covered chair at Dee's Place and drank a soda. He stared at the Bronco pinball game that he had been playing, at the fourteen free games he had left for someone else to finish. He had mastered each of these games, and they no longer held his attention. Learning these games was something that could be done and then forgotten, an accomplishment that seemed trivial.

"How's it going?" Jack Brady, another student, with flecks of premature gray in his hair that made him look older than his friends, though he was just twenty-one, sat on the stool beside Craig and ordered a soda.

"Okay," Craig said, and sipped his RC cola. Learning Vietnamese was not like pinball. As his language lessons progressed he became uneasily aware that he was beginning to feel diminished, shrinking under the weight of his increased knowledge. Day by day in the study of accents and syntax and culture he felt less real. He wondered if this was what some slow crippling disease was like to the person it occupied.

"Stop wriggling your leg."

Craig looked at Jack, shrugged. "Get a new hobby. I'm tired of everybody complaining because I wriggle my leg. I wiggle my leg, so fucking what?"

"Testy, aren't we?"

"I don't know, you testy, too?"

"You pissed or something?"

"Heard you apologized to Co Thuyen because we were acting up the other day. Then you told that bald Green Beret asshole it wouldn't happen again."

"Just trying to keep the peace. I don't want to stand out. My older brother gave me some advice: never volunteer and never give them reason to remember you."

"I thought the idea was to stick together."

"Not when it might mean my ass."

"Somehow, I knew that, Jack." Craig stood up and asked

Dee to add it to his tab, and walked down the hill toward the wharf.

The Red Pony was quiet when Craig ambled in and took his seat at the piano bar and ordered a scotch and water. The bar overlooked the wooden planked wharf, and beyond that Monterey Bay. It was the first tourist attraction delivered to the increasing crowds that wandered down for a weekend or a week, but this was beginning to flourish everywhere in town. He watched strangers wander and pause to watch the attractions: a one-legged trained seagull, a street mime, a folk singer with an open guitar case to receive alms, the sea lions that barked and played on the Coast Guard breakwall. He sipped his drink and said hello to the piano player, Martha.

"Hi," Martha said. "It's been a couple of days. I was beginning to wonder if you'd gotten orders and forgot to say good-bye."

"That's something that will never happen. Been busy tonight?"

"A little slow, but it'll pick up, any requests?"

Craig watched her hands dance along the piano keys, riffling white and then black keys. "Whatever you want."

Martha played "Danny Boy."

Craig was not yet nineteen, but on his first visit when they had carded him, he used a friend's ID card. They had not asked since, and though he suspected they knew his subterfuge, he supposed it was a friendly collusion and one to which he had become accustomed. He had not quite finished his scotch and water when Michelle, the waitress, walked to his elbow and asked if he wanted another drink. "Yes, please," he said, and set some money on the piano bar. He supposed that like most of the men he had a mild crush on Michelle. Though none of them ever behaved as less than gentlemen in her presence, she was frequently discussed in the way one discusses unattainable beauty: besides, her husband was rumored to be big and easily roused to jealousy. He swallowed the last of his old drink and accepted the new with a smile.

Three months of class and study had passed, and the men felt marginally secure in their progress. The teachers still seemed exotic and intimidating to Craig, but he liked them. Most of them had been educated in French schools or in France itself; many were prominent before they emigrated. The classes were conducted in Vietnamese now, except for when a thorny moment of misunderstanding occurred. As patient as stones, the teachers led them through their language.

The students had been assigned Vietnamese names, and they were surprised that they answered to them without a second thought.

Co Hoa Thi, dressed in a blue brocaded silk ao dai over white silk pants, bowed to the class before she began. *"Manh Khoa, Khong?"* she asked.

"Chung ta manh khoa," they answered in unison.

Hoa Thi could have been eighteen or thirty, and this mystery of age added to her allure. She was delicate, so much so that she reminded Craig of a tiny bird. He thought if you held her that her heart would sound like beating wings. He had asked her to sing her national anthem once and she had sung *"La Marseillaise"* in a soprano that trembled with emotion. Embarrassed, she had ducked her head, stared at the floor when she realized what she had done. "I have been too much French," she said softly.

Craig had wanted to cradle Hoa Thi in his arms, and with the memory of that day he wanted to do so again.

"Today we discuss the emperor Le Loi." She handed out a mimeographed sheet to each student. "He is our greatest hero."

Craig looked at the document; the ammonia smell was intoxicating and reminded him of orders. The paper and purple ink seemed so insubstantial, yet these pieces of flimsy paper had come to define his life and his future.

Hoa Thi sat down behind the desk and crossed her legs. She brushed the folds of her ao dai over her legs with her long thin hands. "Le Loi was our hero and his story begins in Hanoi. He was a fisherman and he hated the domination of the Chinese, yet he felt helpless. We were a small country and they were a great one. One day as he fished he was despondent about the state of our country and he cast his net into the lake, and when he withdrew it there were no fish, but there was a great and fiery sword. Le Loi was shocked and confused and this sword frightened him very much. He knew from the beauty that it must belong to a very strong spirit or a god, and he sat there in a stupor. Finally he touched his hand to the hilt and he found a power surge through him, and he feared that he angered the spirits and he might be struck down for his insolence. But as he held the sword he felt such a power that he knew that this sword was meant to be used by him. He returned to shore, and he walked amongst the people and he told his story and he asked them to raise an army to help him defeat the Chinese intruders. The story spread before him, and as he entered villages he found many who had been waiting to join him."

"Like King Arthur's Excalibur," Craig said.

"Perhaps," Hoa Thi said, and continued: "So Le Loi led his army and they defeated the Chinese invaders, and he freed Vietnam. When it was over he took this sword and tossed it back into the lake. The lake swallowed the sword in a flash of fire. The lake is now called the Lake of the Returned Sword in Hanoi." She paused as if tired, then smiled at her students. "Legend tells us that he was a poor fisherman's son, but history tells us that he was the son of a rich and powerful family."

Craig smiled, wanted to hold her all the more for this story. "Do you believe this?"

"Yes, Ong Can."

"Then so do I."

Jack Brady waited until they were straggling down the hill toward the barracks to speak to Craig. "You talk about me being a suck-ass, what about Mr. 'Then So Do I, Co Hoa Thi.' "

"Stuff it."

"Then get off my case. At least when I brown-nose, I rub it in on Americans."

"*Du ong a trong tai trai*," Craig said, and jogged ahead until he was alone.

The men had begun to speak a pidjin language that they dubbed Tieng Monterey: it was an amalgam of Vietnamese and American slang expressions; thus, "What's up Doc?" had become *Cai gi len bac si*? and "What's new?" had become *Cai gi moi*? When a question of guilt came up, they answered in the ubiquitous manner of their own childhoods, *khong toi, khong toi,* not me, not me.

Most of the professors resented their corruption of the language, but Ong Hieu, despite being the eldest, accepted it easily and even created his own phrases. He tried to explain this to some of the other teachers, that these Americans had this in their nature and it was not meant as an insult, but few of them could accept this perfidy. That day, his second anniversary since becoming head of the Vietnamese section, he looked at Craig Nostrum and smiled. *"Guong guong o tren thoung ai la dep nhat a the gioi?"*

Craig laughed. "Mirror, mirror on the wall, who's the fairest of them all?"

"My grandaughter likes it very much."

"Anh xinh o dau?" Craig asked earnestly.

"I was born in Hue. It is the imperial city. The palaces and gates are based on the Forbidden City in Peking. The Perfume River is the prettiest in all of South Vietnam."

"Do you miss Hue?"

"I miss the old Hue very much, but it is disappearing, except from here and here." He touched his head and his heart. "That Hue will never die for me. That Hue was the soul of the Vietnam I knew. My family were in service to the emperors for many years. What do you know of Bao Dai?"

"He was the last emperor. He was installed as a figurehead by the French."

"But he was also the last Nguyen. The Nguyens were good rulers on the whole; they saw the people's hearts. Some were better than others of course. When Emperor Bao Dai abdicated his throne he stood at the noon gate, the emperor's gate, and he spoke to the people. I was there." Ong Hieu's voice was wistful as he spoke; he stared through the dirty windowpanes of the classroom as if they might suddenly reveal the barges of bright flowers that had once floated down the Perfume River. "He spoke to us and said, 'As for us, we have known great bitterness during the twenty years of our rule. Henceforth we are happy to assume the status of free citizen in an independent country,' then he presented his ceremonial sword and seal to an emissary from Hanoi. My mother cried and I held her, but nothing I said could lift her heart. She clung to my arm and she whispered, 'Today we have lost the mandate of heaven and we shall surely perish.'" Ong Hieu looked at his desk, the clutter of papers and folders.

"Do you think you lost the mandate of heaven?"

"It is hard to know these things. During the reign of the Nguyen there were troubled times, but our order was preserved and our ways were followed. Each of us, each in his place, with the proper pieties and humility being shown. You cannot tear the fabric of a country and not have the material begin to unravel. With the Nguyen the altars were maintained, the graves properly tended, the genies given their due. Now we are a people uprooted and torn from our land, and there is chaos. Some have abandoned their altars, some have had to leave their ancestors behind. So which is the right way?" Ong Hieu's voice was soft, barely audible. "Who is to know what one event will bring about the final catastrophe? We cannot know. We cannot lose our culture, our past, and still be Vietnamese. Perhaps the stars have already put the final destruction in motion."

"I'm sorry. The war must be very hard on your people."

"War is hard on all people. We have been at war for a very long time."

"I hope it ends soon, for everyone's sake."

"I wish this as well, Ong Can. Thank you for listening to the ramblings of an old man. Please take your seat, for class must begin soon." Mr. Hieu shuffled his papers, pulled down a wall map, and began to discuss the three Vietnams: north, south, and central. This was not a unified land except in times of national crisis when they were forced to fight off the foreign intruders: the Mongols, the Chinese, the Japanese, and the French. "Ours is a land where a single wisdom has prevailed; the emperor's power stops at the village gate."

Class was over, and Craig and Gerry dawdled as they walked down the hill toward the barracks. They saw an officer approach, and ducked into some trees to avoid having to salute. Military courtesy—either avoiding it or subverting it— had become a tactical game to them by now. Ted Trainer had been the first to suggest the alternate paths where one could avoid meeting an officer head-on. Craig was not sure, when he thought about it, who had been the first to decide to string out along the path so that each officer they passed had to return not a single group salute but individual salutes to as many as fifteen different pairs of hands. On a day not long before, Craig and Gerry had been skylarking down the hill, ignoring everything until a line of eight junior officers appeared, each spaced perfectly apart, and began offering salutes. He laughed with the recollection. "Remember when that zoomie officer got us back?"

Gerry laughed as well, his voice deep and rich. "Who'd have thought that some air force lieutenant would be the one to get us back? Damn, he's one sharp dude. Too bad he's not enlisted."

Week after week the study of accent and tense and tonal marks crowded the young men's minds, and they struggled and practiced and cursed and learned. When Craig asked if the Vietnamese celebrated Christmas he was told that the Christians did, but all Vietnamese, no matter their religion, celebrated Tet, the Lunar New Year. He found that each year bore the sign of an animal, and that he had been born in the year of the boar.

The Red Pony was already crowded when Craig arrived, but Martha had saved him a place at the piano, and he sat down and accepted the drink that Michelle offered with the explanation that it was on the house. He said thank you to Michelle and to Martha, and watched the tourists tarry along the wharf. Some of the locals drifted past in the crowd en route to buy fresh fish.

Monterey had once thrived on the fishing fleet, but the tuna and the canneries were gone, and prosperity depended not on the whims of the bay, but on the whims of tourists. No matter how many times the boats went out, the tuna did not return.

The wharf now had its own society: the waitresses and waiters, the bartenders, the restaurateurs, the fish sellers and fish catchers, the street people who entertained the tourists for a coin or two, an old man who swept the docks each morning, his mind forever lost in World War One. Sometimes the old man, who everyone called Hector though no one knew his rightful name, talked about the gases the Germans used in the Argonne Forest. To Hector, Verdun was just a moment ago, and the armistice still loomed like a maiden's promise of a kiss. To Craig, these were his people; he knew the shop owners and the clerks, the panhandlers and the con men. He felt secure here.

They had sung their way through three musicals, World War Two songs, and a medley of George M. Cohan. Someone screamed that in his day they would have ended the Vietnam war in a week of kicking commie ass. A bottle blonde with frizzy hair and too much makeup with sidling up to an airman Craig knew from DLI. All's right with the world, Craig thought, and ordered himself another drink.

"Your song."

Craig grinned at Martha and sang "Ragtime Cowboy Joe." When he was little this was the song his mother had crooned to him to quiet him. Every time he sang it he missed his family with a sudden intensity and within a day would end up calling home collect. Sometimes when he left the Red Pony he would walk to a quiet spot on the rocks and wonder how any of this had come about at all.

"Let me buy you one for the entertainment you provided."

Craig said thank you, and nodded to the man beside him. He was perhaps thirty-five years old, dressed in a sports shirt, a pair of chino slacks, and a gold chain around his neck.

"What branch are you in?"

Craig shrugged, "I guess it always shows, huh? Navy."

"I did my four in the army. Of course, I started my short-timer's calendar when I was still in boot camp."

Craig laughed, thinking of his own calendar where he carefully crossed off each day as if it were a tree that toppled into his past and brought his future closer to him.

"What do you do?"

"Clerical school," Craig answered quickly, nervously, wondering when he would be able to explain he was a language student, explain what the parameters of his secrets were.

The man nodded sociably and ordered another round. "I need to find a motel down here, you know of any?"

"Anything beats a barracks, but I don't know them at all. There's some at the other end of town and some down toward Pacific Beach as well."

"I know barracks and buffing floors and keeping STRAC lockers. What a bunch of bullshit."

"Roger on that," Craig answered, and began to sing along again. This time with "Sunrise, Sunset."

"Want to ride along while I look?"

"No thanks. I just walk up the hill and I'm home." Craig felt pressure on his left leg, moved a little, felt the pressure assert itself again.

"It might be fun," the stranger said. "You might like a ride."

"Back off."

"Just getting comfortable, you have a problem?"

"Leave me alone."

Finally Craig stood up and moved to the piano bench beside Martha. She winked at him. "Couldn't expect them to leave you alone forever."

"He's a scumball."

"It happens. Sit with me. We're a team anyhow."

Ted laughed when Craig explained what had occurred at the Red Pony. "It's not funny," he said petulantly. "The man put his hand on my fucking leg."

"Welcome to the real world. Everyone and everything here gets Californicated sooner or later."

Craig lowered his eyes to his cards, flipped one onto the table, and took Ted's trick. "Looks like you might be set, old buddy."

"Hey, don't take it out on my bridge game because some queer finds you irresistible."

Craig stared at his cards and led a diamond. He smiled, thinking for the first time that he and Scott Forsberg might actually beat Ted and Gerry.

He won the trick and led a low heart, trump, into Ted's dummy hand. "Worried about the split now?"

"I never sweat the small stuff," Ted yelled, and slammed his card down with a fist.

Craig grinned, and took the next trick with his queen of hearts. "*GAF*, huh? Give a fuck." He laughed. "You are set, asshole. Set, set, set." He wasn't sure when he had first heard the term *GAF*, but the acronym had come to be a noun, a modifier, a verb: a symbol of their general attitude toward the military. He thought that this attitude was perhaps why they had become friends, but it seemed more important than that, and he could not identify the reasons or the moments that had welded them together. "Let's see, vulnerable and doubled. I think we've done it, Scotty, I think we've won."

Craig discussed the victory with Scott and Harry France, and laughed in the retelling of the story of Ted getting set. "I better get some studying done. I haven't even memorized the dialogue yet. Catch you later."

Craig walked downstairs to his own cubicle, opened the book, and began the tedious repetitious task of memorizing the two pages of Vietnamese.

One more time.

Chapter 2

Rain had fallen all night, and at noon there was still a light gray drizzle that splashed over the windows of the classroom building. Co Hoa Thi moved a wastebasket from the corner to the center of the room to catch a persistent leak. She walked gracefully behind her desk once again and motioned for them to begin their discussion again.

Craig raised his hand. "Why is the *Tale of Kieu* so important to the Vietnamese?"

"Nguyen Du was our greatest poet. He served the court of Emperor Gia Long. He had been ambassador to Peking and studied the classic Chinese forms of verse. He wrote the *Tale of Kieu* to teach us of suffering and acceptance and the proper way of things, to teach us of courage, and hope. Many of us read the *Tale of Kieu* as one might read an astrologer's chart, or perhaps you might read the Bible, and from it we take sustenance and we take guidance for our lives."

"He served the Le dynasty, didn't he?" Brady asked.

"Yes, but when the Le fell to the Tay Son rebellion he joined forces with the Nguyen emperors. He wrote his great poem then, but he was without power. The Tay Son rebellion brought back Emperor Gia Long from exile in Thailand. The power was put into the hands of those who had suffered beside him." She looked beyond the men, to the rain, and finally

14

picked up a sheaf of papers and began to hand them out to her students. "There is so much more to Vietnam than we can ever teach you."

Craig's life seemed so familiar to him that he felt no need to examine it; the intimacy sometimes frightened him. He sagged onto his bunk with a lesson book, tired, still damp from the walk down the hill in the rain. He had already listened to Ted complain about his test grades, and Scott about his girlfriend, and Jack Brady launch into his familiar diatribe about the Vietnamese being another burden for the white man. He was tired of listening, but when he tried to speak he found he had nothing to say. He flipped the soft-backed binder onto the desk and closed his eyes. He thought about Sheryl, about the last time he had seen her. It had been at the airport as he left for Monterey. She'd had tears in her eyes, but made a silent farewell with kisses and a long tight hug. He shuddered with the memory, got up, snatched the raincoat from his locker, and walked down the sloping, winding road into Monterey.

Wet and cold, Craig stopped at the Hidden Village and drank a wine cocktail, appreciating the solitude of the small bar and art gallery. Had the rain stopped he thought he would walk further into town to Sancho Panza's, a coffeehouse, but he was also afraid of the place. Too many of the civilians there had long hair and wore beads: they were hippies and they frightened him with their openness as much as with their politics. He ordered another wine cocktail. "Sure is quiet here tonight."

The bartender, actually one of the owners, smiled. "Thought that was what you liked about this place. A chance to get away from the bullshit at the Presidio."

"I know, I get one place and I always want to be somewhere else. I'm one fucked-up sailor, Bob."

"Life's that way, huh? Millie and I were sure we wanted to have this place, to get the hell out of New York City, but what happens? Every chance we get, we want to fly home and see what's happening. That one's on us."

"Thanks."

They talked about the rain, and finally Craig rose and said he was going back to the base. He did not return to the base, though. At the foot of the hill he turned right and trudged through the slop to the wharf and finally walked into the Red Pony.

"It's a day early, isn't it?" Michelle asked, and handed him a scotch and water. "On Martha. Where's all your friends?"

Craig smiled and shrugged, enjoying listening to her French accent, enjoying her flowery scent. "Guess they all wanted to stay in out of the rain."

Craig sang softly, aware at how few others were joining in and afraid to stand out.

"You have a nice voice." The woman who spoke to Craig had frosted blond hair and wore oversized sunglasses even though it was dark. Her pastel-green jersey dress clung to her breasts and hips, and accentuated the roll of flesh at her midriff. Craig supposed she was in her middle thirties, wasn't sure what to say in return, so nodded and sang another song.

Martha smiled. "How about 'Sweetheart Tree'?"

Craig nodded to the pianist, grinned. "Don't you ever get tired of the same old songs?"

"All the time. But mostly I love them."

Craig accepted a refill from Michelle and reached for his wallet.

"It's on the blond lady. She likes your singing." Michelle winked, and walked to a boisterous table of four in the center of the area that held the piano bar.

Craig thanked the woman shyly and sang another song.

"I come to Monterey three or four times a year, and I just love it down here, don't you?"

"It's okay. I guess it's different when you have to be here."

"Army?"

"Navy."

"No ships that I can see. Unless you count the *Te Vega* from Stanford." She laughed, coughed, and lit a cigarette for herself and for Craig. "You do have a nice voice, and a cute ass, too."

Craig blushed, ducked his head a little, and stared at his drink. Unsure what to do next, he finally introduced himself.

"I'm Lydia," the woman said softly.

"Pretty name." Craig grinned suddenly, listening to the music, and began to hum.

"'Queen's Marines,'" Lydia said. "You're not going now, are you?"

Craig shifted uneasily. "No, just moving a little. You know this song?"

As if to prove it she suddenly began to sing, and soon it was just she and Craig and an appreciative chorus of laughter from the other patrons.

Call out the members of the queen's marines,
Call out the queen's old grenadiers,
Call out me mother, my father, sister, or brother,
but for Chrissakes don't call me.

Oh lordy
I don't want to join the navy,
I don't want to go to war,
I only want to hang around the Picadilly underground,
living off the earnings of some high class lady.

I don't want a bullet up me arsehole,
I don't want my buttocks shot away.
I'd rather stay in London,
jolly, jolly, London,
and fornicate me blooming life away . . .

They laughed together, and Lydia took Craig's left hand in her own; he felt comforted. "How did you know that one? I thought I was the only one. I learned it from some Englishman who was here a few weeks ago."

"I was married to a limey once. The song outlasted the marriage. He used to call out for other women in his sleep."

"Is that why you're divorced?"

"*He* divorced *me*, just one of those things. He decided we were incompatible and he liked his partner's wife better. Good riddance to him, that's what I say. What the hell?"

"Sorry."

"Why should *you* be sorry? He was a prick. I miss London sometimes. And Europe."

"I miss everyplace I've been sometimes," Craig said, and it was true. Lately he'd noticed himself feeling wistful and nostalgic, recalling everything with an increasing fondness. "I guess it's easier to miss anyplace where you aren't than to love the place you are." He wondered if this made sense as he said it, shrugged, and sipped his drink.

"I'm sure it is," Lydia said softly, "and I will make you miss this place."

Craig woke disoriented. He supposed that the yellowed wallpaper at the San Carlos Hotel had once been considered elegant; it was now faded and forlorn. The bed was scented with her: Estée Lauder; it was Sheryl's perfume, as well. He found himself alone on the bed, the only proof of her having been there was the mixed aroma of perfume and lovemaking. There was a watch on the pillow, a Timex with a black leather band. Craig picked it up, strapped it on his wrist, and wondered idly if she always carried them with her; perhaps she got a bulk discount, he thought idly, and set the time. He showered, dressed, and walked back from the hotel under a hot sun, the haze still steamy with the recent rains.

He felt swollen and wise, and wished that he could understand these feelings. She had told him that he was a good lover after they had had one quick coupling that ended with his spasms and squirts. The second time was perfect, she had whispered. He whistled as he walked.

"Where have you been all night?" Gerry's tone was scolding, demanding. He stared at Craig in silence and tapped his foot impatiently.

"Out walking."

Ted Trainer laughed and clapped his hands together. "Methinks that the lad got himself some pussy."

"Leave me alone, Ted," Craig answered sharply.

"Got a little, huh? Got laid?" Ted giggled and danced around the cubicle waving Craig's bath towel like a matador's cape.

"None of your business." Craig snatched his towel back and drooped it over his shoulders. "I'm hitting the showers."

"Surprised you didn't say none of your beeswax! Hey, even a blind hog roots up a truffle once in a while," Ted hollered after him.

For six months the men had studied, practiced, and learned together, and now they had formed wary friendships. Each of them had adjusted to his own patterns: their wearisome familiarity had become comfortable; what had been momentous to them in the beginning had eroded little by little to the mundane. Just as an assembly line worker in Detroit might put on the same part, the same way, for eight hours a day for a life-time, they used the same words and phrases over and over, and like the car maker had achieved some level of competence: they were journeymen of language.

Craig ignored the morning herdlike rush to the chow hall and told Gerry he was walking to Dee's Place to get some coffee that he could take to class with him. He said he wanted to study some more before class, but he knew this was a lie—he just wanted some privacy, a temporary shelter from the crowds that were always around.

Typically the morning was an oyster-shell glow of fog that billowed in from the bay, but would burn off by ten or eleven o'clock. Craig got his coffee and walked up the hill, thinking that his life was an engine beyond his control; he trailed it like a kite's tail.

After Lydia there had been others, and when he wrote Sheryl letters he retained a lazy sense of guilt. He knew that he wanted these other women in the simplest way, and he resented it: he thought it was rutting rather than making love. He had tried to explain it one night to Ted, that both he and the older women were fulfilling needs for one another and that somehow this made it okay. Ted had just laughed and said this was the ultimate in rationalization. Craig thought this was true, but he didn't stop, and this is what bothered him.

He looked down the promontory toward the bay and the wharf and the sputter of fishing boats, the bungalows, the rusted skeletons of the canneries, and the sea lions. He watched the teachers begin to straggle down the hill from the faculty parking lot: Ong Hieu with his sharp, cheerful steps, Co Hoa Thi graceful as a green stem, walking beneath a pink parasol, Co Bui walking with her feet splayed to the sides in a measured farmer's tread. These odd moments were the ones that he cherished for their amity and seclusion. He measured the moments until class with his coffee so that he finished only as the last of the students arrived and walked up the stairs to their classrooms.

Captain Egan, a Green Beret, the equivalent of a class student-body commander, puffed his cheeks in and out before speaking to Craig's section, dragging in breaths impatiently. He stared at them with stone dark eyes. "This is a military base, and I have had the last complaint that I am going to tolerate about your behavior. Do I make myself clear?" He did not wait for an answer, but strutted to the center of the room, "Miss Bui says you have been drinking soup in class again, even though that's against the rules. She told me she smelled it just this morning."

The men tittered despite their fear.

"It's not funny. Which one of you is called Vinh?"

Dale Barton raised his hand, half saluted. "Me."

"Miss Bui says that the men kidnap you, they tie you up, and put you in this metal locker here."

Barton grinned ingenuously. "Really, sir? That doesn't even make sense."

"Listen, I don't know what you think you're pulling, but I want it stopped. You hear me? You shape up or your ass is grass and I am the lawn mower! *Is that clear?* Say is now, say, Yessir, that is clear!"

The men responded loudly.

"I don't want to come back here again." Egan wheeled on his heel and marched through the doorway.

Craig waited a moment, then turned to Barton. "Come on, get in the locker. Hankins, you get the rope."

Barton laughed. "Don't tie it so tight this time. Last time I got rope burn on my ankles."

"Just do your part. When it comes to your empty chair you read the dialogue just like normal from the locker."

Miss Bui glanced around the room, and walked immediately to the locker. "Oh, Ong Vinh, why do they do this to you? Didn't the captain come and talk to them?"

Barton nodded, sliding the gag from his mouth easily. "I don't know, Miss Bui. They are just mean to me."

Miss Bui shook her head sadly, and for the first time in these pranks Craig felt guilty. In the beginning he had thought that she was just humoring them, then once they realized that she believed Barton was really being kidnapped, it had seemed funny to lead her along; now he felt dispossessed, part of something ugly and cruel. He walked over and took the rope from Barton's ankles. "We won't do it again. It was just a joke."

Miss Bui nodded solemnly. "I will not tell Captain Egan of this time."

Later Craig told Ted and Gerry about it, surprised how much he missed them since they had been moved to a different section. "We just went too far." He added this transgression to the accumulation of guilt that lately bowed him with its burden. "She really believed it."

"So she's dumb, and you're an asshole for picking on her, so what? Let's get some cold drinks!" Ted shouted.

"You go ahead, I have to write a couple of letters."

Gerry nodded, grasped Craig's shoulder. "Don't take everything so personally, bro. You didn't create sin in the world. Loosen up."

"I will," Craig said, and took out a tablet and set it on his desk and began to write.

In October, not quite three weeks later, Craig spent the night sleeping in the gully that split the east side of the base from the sprawl of adobe houses that bracketed old Monterey. He wrapped his hand in a T-shirt to stop the bleeding from his right hand, and curled against moss and rock and weeds and fell to sleep. He had wrapped himself in a windbreaker that Sheryl had sent him for his birthday.

Craig woke with a bright sun that spread through a break in the canopy of the trees and undergrowth. His hand throbbed with pain, and he thought the feel rhymed with his heartbeat. He tried climbing the wire fence, slid back, tried again, and finally followed the trickle of a runoff to the base of the hill and trudged to the road that led to the base. He kept his hand shoved in the pocket of his jacket. He recalled smashing the latrine window with his fist, drawing his hand back out through the jagged edges and wondering what he had done and why, and finally seeking refuge in running. He thought that when he died this would be his epitaph: He was a runner.

Gerry Norton, having recently completed the negotiation for a 1950 Ford coupe—a sand-pink car with a rasping cough —for one hundred dollars, was looking for Craig to enlist him as a member of the partnership that would own and operate this freedom vehicle. He envisioned the five of them sharing and taking turns with the car. Every fifth weekend would belong exclusively to one of the owners. In the meantime if someone wanted a ride, they could charge half the price of a taxi and garner funds to keep it running. This car had been an obsession with him since he saw the For Sale sign on it in the Denny's parking lot. When asked about it he launched into a complicated explanation of how the time would be scheduled and the ultimate benefits to each of the primary investors.

Now he walked around the Presidio in search of Craig, thinking that if he didn't have the twenty dollars within a few
hours, this opportunity would be lost forever.

Ted puzzled over his own dilemma. He had seen Craig
break the windows in the Russian classroom latrine, had almost called out to him, but stunned by indifference he had
been too slow. Now, just after the military police had questioned him about whether he had any knowledge of the incident and he had denied it, he wasn't sure what would be the
right action. He knew the general rule, solid as a bridge to his
childhood, was that there was a duty to friends, and he was no
fink. But he was also worried. He remembered that when he
was sick with the flu Craig had walked back and forth to Dee's
Place twice daily and brought him soup and crackers and iced
tea. He sighed, and settled into his desk chair, the lethargy of
indecision overwhelming him.

"Twenty bucks, hurry, the man might sell the car."

"We couldn't be so lucky." Craig pulled out his wallet with
his left hand and extracted two tens. He dropped the wallet on
the ground, bent, and retrieved it. He shoved it back in his
pocket. "I'm paid up."

"Something wrong?"

"No. Just tired."

"What about your hand? You hurt it?"

"Just taught it a lesson. Get the car, huh?"

"On my way. Listen, if you want to talk about it later, just
let me know. I made up the schedule and I have the car from
tonight until Monday morning. Your weekend is three weeks
from yesterday unless you want to trade it with someone."

"That's fine," Craig answered, and slumped forward as he
climbed the hill.

"I was worried about you, man." Ted took Craig's left arm
and led him into the latrine. "I saw what you did. You better
let me look at your hand."

"You're better off not involved. There might be some trouble."

"The MPs have already been here. Come on." Ted removed the T-shirt, ran some cold water, and held Craig's hand
under the flow. "The bleeding's stopped. That's a good sign.
Why'd you do something as dumbfuck crazy as that?"

Craig didn't answer, could not answer. He recalled what he
had done, but the reasons eluded him. He shrugged, winced

with the pain when Ted turned his hand abruptly.

"So, big deal, the army can afford windows." Ted placed Band Aids tenderly over the cuts on the knuckles.

"Have you ever been pissed, pissed so bad you had to hit something and didn't know why?"

"I kicked my dog once. I threw up later, I felt so bad. I was nine or ten."

"So did I," Craig said softly.

Craig now walked to class, or rode in the jointly owned car, with an invisible aura: he had become the subject of gossip and speculation, and even those who only knew his name from vague comments talked of him. There was no proof, but he was suspected of breaking the windows, painting a swastika on a particularly aggressive sergeant's locker, creating all manner of mayhem and mischief around the base. Craig did not respond to any questions, but found that he felt a unique pride in the rumors.

Chapter 3

"Leave the doors open and push; once it starts, jump in and slam the doors," Gerry spoke to the other four owners of the illustrious pink '50 Ford they had named Freedom, and sat behind the wheel and turned on the ignition and threw the gears into neutral.

"How come we push and you drive?" Ted asked.

"I thought of this idea."

"For that, you should have to push it alone," Craig grumbled, and took his place at the left rear door.

The car rolled downhill past three barracks, almost to the enlisted men's club, before the starter kicked over and they could jump inside to ride to class. The fact that it was easier to walk to class than to have to push the car to start it every day was not lost on Ted Trainer, and he griped for the entire five-minute ride.

The car had become a chronic problem between the owners. They argued over turns, they argued over the reasons that it didn't start with any reliability at all, over the fact that it was ugly. But like most teenaged boys they took pride in the fact that they had a car, and here on the base they were among the stratified few who could escape and go on dates without finding a girl who liked to walk or had her own car.

"I never owned a car before," Gerry said.

24

"I had a '55 Chevy, the damn thing was a tank. You couldn't stop it and you couldn't hurt it. I sold it to a friend of my brother's and he blew the head gasket within a week." Craig spoke reverently of his car, knowing it was not his any longer, but like a first lover, it retained a special place in his heart. "It even started *every* day."

Co Bui announced her impending marriage in the same quiet, terse way that she taught dialogues. She explained that she would be marrying Ong Ky. Once she was married she explained that they should call her Ba Ky.

Gerry told Craig that he thought Ong Ky looked like someone had rearranged his head with a shovel, and Craig laughed, feeling embarrassed for his cruelty. He expected that Co Bui, already an old maid by Vietnamese standards, with splay feet and not beautiful, must be happy to have found someone at last. Desperation is a cruel master, he told Gerry, and sighed, hoping he was never desperate himself.

The evening settled, and with the last rays of light the men took off singly or in small groups to find their own pleasures for the weekend. Gerry took the car and picked up his date for the Monterey Pop Festival, Ted hitched a ride as far as the Alvarado Cafe and went to the movies, Craig went to the Red Pony and took his usual seat at the piano. Craig wished he had thought ahead, gotten tickets for the concert, but it was too late, and he brooded over his drink.

"My husband is a pig," the woman said drunkenly, and looked at Craig. "A pig."

"I'm sorry," he said without thought, and sang along with the crowd as they ran through a military service medley. He noticed some of the men stood when their service anthem was sung; he sang "Anchors Aweigh," when the turn came, but remained seated.

"He runs around on me all the time. Secretaries, whores, wives of friends, they're all fair game to him." The woman, her brunette hair falling over her eyes, brushed it back with a hand, and continued, "I'm Karen. What's your name?"

"Craig." He looked out of the window and watched the schooner *Te Vega* roll with the tide. Sometimes he imagined himself with such a fine ship, traveling to unknown places, sailing with a full, free wind to push her beyond the world he knew.

"I graduated from Vassar, and he thinks all I am is a baby machine and lump to fuck when he wants a little tail. I don't even think he does it all that well."

"I study Vietnamese," Craig said.

"He's a shit. A total shit."

"There's a war there."

"Where?" Karen asked, then continued to talk as if she had not made the inquiry. "He loves big tits. I've got a nice pair, everybody says so, but he likes humongous tits. He'd love to make it with someone like Carol Doda."

Craig nodded mutely, sipped his scotch, and barely flinched when she began to run her hand down his thigh.

In the room at the San Carlos Hotel, after sex, Craig felt used and silly. Karen's naked thighs seemed immense and threatening to him now. "Lorna told me about you," Karen said softly, and kissed him.

Craig didn't answer, but smoked a cigarette.

Karen stood up; the flesh on her buttocks was dimpled and wobbled when she walked to the bathroom to dress. "Is forty bucks okay?"

He stared at the window and did not answer. He finally said good-bye when she walked out the door. She no longer seemed drunk, and he wondered if she had ever been. He lay down on the bed and closed his eyes and went to sleep.

When he woke on Saturday morning he took a long shower, luxuriating in the privacy, unsure why he felt so depressed. He stared at himself in the mirror, at the scars that ran down his right knee and his left shoulder blade; Know me, know my proudflesh, he thought absently. He hated the scars sometimes, other times they seemed like badges of existence to him. Both injuries had been caused in accidents with horses. His knee had been torn up when a randy stud rolled over on him, the back scar came when he had been thrown and impaled on a fence when he was breaking a colt. He rinsed his mouth with water. He walked out of the hotel and turned toward the base. Home, he thought, it's the only one he had now.

There were not quite three months left to classes, and the early spring brought green to the burnt hills of Monterey and Salinas. Flowers bloomed as brightly as beacons in the yards of the small stucco houses that surrounded the base. Young people began to appear on the streets with flowers in their hair, or garlands around their necks, and they carried them and handed them to strangers and said the word *love*. When the first girl handed Craig a flower he felt defiled when he accepted it; these were surely the people the military kept warning them about. Already he had seen two men lose their clearances because of using drugs. One of them, Kyle, had been having a flashback caused by LSD and had been taken to a hospital. No one could tell him anything of Kyle's fate. He had been locked up for his own good, they said, and then it all became a mystery.

A long time after the concert Gerry was still talking about it: Joplin, Hendrix wrecking his guitar, the Who going crazy. In the audience was love and good marijuana and cheap wine and the promise of a better world, he said.

"You trying for valedictorian?"

Craig looked up from his books. "No. Just doing some studying, Ger."

"That's all you do anymore."

"I have a dialogue to memorize."

"What's the matter?"

"Nothing has to be the matter. Nothing is ever the matter with me. I'm Dear Abby for everybody else, how can I have a problem?"

"You're compulsive, Craigers."

"Don't call me that. I hate it."

"I know." Gerry smiled. "That's why I use it."

"I'm worth more than forty bucks."

"Huh?"

"It doesn't fucking matter." Craig looked at his book, closed it, and began to undress. "I'm going to hit the showers."

Gerry waited patiently, reading a few pages of *Look Homeward, Angel*. He worried over Craig, just as he worried over the others, but Craig was changing and he did not understand these changes. He stretched out on Craig's bunk.

"Thought you were going somewhere," Craig said. He dropped his towel, folded it, and dressed in a T-shirt and white jeans. "Say something."

"How about drinking some Ripple on the beach?"

Craig nodded. "Yeah. That would be good."

They walked the rusted tracks of the railroad that had once

been part of a busy railhead. They bought their Ripple at the liquor store at the fork in the street and continued to a sandy place that bore warning signs—no trespassing, no swimming —and sat down on the rocks to drink and talk. Craig thought that the railroad tracks were the spine that connected the world. He wondered that if these ever disappeared, the world would sputter off like a wounded balloon.

The beach was on cannery row, and from where they sat they could see the dipping tail of the remaining active cannery that dropped into the bay. Above them they could see the tourists stroll past to visit the restaurants, the gift shops, perhaps the bookstore.

"Can't you ever keep still?" Gerry slapped his right hand on Craig's right knee to settle it. "You go a hundred miles a minute even when you sleep."

"I know. I can't help it. Maybe I was meant to be a runner." Craig lit a cigarette, a Marlboro, and smoked in silence.

"Just relax."

"I don't know how. Funny, I keep thinking that if I let down, I might just explode, splinter into a million pieces. Funny, huh?"

"Are you okay, bro?"

"Spiffy. Just fucking swell." Craig tossed his cigarette butt into the water.

"Maybe you've been reading too much Camus. Or maybe too much Brophy."

Craig smiled. He folded himself against a discarded tire, and thought about Larry Brophy. Brophy was another Vietnamese linguist; other than knowing that he was from Wyoming, Craig thought of him as an enigma: Brophy only discussed his life before the navy in riddles and conflicting anecdotes. Brophy was the first one Craig had known who had tried drugs. He liked them, he said. He found some truths there, somewhere in the paisley clouds he saw, he said. They were opposites, Craig and Larry, and Craig wondered how they had become and remained friends. Brophy thought LSD should still be legal, he expounded on the virtues of morning glory seeds baked into oatmeal cookies. "You should get to know him."

"He's trouble. You don't see it, but he is."

"He's a good man, a friend. He got me to read Camus."

"And Kafka," Gerry said. "Maybe that's why you've been brooding so much lately, sulking."

"Not sulking, no way." Craig scowled, lit a cigarette, and took a long swallow of wine from the bottle. "I haven't done drugs, okay?"

"I never asked."

"I just wanted you to know."

"What's the matter, then?"

Craig scooted down in the sand and folded his arms around his knees. "Forty dollars. That's the matter."

"Speak English."

"I'm okay, huh? Hand me the wine."

"You know Brophy's getting a reputation. It might rub off on you." Gerry stared at the winking lights across the bay and wondered if it was Santa Cruz.

"I'm so screwed up on my own that I wouldn't be able to handle drugs," Craig said, and knew that it was true. He was afraid of too many things, drugs, places, people; his fear made him control himself. "I didn't get my clearance yet."

"No surprise, SNAFU—situation normal all fucked up."

"You got yours."

"Maybe I wet the bed less." Gerry grinned. "Don't sweat the small stuff, Craigers."

"I hate that name," Craig said stubbornly. He sipped the wine again, wiped the drippings from his chin, "Maybe it was the sit-ins."

"What sit-ins?"

Craig stared at the stars, "I was a kid, thirteen maybe. I sat in some park to integrate a diner. It was in Pittsburgh, for Chrissakes. Pittsburgh! Shit."

"I'm through with this," Gerry held the empty bottle up, "You want to go to Sancho Panza's?"

"No thanks. Maybe I just need some time alone, okay?"

"Hang in there."

"You, too, buddy."

For a long time Craig sat on the curb of the street and watched cannery row and its denizens. Finally, his energy restored, he walked up the hill to the Hidden Village.

The Red Pony had been his place to socialize, to laugh; the Hidden Village was his refuge. It was an unusual place: part wine bar, part art gallery; low Japanese-style tables with bright

cushions for seats. He ordered a wine cocktail. He wished he
had asked Gerry to come along. Alone, he had to think, he
had to recall this unknown anger, the anonymous fears that
withered him. He knew the pattern of this fear: he wasn't sure
that he could make it here, or anywhere else. In the new
terminology, it was to be a "hacker." You either hacked it, or
you didn't. A hacker was an enigma: a shogun, a saint, a
robber, and a hero. A hacker was the last one standing at a
party and the first one to charge into any situation that pru-
dence would declare off-limits. Everyone told Craig that he
was naive, a rube, a midwestern hick. He knew it was true.
Before he had joined the navy he had listened to a record of
"Battle Hymn of the Republic" and "Over There." He had
teared up for both songs.

"I'm Sara." The girl sat down cross-legged across from
him. She had dark hair and eyes.

Craig blinked, looked down at the table, and finally spoke
his name. It felt foreign on his tongue.

"Your eyes look like the boy who used to be on *Lassie*."

Craig blushed, mumbled an awkward order to the waitress.
"Two of the same, please." He thought of his eyes—be-
trayers, cow-eyes, he'd been told since he was a toddler—and
shrugged. He crossed his right leg under his left to stop the
wiggling and sipped his drink. "Sara's a pretty name," he said
at last.

"I hate it. I think I should be a Michelle or maybe a Cor-
inne. You should be a Holden or a Tommy."

"Why?"

"Names define us. I won't be a Sara. Saras are slow and
stupid and like to dust. I want to fly." She held her drink in
her right hand and tasted it. "Most people have eyes that are
crazy happy, you have eyes that are crazy sad." She took
Craig's right hand in both of hers and kissed it gently.

"I'm not sad. Really," Craig said.

"You are, you know. I can tell. You might not know it, but
you are. You're good-looking, Craig, and I want to know you
better."

"Do you live here?"

"Sometimes. We live a lot of places. Mostly we live in San
Francisco."

"I'm from Ohio," Craig said. "You're beautiful."

"Come to my place. We can have wine and poems."

"Poems?"

"You like poetry, don't you?"

"Yeah."

"My house is built on poems. Celine and Shelley and Yeats and McKuen."

"McKuen?"

She laughed, and kissed him. "'I am the many, and each is a new song for me.'"

Her Monterey house was large and less than a block from the water. It was not quite beyond the imaginary boundary between old and new Monterey. In the living room the furniture was covered with white sheets, and the air carried the musty odor of a house that had been sealed for several months. They walked around the room and opened windows, and Sara lit candles and brought a bottle of white wine and two long-stemmed glasses.

The wine was French and the goblets were crystal. Craig wondered if he had ever been this intrigued or this happy.

"You are wonderful, Paul."

"Craig," he said softly. "Most of the girls around here hate servicemen."

"Most girls aren't me." Sara settled against his right shoulder and sipped her wine. She looked at the book cases, "Have you read Laing?"

"No."

"You should. He knows me, all of the ones inside me."

"He's a psychiatrist, isn't he?"

"Yes, but he's a poet, too. A poet of the soul."

"You're really pretty, Sara."

She leaned to him, kissed him, "'And pluck till times and times are done—'"

"'—the silver apples of the moon, the golden apples of the sun.'" Craig was suddenly embarrassed at finishing the line of poetry for her. Her scent filled him and he thought that she smelled of sea and smoke and soap and wine and woman.

Sara unbuttoned her blouse. "Maybe someday we'll live in Paris and we'll eat goat cheese and drink wine along the Seine and be happy. We could live inside a poem, our own poem. That would be lovely, wouldn't it?"

"Yes." Craig leaned over and kissed her awkwardly, enjoying her taste.

They were naked, entwined on the hardwood floor. The dust felt soft against Craig's skin. He traced her nipples with his tongue, ran his hands over her hips.

They made love slowly, hinged in purpose, gentle in design. Their odors became a single, sweet-sour aroma of sweat and love juices.

There is no way to understand this, Craig thought, no words to explain the way he felt: he thought he might explode, become paltry human dust.

They made their conversation with their bodies, their tongues and their hands. We are a poem, Craig whispered, we are a poem at last.

They lay beside one another, their breathing an easy rhythm that slowly drifted to match the sea sounds. The dust had been swept from the floor by their movements, and clung to their sweat in tiny brown lines like broken veins. Craig looked at the floor, at the dark, damp stains from them, at the sheen of juices they spilled. The spots shimmered with candle-light as bright as dew.

"I might love you," he said at last, wondering how he could love Sheryl as well, and finally pushed the thought from his mind and kissed Sara again.

"This person, this moment, loves you, too." Sarah said, and Craig wondered if she were being coy. "And I love good sex," she said. "I always love good sex."

"Me, too," Craig said as if he had to fill the void with some words.

Sara pulled back. "I want to be alone now."

"Can I see you tomorrow?"

"Perhaps." Here, curled against the sofa, she was on her own ground again, and even before he rose and began to dress she thought of him as a stranger.

"Dinner tomorrow?"

"Please leave me now."

"What's wrong?"

"Sara said leave." She glared at him angrily and turned away.

The house was empty and locked and no matter how many times he knocked, he knew it was futile. Twice the neighbors walked to their stoops to see who was making such a racket, and finally he walked down the street to the beach and huddled in the sand. He set a limit of an hour that he would wait, and when it passed he set a two-hour limit, and so on until the afternoon was gone, eaten in tiny lonely hour chunks, and evening descended with a chill. He walked back to the base in despair.

The rest of the weekend passed, and to get his mind off of Sara, Craig read *Been Down So Long It Looks Like Up to Me*, by Richard Farina, and three mysteries by Ellery Queen.

When Monday's class began, Craig recited his dialogue perfectly despite being paired with Jack Brady, whose timing was awkwardly different from his usual partner, Danny Farris.

Miss Hoa Thi was wearing white, the color of mourning, but she did not explain. When she spoke, her voice was so soft that they had to strain to hear her. "Our culture begins in 2879 B.C.," she said. "A very great dragon fell in love with a beautiful fairy. They were wed and the fairy gave birth to one hundred eggs. The dragon took fifty eggs to the mountains, and the fairy took fifty eggs to the shore. When the eggs hatched, the dragon had fifty sons and the fairy fifty daughters; that is why the mountains are rugged and the valleys are fertile and green." Hoa Thi looked shyly around the room. "That is the beginning of the Vietnamese people."

Ted grabbed Craig's right elbow and whispered, "I was descended from fairies, too. We try to keep it a dark secret, but one of my great-uncles was a transvestite."

Craig shook his head. "Asshole."

Hoa Thi looked at Craig. "Do you have a question, Ong Can?"

Craig turned crimson. "I was just saying that the dragon is important in many Asian myths."

Hoa Thi nodded. "China is the greater dragon and Vietnam is the lesser one. The great Le Loi said, 'Vietnam has never had a shortage of heroes.'"

Jack Brady sniggered and whispered too loudly, "That's why they need us to bail them out."

Craig glared at Jack Brady, turned back to Hoa Thi. "You must miss your home very much."

Hoa Thi closed her eyes. "My home has been destroyed. This is why I mourn. My village is gone."

* * *

Gerry remarked of the Vietnamese, "They have so many superstitions, these myths, but they make sense to me. Weird, huh? I even half believe the dragon and the fairy story." He dropped onto Scott Forsberg's bunk across from Craig and paged through a copy of *Playboy* magazine. "So what happened to your mystery lady?"

"I wish I knew," Craig said bitterly. "She's just gone."

"You up for some cards?"

Craig signed his letter to Sheryl and shrugged. "Who's in so far?"

"Bridge, Scott and you against Ted and I."

"Penny a point, half a buck a set, dollar a game?"

"Those words are music to my ears, bro."

"Just make sure you have cash. Scott and I hate IOUs from fellow lingies."

The four of them sat at a makeshift table made from a piece of plywood set atop two stacked footlockers. Craig sloughed a three of diamonds, still hoping to save his four spade bid. He looked at Scott. "You made a wrong bid, matey, and this is our asses if I can't pull it off."

"I was trying to show support for your spades."

"If you had any points, that would be great." Craig riffed a club lead from Gerry, led back with a low heart to the king in the dummy hand and took the trick. "*Ooooeee*, we're going to make it, Scotty. Now, Ted, did you really double me?"

"I think Gerry was the one that doubled you."

Gerry frowned. "Hey, you said go ahead and do it."

Craig grinned. "I love it!"

"Quiet, douchebag, I want to eat my pride quietly. And tell your brother scum to quit grinning like the Cheshire cat." Ted finished off his Coke and belched.

"You have lots of class, Ted; problem is, all of it's third." Craig gathered the cards and handed them to Gerry to deal. "From the top, huh?"

The game was friendly but fiercely competitive: none of them were graceful losers. When they finally settled up and Craig and Scott paid off eight dollars and seventy-six cents to the others, Craig walked off sullenly to his cube and lay down.

Three weeks remained until graduation and the rains had stopped. Craig's clearance had still not been approved and he brooded over this daily, complained to his friends, checked incessantly with the security group officer, and finally, since there was nothing else to do, he waited for it. As Ong Hieu had told him, any portent could be the engine to bring catastrophe, and so he forced this one from his mind and enjoyed the weather, thinking these last days were much finer than the first ones.

Chapter 4

Probably the last three weeks were the hardest as they prepared for final exams. It wasn't just the examinations, but also the insecurity of waiting for orders once again, and the rising tensions that grew between even the closest of the classmates: even the smallest of quirks seemed intolerable now.

Gerry, Ted, Craig, and Scott and four others were all skylarking, grab-assing in the aisle of the barracks, shooting shaken-up Cokes at one another, until Chief Diebold called them down and made them GI the whole barracks, including new paste wax without any help. Each blamed the others, each one glum and unyielding.

"I hate this fucking place!" Ted screamed out and kicked the mop bucket across the aisle into a corner. Spilled, the dirty water spread like a lake and the others pitched in to swab it up.

"I want to know how I get out of this chickenshit outfit," Gerry yelled.

"Get orders," Craig said softly. "I wish I would."

"Luc luong dac biet," Ba Thuy said. "Special Forces."

Craig repeated the words, as did the others. He liked the sound of these words, each one using a low glottal stop that

36

allowed for some acting on the men's part. Ted grabbed his belly and said he had gotten a hernia.

Two weeks now, Ba Thuy thought to herself, and she would miss these men, her first class. She held the vague hope that this got easier from one time to the next; that the men seemed less individual, perhaps could be forgotten easily. She continued the lesson from the book, but her mind strayed frequently to the hearts of her students, and she hoped that they would be good men.

"I'm going to the Philippines," Gerry yipped, holding his orders over his head. "I got fucking orders!"

Ted had orders to the Philippines, too. Scott, wondering why his French skills would be important there, got orders to Ford Meade, Maryland. Hawley got orders to the USS *Oxford*, and Manley to the USS *Jamestown*. Craig listened to the litany of orders, the promise of tomorrow, and felt cowed and angry and small.

"I don't care where they send me. Just give me orders," Craig implored.

In the last gray hours of twilight, on the Monday before graduation, the communally owned car, Freedom, died on the main street in Salinas. No amount of coaxing, pushing, swearing, and cajoling could spark life in the engine, and even when Ted kicked the front bumper and Craig slammed a fist into the left rear fender, the car remained resolutely dead. She's really dead, Gerry said unnecessarily, and the other two groaned agreement. They debated, argued, finally all agreed that the only thing to do was to just leave it behind, hitchhike to base, and hope that they were gone long before anyone identified the car as theirs and forced some tickets or towing charges onto them. Craig agreed reluctantly, knowing that on seventy dollars every two weeks, any debt burden was too much for them.

So the three of them, cheerful and silly, walked down the street, had a beer, and began the arduous task of getting someone to drive them back to Monterey.

"Write, huh?" Craig asked this of Gerry, felt awkward with the question, the coercion of eliciting a promise. "I will—you too, promise?"

"Cross my heart and all that dopey shit."

"You'll get orders soon."

"So they say. Situation normal, all fucked up."

"SNAFUs aren't that strange in the navy, matey."

"I feel like shit, being left behind again."

"It'll get better."

"I hope so."

"Keep in touch," Gerry said again, knowing he was prolonging the good-bye to his friend, knowing that he had to get his gear and catch the bus soon or he would miss the flight. He finally clapped both hands on Craig's shoulders, "Hang tough, bro."

"You, too." Craig broke away first, and walked back to the yard detail he had been assigned without looking back once. He knew what he would see: Gerry receding into the curve of the hill, until once beyond the horizon he would disappear once and for all. Craig picked up his hoe and began chopping the dirt at the base of a jacaranda.

Gerry had not been the first to leave, nor was he the last, and Craig said good-bye to each, though with each he became less insistent on keeping in touch, steeling himself more for their departures while he still waited for orders. Ted had told him not to sweat it, don't sweat the small stuff, but he worried, and with the worries he drank more, and once after a long night at the Red Pony he had fallen into a ditch and slept the night through curled amidst the ferns and moss and bugs.

"You seem sad, Ong Can." Ong Hieu, eternally optimistic, as only the ones who know devastation and loss can be, passed a plate of *cho gio*, spring rolls.

"Thank you for inviting me to eat with you and your wife," Craig said absently, happy for the company, eating well, and reluctant to leave. "Everybody else has orders."

"You want to leave Monterey that much?"

"No. I just want to get on with my life. I need to know where I'm going."

"Vietnam," Mr. Hieu said softly. "We had your chart cast by Mr. Liu, and he says you will go to Vietnam."

"I wish he'd tell the navy, then."

"It will come. In three days' time, he thinks. It is very hard to know the exact time, though."

"You didn't have to do that."

"I am happy to do so. You are a most good student."

"Thank you. Even when we used to leave early on Friday afternoons?"

Mr. Hieu smiled, revealing two gold-rimmed front teeth, "Even then. Every time I said, '*Hom ngay chung ta di xe phim*,' I knew that you translated that as '*Hom ngay ve nha som*.' Today we go home early. I would not watch military films either. Did you enjoy the beach?"

"Better than some newsreel from nineteen fifty-four."

"I agree. Some tea, please?" Mr. Hieu poured green tea into a small cup and set it before Craig. "Tea is better than scotch sometimes, *non*?"

He hated the way he felt, the dullness, the throb at the base of his skull. Craig struggled free from his blanket anxiously.

After showering and dressing he walked first to get some coffee, and then to the headquarters company office, but there were again no orders. He accepted the news with a soft curse, and walked to X Division, the holding company, and listened to a paunchy sergeant tell him how to trim weeds and shrubs and hand him some tools. Holding companies were the military equivalent of purgatory, and Craig, like the others, went about his tasks in a dawdling manner, holding to a lazy hope that this would end soon.

Denny Baskins, a linguist in the class behind Craig, had become first a casual acquaintance, like some of the others in his class, and like a few had gradually become a friend. He stood at the end of Craig's cubicle. "How are the weeds doing?"

"Funny man. Don't expect any help with your dialogues next time, huh?" Craig collapsed onto his bunk, sweaty and sore. "Thought you and Corey and Mimana would be off partying for the weekend already. You cut out during the movie, didn't you?"

"Naturally. Think I'd really watch some movie on how they won Dien Bien Phu again?" Danny sat down in the desk chair and propped his feet on the empty bunk across from Craig. "I got a new cubemate. He's in two classes behind me, name's Mark Mitchell."

"Something you get used to here is new cubies. I think I had four since I've been here. So where are the other two members of your band of rebels?"

"Mimana had to catch a bus to visit his cousins in San Jose

and Corey Lane is just drifting around town, I guess. He walked to the bus station with Joey, and said he was going to walk awhile and meet me back here to hit the enlisted men's club."

"I know, fifteen-cent drinks at the EM club tonight. How well I remember Friday happy hours." Craig smoked absently, wondered if, when he finally left, these men would miss him the way he missed Gerry and Ted and the others. At odd moments he even found himself missing Jack Brady. He thumbed through his mail, set the letter from Sheryl to the side to read later, ripped open a short letter from his youngest sister, and read it quickly. Everyone was fine, she said, and he supposed that they were, but the ache of homesickness returned every time he heard from any of his family. "I'm going to grab a shower."

"You want to grab a few brews with us?"

"Maybe. Let me clean up and get on some civvies and ditch this uniform and we'll talk about it."

"Okay." Danny leaned back and closed his eyes.

Corey Lane was also in his cube by the time Craig returned. He said hello to Corey, hung his towel on the rack in the locker, and put on white jeans and a red striped T-shirt. "So, we going to get some beers?"

Corey looked at the floor, finally spoke. "I heard some news about Sara."

Craig wheeled around, "What?"

"She's in the hospital. They said she tried to commit suicide in the bay this morning."

"I'm going to see her." Craig didn't wait for any response, but strode out of the barracks and half jogged down the hill into Monterey.

Until now the only time Craig remembered being in a hospital was when he was seventeen and had knee surgery. He'd had his tonsils out, but had been too young to recall it, and the time his father had been hospitalized, he had been too young to be allowed to visit, so could only wave to his father's room window from the lawn.

It was finally a young nurse who took pity on him and answered his questions as best she could, explaining the whole time that it was against hospital policy to give out information other than to patient's families. Sara had been admitted after she attempted to drown herself. She had also had a spontaneous abortion of a twelve-week-old fetus.

Craig felt staggered, nodded dully to the woman and thanked her. A baby. He thought about their lovemaking, felt a flush of guilt akin to criminality. He waited until Sara had been taken to her room, and walked down the hallway.

"You can't see her." The orderly was adamant, and the older man at his side nodded a voiceless agreement.

"I have to," Craig said.

The older man finally spoke. "I'm her father, and I don't want anyone to see her, especially one of her ex-boyfriends."

"I loved her."

"You loved the illusion of her. Sara's very sick, she's been having manic episodes for months, and she wouldn't allow us to get her help. This time she's getting help. From here she'll be transferred to a psychiatric hospital. I'm sorry, son, but I can't take a chance on anyone upsetting her, or her conning them into helping her make a break for it again."

"I don't understand any of this, I just know that we had something special and I want a chance to see how she's doing, to let her know I'm here for her."

"I'm sorry, I've given you more explanation than anyone else, but I won't change my mind."

Craig, drunk, shuffled along the beach, walking into the surf and back out without taking off his shoes or socks, and finally, his depression unabated, walked back to the barracks and collapsed on his bunk.

In the morning, pained with a hangover, Craig refused to talk to anyone about it despite Corey and Joey Mimana both questioning him and urging him to speak. When they finally gave up, Craig walked to the wharf, bought a cup of coffee and sat on the roof balcony of Rappa's for the rest of the day and watched the boats and sea lions.

"You got orders, huh?"

Craig nodded to Joey, smiled for the first time in more than a week. "Fort Meade, Maryland." He shook his head. "More classes, they said. Then I go to Coronado for something called SERE school, and by then I'll have final orders, they said. I leave tomorrow."

"It's going to be drunk-out tonight."

"That it is, buddy, that it is. Red Pony time. ETA is five o'clock P.M."

"I'll get Corey and some of the other guys."

"Just bring money and a thirst."

A seabag, two suitcases, and a manila folder with orders in it: Craig's life had become this simple. He checked his bags through on the flight, and waited impatiently for the announcement to board the plane. Joey Mimana and Corey were with him, both of them silent, and he could not bring himself to talk, either. This was his second duty station, the second time he had made friends, been left, or left them in return, and he didn't know what he should feel or do, other than adding them to the list of people he already missed. Finally, his throat tight and dry, he said, "Keep in touch, huh?"

"Sure," they both answered.

"I'll write when I get settled."

"Me, too," Corey said, scuffing a toe into the floor.

Promises made, and promises broken, Craig thought. He hadn't heard from one of the men who separated from boot camp, and had yet to hear from the men who had left him behind in Monterey. "I promise," he said without any faith in his words at all.

After boarding the plane and taking his seat, he looked out of the window at the terminal. He could no longer distinguish his friends from the blur of faces and he felt better for this. The plane taxied out toward the runway and he thought he might not be able to handle the wait until the No Smoking light went out.

The stewardess woke him; she said that he had been crying in his sleep and she was worried. He accepted a drink, a scotch and water, and shrugged. It wasn't for his friends; he remembered the dream, vividly. He had dreamed of a seaweed-covered fetus that had eyes just like his own.

The Building. After only his first day he began to refer to the National Security Agency building by the same simple epithet that everyone else used. The Building. Craig walked its corridors as if they were church aisles, afraid to talk to anyone, unsure where all of these people actually worked. He had a blue foil badge that aligned him with B group; he had no idea what the other badges meant, or what groups they were assigned. He walked into his classroom and took a seat in the middle of the rows, took out his new tablet and doodled while he waited for class to begin.

"I'm Jim Laurence," the instructor said. He was a naval petty officer second class: a CT2 with combat ribbons that spread over his left breast. His hair was sandy, shades lighter than Craig's, and he was thin with a sallow complexion that was tinged toward yellow. Before he began to teach, while still introducing himself, he said he had malaria. He warned that anyone who ended up in Vietnam should take the small yellow pills that were a malaria prophylaxis even if they got the shits from them. "Here you're going to learn some basics about equipment, language, and possible missions. From here directly to other Naval Security Group detachments, some on ships, some not. Mostly we're going to familiarize you with some of the terminology and the idea of radio/telephone intercept." He had a practiced voice when he spoke to them, seemed casual and right. "How many of you had some Vietnamese instructors that you considered friends?"

Many of them raised their hands.

"That's the last time you'll feel that way. Within hours of graduation the North Vietnamese and the Russians had a complete roster of your names. It's the way it is."

"Are you saying that our instructors were spies?"

Laurence shrugged. "I'm just saying that you're prime bait now. The information gets out, we don't know the sources. From now on, you have to be leery, you have to watch out what you say, and you have to maintain some discipline about security matters. You've been given top-secret crypto clearances because your government trusts you. You have to protect and retain that trust."

If Scott Forsberg and Harry France hadn't been assigned to the same barracks, Craig thought he would not have been able to handle the constant changes of his life. He and Scott became roommates, and it was almost like Monterey again as he settled into the pattern of going to class. Though both Scott and Harry were French linguists, Craig found their company settling and safe. Harry was assigned to duty at the NSA building itself; Scott, like himself, was waiting for further orders. "Can I borrow *Totem and Taboo* for a couple of days?"

"Have at it, Craig. You think you can read Freud in two days?"

"Either that or give up on it. I'm easy."

"Lend me *Lolita*, okay?" Scott grabbed the book from the desk they shared. "I need some good sex stories."

"Where's Harry?"

"He split for Baltimore tonight. He's watching an Orioles game."

"The Texan digs the birds, huh?"

"He digs the ladies that go to games, I think."

"I've sworn off since Sara," Craig said softly.

"Believe me, it happens again in time. Good thing that all of the Waves I meet are either officers or ugly."

Craig laughed, flippeed open the book, and dropped to his bunk to read.

The days passed easily, and though Craig found the classes puzzling in their generalities, he liked them, and he liked Jim Laurence. They talked about radio frequencies and signals, proper communications dialogue, the types of intercepted conversations and codes that they might encounter. He learned the differences between single-channel and multi-channel communications, and that the Vietnamese followed the Russian order of battle. He found that each piece of the puzzle made him more confident, and that he was able to keep up with most of the others. In fact, he found that finally life was getting easier for him, and this fact made him feel both better and more scared.

"What're you doing?" Craig looked at Scott and the suitcase that was open on the floor.

"Packing. That's an English word, maybe a zip linguist wouldn't understand it."

"Funny, what's happening?"

"I got some TAD orders."

"TAD?"

"Temporary additional duty. I'm flying out to join some ship called the *Liberty*. Three months and then I'm back here."

"I'll be gone by then."

"Yeah, so it goes, huh?"

"You need any help?"

"Well, I could use a drinking buddy in a couple of hours to give me a send-off, and maybe someone to make sure my stuff is okay while I'm gone."

"Protector of porno and drinker, that's me." Craig grinned, feeling inadequate with words. Knowing two languages, three

if you counted three years of high-school French, he felt iso-
lated from even his native tongue. He shrugged. "Meet you at
the club?"

"You got it."

The class was in progress, and Craig felt the strain of his
night out with Scott and Harry. He jotted notes on his tablet,
raised his hand twice to answer questions, and another three
times to ask them. Of the men he had known in Monterey,
only Jack Brady was present with him now, and the two of
them spent their spare hours in "Boomtown" playing the slots,
drinking, and playing pinball. The pinball and the slots both
paid money, and Craig was good at pinball and lucky with the
slot machines.

When class was over Craig went with Jim Laurence and
had a cup of coffee in the NSA coffee shop. "You might make
it to Det Tango," Jim said. "If you do, then look up Andy
Jenkins and tell him I said hey. He's ace."

"What's Det Tango?"

"One of the places you might go, but that's all I can say
right now."

"We have our clearances, why is everything still secret
from us?"

"Need-to-know basis."

"That sucks."

"As they say, the navy's like a big fan that sucks in one
side and blows out the other."

"I feel like a fucking criminal."

"You're doing fine."

Midway through the course, after the first examination,
Craig was doing well, felt good about the lessons, but already
began to feel a nagging desire to move forward from here. He
had begun to hear from some of the others: Thornhill was on
the *Oxford*, Harris on the *Jamestown*, Ted and Gerry were
both some place in the Philippines, called San Miguel. He
studied hard, drank beers with Jack Brady and sometimes
Harry France, and twice he hitchhiked to DC to see the
Smithsonian.

Barely two weeks before graduating from the course Craig
was called from the room by Jim Laurence and taken into the

second-floor hall. "I know this isn't a good time or place, but none are. Scott's been killed."

"What are you talking about?"

"The Israelis strafed and bombed the *Liberty*; several men were killed, lots more wounded. Scott was KIA."

Craig, stunned, shook his head and finally said, "Oh my God," and leaned against the wall to try to sort out his feelings. He took several deep breaths.

"You're off the rest of the day. You need to meet the chaplain in your cubicle, and help pack Scott's things."

"Shit."

"I'm sorry, huh?"

"Thanks. I mean, shit, I don't know what to do. I never thought anybody was going to die. Nobody I knew."

"I know." Jim patted Craig's shoulders and excused himself to return to the class.

The chaplain was thin and pale and had thinning hair and a demeanor that was mild and solicitous. "We need to sort out what belonged to Scott and what is yours, we need to send his personal belongings home."

Craig nodded, swore under his breath. Dear Mr. and Mrs. Forsberg, we can't return your son Scott, but we are sending you his skivvies. Craig stacked some letters from Marsha, Scott's girlfriend—a handful, really. Then he began to sort through the books piled on the desk: erotica that they both laughed about, serious books, classics, some westerns and mysteries. He took his copy of *Look Homeward, Angel* and handed it to the chaplain. He left all of the erotic books. He added some college brochures that Scott had gathered trying to plan for his return to civilian life. On the whole it all seemed paltry and meager.

"How about this?" The chaplain held up a red plastic ashtray from Gino's. "This his?"

Craig looked at it, remembered the night that they swiped it from the fast-food hamburger place that took its name from Gino Marchetti of the Colts. "It's his."

"Maybe you want to keep it as a souvenir?"

Craig blinked, slapped it away from the chaplain, and watched it bounce on the floor. "Just get away. Get out of my cube."

"I know how upsetting this can be."

"Go away."

"Maybe you'd like to sit down and talk to me."

Craig paced the floor, his pulse pounding at his temples. "A fucking ashtray? You want me to have a fucking plastic ashtray instead of my friend? Why can't you bring Scott back?"

"Settle down, son. Let's talk a little."

"I'm not your son. I have a father already."

"Maybe I can help."

"What you can do is get the fuck out of my cube!" Craig slammed his fist into a locker and rushed out of the cubicle himself and ran down the aisle until he was outside.

Over beers that he used to toast Scott and the good times they had had, he remembered his friend and missed him with an intensity that surprised him. He did not cry, and it puzzled him that he could not bring himself to tears. He had tried to find Harry France, but nobody knew where he was. He had always thought that Harry and Scott had shared a closeness that was special, and within which he was accepted, but only to a certain point. Harry always remained an enigma to him.

"Better slow down. You get too drunk and I'm supposed to put you on report."

Craig looked at the bartender, a young soldier with bristly red hair, and grinned. "Just so you don't send me to a ship."

"You okay?"

"Right as the fucking rain, man, right as rain."

A day later, Craig and Harry sat at the same table with a pitcher of beer. Craig could not forget Jim Laurence's kindness or his concern, but it unnerved him.

Harry was more taciturn than usual. Craig noticed that the other man had lost some weight, that his round freckled face had become a little drawn. When Harry spoke it was with a Texas drawl, and his words sometimes came so slowly that others had an impulse to finish his sentence for him. "God, I miss him." He'd said at last.

Craig nodded. "I leave here in two weeks. I still can't believe that Scott's dead."

"Going to Vietnam?"

Craig shrugged; it was a question they asked themselves and each other daily. Even Jim Laurence seemed reluctant to answer it. "I don't know."

"Momma Navy loves to keep us squids guessing, huh?"

"It's a grade-A bitch."

This was the most time that they had spent alone and each of them felt awkward. They spoke of Monterey, of the good times there, and they talked about Scott: the way he talked, his breathless enthusiasm for so many things, his odd halting walk. "I forgot to pack some of Scott's dixie cups," Craig said at last. He held up two of the navy hats and handed them to Harry.

"I'll take care of them."

"I better get some sack time, we have a test tomorrow."

"I've had enough anyhow." He thanked the bartender, then spoke to each table of men that they passed. Harry was usually so laconic, Craig was surprised and asked him about it.

"Never know when you might be running for sheriff."

Mr. Gordon was the first black man that any of them had seen in their section. He was medium height, wiry, and wore a blue suit that had been well tailored. Laurence had told them that Gordon was a high-ranking civilian at NSA and that they might see him again.

"Seven more days and you'll be on your ways. Most of you should have orders already. I'm here to try to explain the informal relationship that exists between NSA and the various service security services, whether it's the Naval Security Group, the Air Force Security Service, the Army Intelligence agency, whatever. You will be assigned to various collection platforms, airborne, seaborne, some on land, and the data that you collect will end up back here at some point for our analysis and to create intelligence reports that are shared by all of the agencies. A lot of the data from Southeast Asia will end up being sent to JPRC in Japan, and from there will be forwarded to us. Each of your missions is important to the overall war effort in Vietnam. No one mission has an exclusive value that the others do not. It's with the parts that the total becomes effective and accurate intelligence. In other words, we need your maximum efforts, and we need you to understand that secrecy is important. Don't discuss what you do with anyone else. Perform your jobs and don't brag about them. What each of us does is important, but we're not like a field grunt that can brag how he took a hill. Our hills are all classified and our tasks have to remain among us. Some of you might become heroes, some of you might even die. But you won't get that credit, the new releases, we can't allow our personal pride and ambition to interfere with the mission."

Craig listened half-heartedly, already thinking about his orders. The discussion was casual, almost lazy, and most of the men were preoccupied more with their futures than their presents.

Thin sunlight broke through a hazy sky. Shadows already stretched out over the courtyard between the barracks, and those men out sunning had begun to stir themselves from their positions. Craig looked at them through the window, taking a break from his book. He was reading *Demian* by Hermann Hesse.

There was some shouting beyond the doors that separated his bay from the heads and the other sleeping bay that lay beyond them. He couldn't make out the words, but he heard an urgency that scared him a little. He looked at the partially completed letter to Sheryl and scribbled his name and love at the bottom and promised to write more soon. At last, uncomfortable with the curiosity, he walked down the aisle and pushed the door open.

"Hold it. Nobody allowed in the latrine."

Craig stared at the SP, a big blond kid who looked like an oxen to him, and asked why.

"Some stupid squid offed himself in the head. Hung himself in the shitters. Leave it to a fucking CT."

CT, communications technician, Craig's rating. He looked at the floor, staring at the SP's shoes. "Who?"

"Don't know yet. But he hung himself with a belt that had a brass buckle that said Texas."

Craig leaned into the doorjamb. He knew it was Harry. He had seen the belt buckle too many times before. "Oh, no," he said softly, and began to back away from the doorway.

"You okay?" the SP yelled.

Craig didn't answer, and continued to back up until he was outside, and once in the evening air he walked all the way to the bars in Boomtown without trying to hitch a ride at all.

"You're AWOL," Jim Laurence said.

Craig looked at him, blinked, and nodded at last.

Laurence hugged Craig suddenly, held him tightly in his arms. "Shit, I'm sorry. I told them I gave you some personal time for good work. You got to come back now." Jim looked at the seedy bar, at the young man, and just shook his head, wishing his life were different, but knowing that it wasn't. "Are you okay now?"

Craig nodded, thinking he would never be okay again. He had finally cried, for Scott and Harry both, tears that never seemed to end. He caught his breath. "I can do this job."

"I think so, too. I wouldn't be here otherwise."

Suddenly aware of the smell of booze and body odor he reeked, Craig stepped forward. "I need a shower and some rack time."

"You want to talk about it?"

"No," Craig answered. Someone with grief might sometimes forget their pain as they talked: he wanted to remember. He just wanted time to pass and let everything atrophy into his history.

Craig stood outside the barracks with his baggage. He was surprised that Jim Laurence waited beside him.

"If you get to Det Tango say hey to Andy Jenkins. He's the ever-loving best."

"You told me before, I'll remember."

"They had to keep it quiet, you know."

Craig shrugged, not knowing this at all. He knew that since Harry's death it had become a myth, a story that people told without detail, apocrypha from the barracks. No one was even sure who had actually died any longer. He sighed and watched the gray bus pull over to the curb. "That's my ride," he said as he hefted his bags.

"Good luck."

"Yeah, you too."

"You need to let loose a little more, Craig. Just some free advice. You have to handle things."

"Right on," Craig answered, and climbed up the steps to the bus.

Chapter 5

Coronado Island had two landmarks: the Hotel Del Coronado and the naval amphibious base. The first, a bit rundown, had been the playground of the rich; the second was home training base for the navy SEALS and a host of other sailors. The island lay across a long low bridge from San Diego, and on a clear day you could see the coronets and towers of the hotel from the city. On the base navy SEALS, UDT men, jogged past everyone under full gear, sweating and swearing in the hot sun.

Craig Nostrum had spent two weeks' leave before coming to Coronado, one of them with Sheryl. They had spent long days sitting beneath an oak tree in her backyard, and they made love for the first time. Without talking about Scott or Harry, in her bed and her kindnesses he had begun to heal. Stepping onto the grounds of the base he felt strong and wise.

"Move it!"

Craig stepped aside and let a line of men in trunks and backpacks run past. He walked to the chow hall, got a cup of coffee, and sat down at a table. He wasn't sure what the school was about, rumors had been too diverse, but he decided that SERE school probably stood for survival, evasion, resistance, and escape like the last man had told him. He knew there was weapons training involved, and he knew that this was a prerequisite for going to Vietnam. When he thought of this, and all of the times that officers and chiefs had assured him that he would probably never see Vietnam, he understood the first skeins of his naïveté were being destroyed.

A marine gunnery sergeant was teaching the weapons portion of the class. Gunny Boros explained that he had done two tours in Vietnam. He taught them how to field strip and clean and reassemble M14s and M16s and .45s. He taught them about grenades and launchers and machine guns. In between they attended classes where they memorized the American Code of Conduct. Name, rank, serial number, and date of birth, Craig thought when they asked him about it. Craig Nostrum, PO3, X38 00 68, U.S. Navy, September 23, 1947. Give no other information, that was what he recalled most. That, and to always try to find ways to resist the enemy captors, and to seek escape for yourself and your comrades.

"Today, ladies, we will actually shoot an M16. Now, if you can get your lazy asses in gear, we can hit it."

"We get our own guns?"

Craig looked at the questioner, a short kid from Alabama, and groaned.

"You were born with a gun, boy, unless you're missing some very essential equipment. This here is a rifle, or a weapon, but it is never a fucking gun!"

The young man next to Craig nudged his elbow. "You have to learn that little ditty?"

Craig laughed. "This is my rifle and this is my gun, my rifle's for fighting, my gun is for fun." He recited it in the same singsong voice he had learned it in boot camp. He recalled Chief Petty Officer Byrnes imitating masturbation when he spoke the word *gun*. Only after he had spoken did he notice that the other man had bright gold ensign bars on his collars. "I thought only enlisted men had to do this shit."

"Ask anyone who went to OCS and they'll tell you that the only thing lower than whaleshit on the bottom of the ocean is a seaman, and the only thing lower than that is an ensign. I'm Todd Carey, by the way."

"Craig Nostrum, PO3, which means I'm just about even with whaleshit by now."

"What's your rating?"

"Communications technician."

"A real live spook, huh? I didn't think you guys went to the 'Nam."

"I got it on my senior trip. I wrote the best essay."

"You two finished with your private circle jerk?" Gunny Boros stared at them and began issuing weapons.

"What do you do?" Craig asked.

"Helicopter pilot. They tell me I'll be flying on sea and air rescue missions over there. But who knows? The navy's never been known for honesty, huh?"

"Not the momma navy I know, sir."

"Call me Todd, okay?"

Craig loved the M16 from the first time he fired it. Until then the only shooting he had done was with a .22 caliber pistol or rifle when he shot rats and crows and other farm pests in Ohio. He fired well enough to qualify on the first attempt, but asked to fire again.

"You like that weapon, boy?"

Craig cringed over being called boy, but answered anyway, "I do, Gunny, I really do."

"Last time I said I do I got married. In fact *every* time I said I do I got married. Three times so far. If I was you I'd just learn to say yes sir, or maybe okay. Fire away."

They rode in the back of a half-track to the desert on Camp Pendleton. Under a hot morning sun they scuttled off the truck and formed ranks for Gunny Boros.

"I would suggest that you ladies buddy up. Find a likely pal and you hang with him. You'll need him sooner or later, and I don't like having to stalk the desert trying to find some asshole that gets hisself lost."

Craig stood still, wondered what to do, until Todd Carey grabbed his shoulder. "You and me, buddy, okay?"

Craig nodded thankfully. "We're a team, sir."

"I said to call me Todd, huh?"

"Okay."

Gunny Boros handed out silk parachutes to each man. "The desert is hot right now, but come nightfall it will get colder than a well-digger's ass, believe you me, girls."

"I think he's an asshole," Todd said.

"Me, too, but I kind of like him."

"I got a weird buddy."

"I do, too," Craig answered.

They walked hard and long under a noon sun. The men stopped along the way to cut off the pink flowers of cacti and eat them despite the prickles being left in their mouths. They drank water from their canteens only sparingly since they had been warned that there would be little chance of replenishing them in the three days left to them.

Their feet hurt and their backs, and some complained about blisters and sunburn, but nothing slowed their march through the desert. They bitched and complained in whispers, more afraid of the gunny's wrath than the sun. Gunny Boros was without sympathy when one man fell from heat exhaustion. He told them that he had warned them about dehydration. "We'll be making camp soon," he said at last.

"I'm going to make it, just to show him," Craig said.

"Then two squids will make it," Todd replied, and picked up his pace to match the gunnery sergeant's.

Craig turned to Todd. "Catch something to eat? He's got to be kidding us. I haven't seen anything edible all day."

Todd shushed Craig with a finger to his lips and pointed to a rock. A rattlesnake sunned himself there in the afternoon heat. He mouthed the word *dinner*.

Craig nodded. "I've been catching snakes all my life. I'll pin his head and you cut it off."

"You eat snakes as a kid?"

"I collected them as pets. That's why I want you to cut the head off. I couldn't kill one."

More soundlessly than he thought possible, Craig stepped behind the rock, took a forked stick and pinned the snake's head. The snake stared with dull eyes, rattled for a brief second before Todd beheaded it.

They took the snake to the gunny sergeant. Others had caught rats that the gunny exchanged for white rabbits. He explained that in the jungle they would eat rats, but here they wouldn't take a chance on infections and intestinal disorders. The kid from Alabama asked for and received the snakeskin which he said he would use to make a belt.

The rabbits were cooked in a thin stew of indigenous plants and weeds; the snake was cooked over the fire, cut into small pieces, and shared with all of the men. Craig was surprised that it tasted like chicken. He had to kill one of the rabbits with a blow to the neck; the gunny had insisted, ordering him to do it. It took three tries, and he still felt badly.

"This isn't half-bad," Todd said, and chewed his stew. "You better slow down and appreciate this, it's all we get for a while."

"I'm from a big family, you always eat fast. Otherwise the others get more than you do."

"I'd still slow down. I hear the POW camp isn't any fun at all, at all."

"You know anybody that's been through it?"

"My older brother, but he won't tell me shit. He thinks this is like some fraternity hazing that I have to go through on my own."

"He in 'Nam?"

"Back from 'Nam now. He's selling medical supplies in Iowa."

Craig nodded, and slowed his eating. His own older brother was indistinct to him; a hero to him, but so much older he did not think that they were friends. He remembered best when his brother came back from the army. He taught him to shoot craps and won the hard-earned and hard-saved sixty-five cents that constituted a fortune in his six-year-old world. He knew there were differences between them: Chuck was a prodigy, and quick to fight as well; he was pessimistic and worldly. Craig thought he was none of those things; he had made it through school, done well in subjects he liked, and failed those that bored him. He had fought only twice, and won only one of them, though the victory was a conundrum for him—in winning he had lost his best friend, and hurt him badly. He had not been able to stop hitting until someone pulled him off. He thought about Chuck, about his need for his brother's approval, and recalled the times when he was still six or seven that Chuck would lift him on the garage roof and let him jump into his arms. He loved it, but his mother put a stop to it with only her tone of voice. In any warning she merely used the child's full name and received compliance. Craig well remembered hearing, "Craig Joel Nostrum," and knowing it was time to obey.

"My brother was in the army during the Korean war," he said.

"Must be a lot older."

"Big families are like that. We have six kids."

"Just the two of us," Todd replied, wondering how it might have been to have more siblings.

"Makes the barracks seem like home sometimes; actually, sometimes it's quieter than home." Craig smiled suddenly, "You know when my brother was in England he had a great time. Anyhow, one time he picked up this girl and screwed her in the back seat of a taxi. He went back to base, stripped, and went to bed. The next morning he was at headquarters company and looked at the bulletin board and there was a pair of bloody skivvies pinned to it with a note, 'Chuck Nostrum screws only virgin in London.' It seems the lady was on the rag."

The two of them laughed together.

By the time they finished eating, the temperature had already begun to drop. Despite disbelief, the men began to complain about the cold.

"Time to make some shelter," Todd said, and looked for a likely scrub tree. "My idea is this: We can freeze separately or freeze together. So let's use one parachute to make a tent and the other to wrap up in."

"Be a little cozy sharing one parachute," Craig replied.

"Cozy or cold, your choice."

"Cozy's nice, I guess." Craig laughed. "Come on, you're the ensign here, take charge and show me how to build this palace in the desert."

"I will."

Craig marveled at the lean-to. Weighted with rocks it withstood the high squealing desert wind. Todd and he were wrapped cocoonlike inside the second parachute. "Isn't this where we're supposed to tell ghost stories?"

Todd laughed. "Sure did when we were kids. I used to go across the street to watch scary movies with my best buddy and we'd be so tough, real macho, except when it came time for me to go home I always wanted his dad and mine to stand on their porches and make sure I made it."

Craig laughed with his own memories of reading Bram Stoker and Bradbury and so many others and then always looking beneath his bed to see if there was really anything there waiting to get him.

"Tomorrow's going to be tough."

"And the tough get going."

The two of them giggled like young boys, and somewhere in the keening winds and the shared stories they fell to sleep.

"First phase is over, ladies, and now you get to show us how well you can evade the enemy. You start from here with your compass, and you try to get to point X. In between, there are going to be some men trying to make sure you don't get there. The three men who hold out the longest, and, of course, anyone that makes it to point X, get some sandwiches and Kool-aid. Now get moving and do your best."

Craig was captured within ten minutes, and Todd within five minutes of him. They were not the first to be loaded onto the stake-bed truck surrounded by guards with khâki uniforms with red stars over their breasts. They waited impatiently, and whenever they tried to talk to one another one of the guards ordered them to be silent. They lapsed into a restive silence and waited until the guards finally climbed aboard and the truck wended its way through the scrub oak and pine to a fenced camp.

The camp was in a wide clearing with manned watchtowers, and they were herded through the main gate with sharp commands and rough shoves. When one man fell the guards kicked him twice before helping him up and pushing him back into the throng of prisoners.

The camp commandant, his boots brightly polished, stood in the open area where the men were gathered together. Behind the men were low bunkers that served as their housing, though none of them had been inside them yet. The commandant spoke at last. "You will now strip off your clothing except for your undershorts and toss all of them into a pile here. Then each of you will present himself to me. I expect you to salute and then kneel before me while I introduce myself."

"You're shitting me," Craig said. From out of nowhere he felt a slap on the back of his head and heard a guard shout at him, "No talk. You strip."

The men did as ordered; forty pairs of pants and forty shirts were thrown into the air.

"I am Commandant Nero, what is your name?"

"Nostrum, Craig J., X38 00 68, U.S. Navy, born nine twenty-three forty-seven."

"Where are you from?"

"I'm sorry but my country will not allow me to answer that question."

"I gave you orders to kneel."

"No, sir," Craig answered, but a guard twisted his arm
until he dropped to his knees.

"You see? We have ways. You will talk."

Craig stared at the ground.

The stripping, the kneeling, the lack of any amenities were
all part of the intimidation, the depersonalization process that
they had studied in class. When any of the men got close to
one another they noticed the sour fetid odors of the unwashed,
and each man thought the other smelled, but seemed nearly
immune to his own aromas.

"Interrogation."

Craig nodded to the guard and stood up from his task of
stacking and sorting stones in the dirt yard. He had spelled
FUCK YOU with the stones, but so far none of the guards had
noticed.

Craig knew as he trailed the guard that the object was to
attempt to escape, but he saw no paths open to him at that
time. He followed without submissiveness, twice kicking dirt
into the guard and getting slaps in response.

"In here," the guard said, and shoved him into a small
office. There was an interrogator across the desk from him
and Craig stood at attention.'

"You are from Ohio, Craig Nostrum."

"My name is Craig Nostrum, serial number X38 00 68, I
am an E4, and I was born nine twenty-three forty-seven."

"I am being friendly, why are you not friendly? I am Major
Bu."

"My name is Craig Nostrum . . ." Craig spoke through the
familiar litany again, was knocked to the floor and dragged
out of the office to another small room. The guard forced him
inside a small black box where he had to fold himself to fit.

It was dark, uncomfortable, and Craig's bad knee throbbed
with pain. He could not change position at all and he felt
knotted and sore. He tried to empty his mind, to fantasize, but
it wouldn't work. He knew he was stuck in the place that he
had always feared most. The walls of the box seemed to close
in on him. He sweated profusely.

"That you, Craig?"

Craig looked at the air holes between his box and the one

beside it and saw a finger poke through. "Todd?"

"In the flesh. God, I hate the dark; silly, isn't it?"

"Not so silly, I'm going nutso in here."

"You okay, though?"

"My legs are killing me."

"Try to concentrate on relaxing. Do it easy. Think about floating and then think of each part of your body relaxing. Start with your feet and work your way upward. Just relax. Think about nothing except relaxing. Listen to a waterfall, or maybe a river rushing past. You're beginning to relax. Feel it. Feel your muscles loosening."

Craig listened to Todd's voice, felt himself feeling better, thought about Rocky River after a hard rain, the way it coursed and rolled.

Craig heard shouting, slaps, and finally silence, and knew he was alone again.

"What happened to Todd Carey?" Craig asked his interrogator.

"You will answer questions, not ask them."

"My country will not allow me to answer any questions."

"Would you like a cigarette?"

"Yes."

"Then tell me about yourself."

"My country will not allow me to answer questions."

"You are foolish." The man slapped Craig twice, then knocked him out of the chair and kicked his side. "We can do anything we want to you. Do you want to be hurt?"

"My name is Craig Nostrum . . ." Craig recited it all again and was hit again, and recited again.

"We already know where you are from. You will talk, you know. We can make you talk."

Craig stared without response, felt another fist to his head, and was finally dragged off back to the main compound.

The questioning seemed endless, but Craig could tell from the position of the sun that little time had actually passed, and the thought depressed him. Time seemed irrelevant already, something they had warned him about in class: but the teaching and learning did nothing to prepare him for the reality. He took a position on a small hillock to watch for enemy aircraft at the orders of a guard. By enemy, he knew that they meant

the U.S., and despite knowing this was all a parody, he began
to hope that he would see one.

"What happened?" Craig blinked from the semidarkness of
the bunker and accepted a sip of water from a tin can.

"You passed out. Heat stroke. Think you can save some of
this water? It might help some of the others if they can have
some. We can hide it here under the bunks."

Craig nodded to Todd. "You're okay?"

"Yeah. They slapped me around a little, put me back in the
box. Guess they know I hated it."

"Anybody cave in yet?"

"I heard one guy did. He just went nuts in the box and said
he'd sign anything they wanted."

"I just hope it wasn't a CT, we take enough shit as it is."

"A marine, I think. Just try to get some rest."

Night crawled over them with the same high cold wind as
the previous days. Craig was manacled to a barbecue where he
was preparing a meal for the guards. The aroma of the food
was tempting, dangerously so, he thought, but he did not give
in. Steak, beans, corn.

"Perhaps if you do good job we give you some."

"No thanks. Feed all of us."

"You fool. Others would do it."

"My name is Craig Nostrum—"

"Shut up, foolish American GI."

Every time the guard walked away, Craig bent with his
knees and tossed another handful of dust into the food. He
told himself that he shouldn't do it, that those men were just
doing their jobs, but he did it anyway. He did not spit into the
beans, though he thought of it. Behind him he listened to the
giggles of the guards, the sounds of soda cans being opened.
He tossed in more dirt.

"Everyone up, outside!"

The men were startled from sleep by the scream of orders.
Craig knew he had slept, but not for long. He rose groggily
and followed the others outside to form two ranks before the
bunker. He looked at the bright lights from the watchtowers
and the flickering of shadows in the barbed wire.

"We have been benevolent, but three of you have tried to

escape. They are being punished now. But still, we try. We are allowing your commander here to lead you in some entertainment so that you can feel more at home."

Sleep deprivation, another of the tricks. Craig thought about this, wondering how this would be in a real POW camp. He glanced around looking for Todd and finally asked one of the other men.

"He's back in the box. They caught him trying to crawl under the fence."

Craig nodded, ashamed that he had not been with him, angry that he wasn't asked.

The senior captured officer, Lieutenant Commander Graham stood atop the bunker and held up his arms. He began to sing in a soft voice, until everyone joined him and the music was a crescendo of "God Bless America."

The commandant began to yell at them to stop, and finally shoved Graham from the bunker into the dirt. The naval officer rose without help, but there was blood on his face and arms from the rocks.

Craig felt someone touch his shoulder and turned to see Todd Carey. "You asshole, you should've had me along."

"You already passed out once. Besides, it didn't work. Maybe all these trips to the box will be good for my psyche later."

"I heard two men did make it out, that true?"

"Three. Two squids and a grunt. They made it from the south end."

"Good," Craig said. He felt a sharp punch to his back, felt his arm twist backward, and was dragged off to the box again.

In midmorning it was over. The guards had turned from enemies to instructors, and the commandant replaced his khakis for a marine camouflauge uniform and major's insignias. They handed out coffee and cups of oatmeal.

"When you get back to Coronado your first urge will be to hit the geedunk and eat everything in sight. Don't. You're going to get sick. Your stomachs have shrunken up, and you need to eat a little at a time."

Craig sipped his coffee and handed his oatmeal to Todd.

"Eat that, you need food as much as any of us."

"I wouldn't eat oatmeal as a civilian, I sure won't eat it now."

"You've got to be starving, I still am."

"I'd rather starve than eat that shit. Have at it." Craig walked up and got a refill for coffee.

"Thanks, huh?"

"For what?"

"Everything, my man, every fucking thing." Todd said.

"You okay?"

Craig lifted his head from the cool porcelain of the toilet bowl and sighed. "I'd feel better if I just died."

Todd grinned. "They warned us. You were the one that insisted on eating two cheeseburgers, some fries, and a milk shake."

Craig gagged again and spit up into the toilet. "Don't remind me, huh?"

"We made it!"

"Yeah, Kemo Sabe. I guess I'm better at not listening than I am at listening, though. God, I feel like hell."

"But we made it!"

"That we did, Todd, that we did."

"Two beers and I already feel loopy." Craig clinked his mug against Todd's. "To making it."

"To making it," Todd repeated. "I hope they don't find out I'm really an officer. It feels strange to be in an EM club."

"Better than me trying to pass as an ossifer."

"Smile when you make fun of my brethren and me."

"I will. You're really an okay guy."

"Just doing what I can to make enlisted pukes feel at home."

"Keep it up and wear some beer, matey."

"No way."

"Keep in touch, huh?"

"Sure. I'll give you my parents' address and they can forward mail until I get settled in."

"Same here."

"You'll write, promise?"

"Promise."

Craig climbed aboard the airliner at Travis Air Force Base, his orders pressed in his right hand. He looked at the terminal, at the others who were aboard. Their destination was Clark

Air Base in the Philippines, and beyond there each would take his own direction.

Craig's last view of California was from an airplane window that showed the brown hills and the blue surf of San Francisco bay.

Chapter 6

A single paved road, a half-dozen bars, a sari-sari store, two brightly painted and bejeweled jeepneys, two shore patrolmen: the barrio of San Miguel was that small, and seeing it for the first time Craig thought that he must not yet be there, it seemed so insignificant. The rest of the village sprawled out on dirt roads: nipa huts, small cement-block houses, carefully tended flowers, gardens, trees, and, beyond the village, the bright white strip of beach that ran for miles along the island of Luzon. Unlike most of the barrios there was no cathedral in San Miguel, and the closest was the cinder-block Catholic church in San Antonio.

The barrio had begun as a small fishing village, and the original thatched huts remained as decaying ruins near the water. When the base was built, the village began to sprout in response. The bars, some owned by Filipinos, others by Americans who had remained behind when their tours of duty were over, were so close to one another that they seemed a single entity, though each fought competitively for the sailors that took liberty there. The names of these bars became familiar easily: The Nautilus, the Playboy, the RRB, the Pink Club, the New Jungle Place.

The jeepneys, so gaily decorated, had been army jeeps during the world war, and had become the most common form of transportation, something less and more than a taxi. You could hire a jeepney by the mile, the city, or the day. The drivers were maniacs that used their horns as a common language between them. Besides the jeepneys and the gray navy vehicles, there were no cars in San Miguel, and the most common form of hauling market goods was still a cart drawn by a lazy, huge carabao, the Asian oxen.

Everyone, including the Filipinos called this place the crossroads, or more often simply the Roads.

Jesus Obrego, called Jesse by his friends, was a man who wanted nothing more than to find a way to get rich amid the wealth of the Americans. He ran numbers and errands, rented his carabao out for picture-taking sessions, had even offered to arrange for broken kneecaps and other injuries for an appropriate sum. At the moment he was working as a bouncer at the New Jungle Place and wore a UCLA T-shirt and Levi's sent to him by a cousin in San Francisco. He stopped at the table, solicitous as was his nature, and inquired, "Do you want another San Magoo beer?"

Craig nodded and accepted another cold San Miguel beer from Jesus and thought that everything here, even the beer, was steeped in mythology: everyone passed the same rumor, that MacArthur and his family owned the brewery and the bus lines called Victory Liners. This story was repeated so often that it had become the known truth, despite being erroneous. Everyone said MacArthur had received these companies as gifts for his having saved the Philippines. "Have you bought your jeepney yet?" Craig asked. He knew that Jesse wanted a jeepney more than anything—that he considered this would be his first step in becoming a somebody in Zambales Province.

"Not yet, maybe soon." Jesus wiped the table with a rag. "Do you need protection?"

"Not that I know of."

"Many times marines get drunk and they beat up CT sailors. Ask around and you find Jesus gives number-one protection and number-one payback. Half-price for you."

"No thanks," Craig said, and waved a hand toward Gerry Norton as his friend walked through the door. "Get another cold one, okay?"

"Ziggy now, Craig, chop chop." Jesus laughed and walked to the bar to get the beer.

"What's new, *kaibegan*?" Gerry asked, and slumped into a chair at the table. He thanked Jesus for the beer when it arrived and told him to put it on Craig's tab.

"Not much. Roger's pretty hard on the old ego. All the schools before now seem easy compared to this."

"None of the others really make a difference. This is what we really do." Gerry looked at a bargirl named Felie and smiled. "She is a knockout. I tried my best to get her to bed, but she says she waits for a husband. Lucky one, no doubt."

"Will I ever catch on to this shit Roger teaches?" Craig asked and ordered two more beers by signaling with his fingers.

"Yeah, it gets easier, just make sure you get it down pat, because we always need good lingies in Da Nang."

"You think that's where I should go?"

"You don't have much choice. It's up to Roger and the powers that be, but it beats the shit out of being sent to some tin-can destroyer that bobs around the Gulf of Tonkin."

"You really like it, huh?"

"What's not to like? Booze, beer, beaches, the only thing missing is broads, and it seems like every time I find one of them here, I end up dripping with clap."

"Who was it this time?"

"The numbers compel me to say who knows or even gives a flying fuck. I don't mind being so easy, I just wish they'd wear neon flashing signs that say Clap Here."

Craig laughed, wishing he were through with classes and finally doing a real job. He thought about Roger Tripp, his teacher, mentor, perhaps his friend. Roger was small and had dark bright eyes that darted endlessly and seldom settled on anyone or anything for more than a few seconds. Roger, who was Gerry's friend, and who told so many conflicting tales about his past that no one knew which one was the right one: he was rich, he was an orphan, he was from Cincinnati or he was from Carmel, California. "How long before I get out of here?"

"This bar? Depends on when you get tired of warm beer. The PI? Then it's up to Roger. A few weeks, I guess. I was here for six weeks. I leave for Da Nang tomorrow again."

"I guess that was another lie, that we wouldn't end up in Vietnam," Craig said softly, looking to see if anyone was listening.

"That's the easy part. The real lie is how long you stay.

You know that after thirteen months you can rotate home, right? Well, we get assigned to Da Nang as TDY duty, so we come back here every three or six months for a couple of days and so our time in-country never adds up to thirteen months. Real bitch, huh?"

"Really?" Craig smoked his cigarette and thought about this. "How long can we be there?"

"Jenkins has been there more than two years. Laurence, the guy you met at NSA, was here for almost three years. He didn't get home until he was ready for discharge."

Craig was surprised at the changes in Gerry since Monterey: he was louder, more boisterous, more confident. He sipped his beer and listened to the jukebox blare out "Hey Jude" in what seemed an endless repetition. "You mean we could just stay there?"

"Give the boy a cigar. For us, getting home in thirteen months is just another of the great lies: the check's in the mail, I'll respect you in the morning, and I won't come in your mouth." Gerry grinned. "You can even add a couple of more: I love you no shit, Joe, and I don't have VD clap, GI."

"Guess I have a lot to learn."

"So did I. But you do learn it."

Craig wondered about the drunken good-bye party he and Roger had thrown for Gerry, whether feeling this bad was worth it, but he forced it from his mind and tried to think about the lessons at hand.

"Everything we've been going over up until now has been easy, a review, now we get serious." Roger stared over his students' heads, made a slight gesture that resembled a shrug, and an eraser exploded chalk dust over the back wall of the classroom. "From now on, it's *chu y canh gioi*. Pay attention and be alert. You've seen that the lingies have a kind of GAF, give-a-fuck attitude. That's fine when you've already made it. Now, *you* can't afford it. We are here for one reason only, and that's to save American pilots. You do this well and you can piss on the captain's grass. You fuck it up and you'll be chipping paint over the side of a rusty tin can for the rest of your fucking days. Did I make myself clear?"

Jack Brady raised his hand and asked the question each of them had asked since the beginning: "What exactly will we be doing?"

Roger stared at each of them individually, his eyes as hard

as stones, then looked back to the wall. "We listen in on the North Vietnamese communications system. There are two separate protocols: tac/air and SAM. You've already been taught about single-channel and multi-channel. You either listen to a single voice, or to multiple speakers. Tac/air is single-channel, SAM is multi-channel. You make part of the choice of which job you do, but most of it rests with your talent, and fate, and what we need at the time, and if you get along with the 'old guys,' like me. 'Old guys' is a term that represents the men that have been there and done the job and done it well. You might think it's a clique, but it's a way of life and it works. Senior men are the ones that have paid their dues and they know what's up."

"Eat shit," someone said from the back of the room.

"Get it out of your system, asshole. Tomorrow's fuck-up might cost some flyboy his life." Roger paced the front of the room and pointed to a chart he had hung on the blackboard. "Tac/air operators listen in on the communications system of the North Vietnamese Air Force. They work alone. They listen and they translate it immediately to paper; we call that transcribing. On the flight there is an evaluator, an officer in charge who watches what's happening and sends out spot reports when necessary. SAM operators listen to two channels, and they work as a duo. One man listens to the tracking side of the surface-to-air missile sites, and the other listens and translates the multiple voices that we consider the control segment of a launch. He has to know each voice well enough to identify it with a letter of the alphabet; there can be as many as ten or twelve speakers at a time. While all of this is going on there are ditty boppers, Morse-code operators that are copying the grid coordinates of all aircraft over North Vietnam. There's a plotter who is drawing all these flights, at least the important ones, on a map; there are T-branchers, radar intercept operators who are recording radar signals from the North Vietnamese; and an O-brancher who sits in his spaces and sends out messages at the evaluator's direction. So there's lots happening in a small world. You have to be good to handle it."

Craig raised his hand. "Can we translate all of this fast enough?"

"Not really, but we use abbreviations, codes, shorthand. We catch the gist of what's happening and that's what matters."

"How do we know all this?"

"You learn it. You just do it. It happens." Roger held up his hand. "Now you get a twenty-minute break. When you come back I bust your balls. Have fun while you can."

Craig walked to Roger while the others filed out of the room. "You sounded like Billy Sunday."

"Don't confuse that we're friends with your performance here. The two issues are mutually exclusive. From here on out it's strictly the best man."

Jack Brady smoked under the rustling fronds of a palm tree. He looked at Craig from half-crossed eyes and smirked. "You sucking up to Roger like you did those zip teachers in Monterey?"

Craig lit his own cigarette and frowned. "And other than that how was the play, Mrs. Lincoln?"

"What kind of asshole comment is that?"

"Just that you always look for the bad side, Jack, and sometimes there just isn't one."

"You always thought you were a hot shit in Monterey, but that won't happen here."

"I never thought of being a hot shit at all."

"Don't think you're so good."

"Fuck off, Jack, just fuck off."

Roger, intense, walked to the blackboard, strutted like a martinet. "We've taught you to speak Vietnamese, and now you have to learn to think in Vietnamese. But keep one thing in mind: no matter how Vietnamese things sound, it's basically the Russian air-defense system. Don't ever lose sight of that. Those pilots, those MiG controllers, those SAM site officials, are all Russian with epicanthic folds in their eyes."

"Russian," Brady said. "Fucking Russkies."

Roger shook his head. "Everything they do is based on the Russian systems and the Russian order of battle. The enciphered grid systems that they use to track our planes, the commands they use to fire missiles, the structured ground-controlled intercepts they use to attack our planes with their fighters—all of these are from the Russians. GCI is ground-controlled intercept, a MiG fighter sent after one of ours, right? A GCA is ground-controlled approach, a ground tower is guiding a landing for an NVN airplane. That could be a MiG or an IL-28 light bomber, or a passenger plane. If you

end up in Da Nang, at Det Tango you'll have access to a lot of
material, MiG manuals, situation reports, you need to use
them." Roger slapped a tape into a recorder. "Put on the earphones on your desk and write down everything you can from
what you hear. Use abbreviations if you want. In fact, I'd
recommend it."

Roger stopped the tape and pointed at Jack Brady. "What
did you hear?"
    "Hoi an bao nhieu, hoi an 310."
    "What's it mean?"
    "I don't know, we just started."
    Craig raised his hand. "What is your heading, heading
310."
    Roger nodded, "The NVN Air Force has this bad habit of
using the same or similar cover names for all of their functions
and they think somehow it might fool someone. They usually
use *ca fee* for fuel. *Toc do* for speed. Listen to the rest of the
tape and do the best you can."
    Brady glared at Craig Nostrum, and Craig flipped him the
middle finger of his left hand.

The days of class passed like volleys of words: Roger
pitched in Vietnamese, the students returned his serve in English. Each day differed from the one before it in the com-
plexity of the assignment, in the details, in the fact that the
tapes they listened to had more static to interfere with their
translations. Roger was tough on each of them.
    "The SAM sites, SA-2s, are controlled from a van that is
equipped with radar. The thing to remember is that they can
shoot down any fighter or bomber that we have."
    Craig looked up from his notes. "Does that mean we have
some planes other than fighters and bombers that aren't vulnerable to SAMs?"
    Roger laughed. "I phrased that wrong or you picked up on
it too fast. Anything other than the planes you know about
now will become important only after you've been assigned to
a duty station. Don't ask questions."
    After the assignment of listening to and copying the
traffic from a SAM site tape, Roger stood over Craig's
shoulder and said he had it wrong. "There's four speakers
and you show six different voices. Listen to the ca-

dence of the language first and then the voices."

"I thought I did," Craig said. "This is a bitch."

"Welcome to the real world," Roger replied.

"You're really going to be good at tac/air," Roger said, and sipped his rum collins. He turned his head and watched as men fed dimes into the slot machines. The machines dinged their responses in losing and winning. "You might be one of the best."

Craig nodded, puffed his chest out as if it mattered. "I hope so."

"It's up to you now."

"It always has been, huh?"

Roger grinned. "Always."

After the examination, the class was quiet. "You'll know by your scores if you are performing well enough," Roger said as he handed back the papers. "This should tell you whether or not you have a tin ear. If it doesn't then someone else will let you know. We need good linguists, but we can't handle any hammers."

"God, there's a lot of static on this tape. How're we supposed to hear through this?"

"There's always some grass on the tapes. Listen *through* it. You concentrate and hear the rhythm of the words. Pick a word, a phrase, pick it out. That's how you do it." Roger rewound the tape and began again.

The first voice Craig heard he did not understand at all and wrote down *XG*, the acronym of an unlimited number of garbled words. For the next phrase he scrawled out his English transcription and made two phonetic notes to represent Vietnamese words that he didn't know. Suddenly, like a satori, he realized that he loved this work.

Roger turned off the tape and walked behind each man and reviewed his hand log. He offered comments, some kind and some biting; to Craig he said only that he could do better next time. "Now I play it again, and try harder. *Listen!*"

Bill Albert and Smith Goodrum were gone now, and Craig missed them. He had met them at the recreation center, and they had bowled and drank and kidded together. He sagged into his chair at the pool and wished they were still beside him. He spread out on a chaise lounge and splashed some of Jesse's special coconut oil across his chest and belly and legs.

"The R-beats thought they pulled one over on us by getting the day shift." Jack Brady smiled and helped himself to Craig's suntan lotion. "Ditty boppers don't have any sense at all."

"Nobody does," Craig replied. He couldn't imagine being a ditty bopper, an R-beat, himself. He couldn't think of listening to an endless blip of dots and dashes for Morse code that meant nothing until plotted on a map. He thought about the R-beats and wondered how they ever stayed sane at all. All those dots. At least in listening to voice traffic you knew what was going on. Too much so, perhaps.

He ordered his first beer of the day though it was only ten A.M.

Nitz worked at the enlisted men's club—the Starlight Club—and Craig had slowly come to be her friend. It was because he had become her friend, and the friend of her brother Efram, that he now found himself seated on the porch of their house in the barrio and drinking a glass of a potent Filipino wine.

The house was of a bright reddish wood that Craig would have called rosewood, but was not sure at all if this was right. Bright flowers bloomed in the gardens that spread in circles from the front of the house to the gazebo.

"We are pleased you can visit," her father said.

"Thank you, sir," Craig answered. "I can't believe how beautiful your country is. I've never seen so much white sand."

"It is so. We have much to be proud of here. But soon the rains come and they are bad rains. I can feel it."

"More rains?"

"Monsoon rains. They will come with the wind. It is this way here."

"A storm?" Craig asked.

"Typhoon," Mr. Abaya said resolutely. "A big typhoon come soon."

"When?"

"Tomorrow? The day after? Typhoons come in their own time. But they do bad things."

* * *

Rain fell all that night and into the morning. Mr. Abaya was right; a typhoon was coming and heading in fast. Classes and liberty were cancelled and everyone was confined to base.

Typhoon Emma.

The speakers in the barracks announced the secure situation and then began calling out names to report to the master-at-arms shack, the officer of the day's office downstairs. "The following names lay down to the master-at-arms shack," the voice said.

"That's you, buddy."

Craig looked at Jack Brady. "Huh?"

"They just called our names. Better move it out."

"Bullshit." Craig lowered himself from his bunk and trekked down the stairs behind Brady.

Chief Masters, a short, chubby chief petty officer with sandy receding hair, stood in the center of the hallway and looked at the men he had assembled. "You men are going to get out there and secure everything that you see break loose tonight. If it doesn't salute, then you nail it down, hold it, or bring it back in the truck. This is a real bitch of a storm coming."

Craig nodded, rubbed his nose.

"You trying to be funny, boy?"

Craig looked at the chief, at his round bovine face, and laughed. "Not here, Chief."

"What's that mean?" Chief Masters knew Nostrum was a linguist, and he considered them his personal penance though he could not understand why he deserved this. "You just do what I say when I say it."

"No problem, Chief."

"We have to protect the lives and property on this base. Nothing is too good for our men."

"And nothing is what we get," Craig answered.

"You trying to be funny, boy?"

"Just commenting that this is a stupid maneuver."

"What do you *do*, boy?"

Craig grinned. "My job, Chief, what do *you* do?"

Masters face reddened and he shouted for the men to stop laughing. "You, you, you," he stammered. "You, you, you . . ."

Craig nodded, took Jack Brady's elbow, and walked outside to the truck they were supposed to use.

"You really screwed that up," Jack Brady said once they were in the gray truck.

"What?" The wind and rain were so loud that Craig wasn't sure what he had heard. "He's a jerk."

"Causing trouble isn't going to make this any easier."

"It was nothing."

"Bullshit. You pissed him off."

Craig sagged into the passenger's seat and groaned.

A tree limb smacked the hood and bounced.

"Great driving, sport," Craig said.

"Do it yourself, then," Jack said as he pulled over to the curb.

"Fine," Craig said, "I've got to be better than you."

Craig liked driving better than riding in the storm. They stopped and pulled debris from the yards, secured what they could against the winds and rains. Soaked and tired, they moved from one area to the next.

Shingles stripped from roofs by the winds cracked against the truck like bullets. Trash cans banged and buffeted around the grounds.

Twice they stopped to pull tree limbs from the road and set them to the side.

They rode in silence for the most part, occasionally gossiping of one thing or another.

"I'll get it." Jack walked toward a trash can that had broken loose and become flattened against a palm tree.

"Look out!" Craig jumped out of the truck and shoved Jack down as a tree limb ripped free and hit him a glancing blow to the shoulder and the left cheek of his face.

"Thanks," Jack said. "You're bleeding." He looked at Craig's cheek. "You got cut."

"I know, I can taste the blood. Let's get out of here." Craig took a handerkerchief from his pocket and held it over his cheek and climbed back in the truck. "This is nuts to have people out in this."

"Masters wants all lingies dead, but doesn't want to take the fall for murder. This is his next best option. Notice that only lingies were assigned to this shit." "Yeah. And you're number one on his list.

Khong dam, Craig said, saying the 'Thank you' carefully to avoid his earlier mistake of saying 'Don't fart.'

*　*　*

"The chief sure does have a hard-on for you," Roger remarked over a rum collins. Four drinks were in front of each of them at happy-hour prices. Behind them was the *chinkachinkachink* of the slot machines that swallowed and vomited dimes. On the jukebox someone had played Janis Ian's "Society's Child" for the third time straight.

"Just part of my charm," Craig replied. He mused over the deteriorating relationship with Chief Masters, but found no way to alter it. They had fought from the first introduction; each seemed as committed as the other in pushing back and forth.

"Mindless behavior is expected here, tolerated, just don't let it interfere in the work," Roger pursed his lips. "I heard you were out chasing the bargirls the other night."

"International-relations seminar I was conducting."

"I thought you would be better than the rest of them, but I thought the same of Gerry. I think man is supposed to be better than that. Moral man. Human nature seldom fails to disappoint me."

"It's the way things are here. I'm no worse than anyone else."

"Have you read *No Exit* by Sartre yet?"

Craig shrugged, embarrassed by the question, and the lecture on behavior. "No, haven't had time."

"Not with all those international relations to worry about, right?"

"I'm sorry, okay? I'll read it soon, I promise."

"You can leave this experience better than when you came into it. You've already read more good books than you were exposed to in that podunk town you were raised in," Roger spoke petulantly, glared at Craig, and finally returned to his drink and recounting of a story about Andy Jenkins and how he had caught one of the first MiG-21 flights out of Phuc Yen airfield in North Vietnam. He repeated the story in hushed tones, careful to stop whenever one of the Filipino waiters or a stranger came near the table.

"*Salamit Po*," Craig said to Nitz, and pushed the empty bowl away from his place at the table.

"You're doing well with Tagalog," she said.

"You're doing even better with your English."

"I have done this longer."

"Thank you." Craig accepted the beer and took a long

swallow. The enlisted men's club was nearly deserted at this hour, and he and Nitz always practiced their mutual language lessons before class while he ate. "Have you read the book I gave you?"

"I did not like it. The pony dies. It is sad."

"Steinbeck is a good writer. I like his books."

"But next time I want something happier, okay?"

"Sure."

"Did you read the story I gave you?"

"No."

"You do not like romances, right?"

"Right," Craig answered.

"Next time I bring you a scary one. We like love stories and ghost stories, too."

Chief Masters had his arms behind his back and rocked front to back from toe to heel. His uniform was as tight as a sausage casing against his stomach. "I hear you've been hanging around with Huks, Nostrum."

"I have some Filipino friends, but they're not Huks. Huks are Philippine communists. There's a big difference, Chief. Besides, the Huk movement was crushed by Magsaysay."

"I don't need a history lesson from you of all people. I'm telling you that it's not a good move to hang around with them, whatever you call them. There are more spies and creeps here than anywhere in Asia."

"They're my friends and they aren't spies."

"Fraternization looks bad on the old report card. Loose lips sink ships."

"And a stitch in time saves nine," Craig answered.

"You getting smart with me, boy?"

"Chief, my opinion is that getting smart with you wouldn't be fair at all."

"I don't like you now, and I'm getting to like you less every day."

"I grow on people, Chief, honest." Craig walked away and controlled his urge to throw a punch.

"You're drinking too much," Efram said. "Too many drinks bad for you, bad for me, too. Club say no let sailors get too drunk."

"Just bring me another one."

"You have class tonight."

"I know." Even as he knew he was getting troubled, Craig could not identify or name its source. The drinking helped him calm down.

Two weeks later Craig stood at a urinal and another man, a stranger, stood beside him. He smiled. Craig finished urinating, glanced at the stranger again, and ran from the barracks. He could think of no reason, and when he looked behind him there was no one, but he was sure that this man was after him. Craig finally dodged into the dugout at the baseball diamond, curled himself into a fetal position, and fell into a troubled sleep.

Even though he was embarrassed by the tears, Craig could not stop crying. His hand trembled, and he pressed them both under his buttocks to still them. The corpsman told him that a doctor would be along in a few minutes, and left him alone in an office.

The room was small, and a gecko lizard sang on the screened window. Craig stared at the framed diploma on the wall, at the cluttered desk.

"I'm Doctor Paulson."

"I don't know what's wrong. I'm nervous, I'm hallucinating, I can't stop crying. I can't control myself at all."

"You're looking for a psycho, right?"

"No sir. I can't sleep, I just want to be back to normal."

"I've heard most of the dodges before, you know. I don't fall for all of that. I've seen every screwball trick in the world, Petty Officer . . ." He leaned to the medical chart, "Nostrum."

"I just want some help, something to calm me down."

"Think it's easy to bluff a doctor, that's the way most of them think."

"I want some fucking help!"

Craig was screaming one moment, and the next found himself sprawled onto the floor, his face still sore from where the lieutenant made contact with his fist.

Paulson stood over him. "You were hysterical. It isn't going to work, no discharge from me. I'll give you some tranquilizers, but remember this: Every time you take one, you are admitting you can't hack it and that you need a crutch.

You are a cripple as long as you swallow them."

"Yes," Craig whispered.

The doctor tossed a vial of pills at him. "Now get out of my sight."

Craig was sprawled across the floor of the shower still clothed and the cold water was pounding on him. He blinked and saw Roger Tripp standing over him. "What happened?"

"You sure you want to know?"

"Please."

"Let's see if I can reconstruct it; you took a couple of pills, then you got drunk, then you broke a glass in your right hand. About this time you gave the rest of the pills to Efram to throw away and started shouting that you weren't a cripple. That was the point where you ran out of the club with Efram shouting for you to go to the dispensary. Then, still drunk and bleeding profusely from your finger, you came to class, prayed blood all over the wall and Chief Master's desk, and proceeded to sit down and listen to a tape. You copied and translated the whole thing. No one else could figure it out, and you know why? It was Russian. Am I going too fast for you?"

Craig closed his eyes, remembered only the pills.

"Then you got put on report, and then you proceeded to tell all of us to fuck ourselves, and then I hauled you back here and threw you under the water about twenty-five minutes ago. Why in the hell didn't you tell me you were having some kind of troubles?"

Craig shook his head. "I didn't know what kind they were."

"You ever try any LSD, any of the other hallucinogenics?"

"No. This was just weird. I was paranoid and scared and I kept crying and Paulson slugged me. Shit, I don't know what's going on, myself. I want to get out of here."

"I'll see what I can do."

Craig leaned his head against the tiles. "Please get me orders, just get me orders. I know I can do the job and I need to get involved in something."

"Det Tango needs a lingie, and I can probably swing it by telling the executive officer that he can save himself a captain's mast by shipping you out. But if you fuck up, you leave me hung out to dry and your ass is grass."

"I can do it. I won't let you down. Just get me out of here, please?"

Roger shook his head, his voice soft. "Okay. You get cleaned up and pack and I'll get working on it. For Chrissakes get your head screwed on straight."

FLIGHT ORDERS FOR THE WEEK

ALPHA CREW	BRAVO CREW
CRAIG NOSTRUM	DAMON ARNEAULT
WILLY AMES	STEVE MARSHALL
GERRY NORTON	GARY KRAFT
TED TRAINER	GEORGE LEWIS

CHARLIE CREW	DELTA CREW
TIM MCELROY	ALAN ERICKSON
JACK BRADY	BOB LEIDNER
RAFAEL GARENA	JERRY EMERICK
TOM LABINSKI	DANNY BASKINS

ALPHA CREW: EARLY, EARLY, EARLY, OFF, LATE

BRAVO CREW: AFTERNOON, AFTERNOON, LATE, LATE, OFF

CHARLIE CREW: LATE, OFF, OFF, AFTERNOON, EARLY

DELTA CREW: OFF, LATE, AFTERNOON, EARLY, AFTERNOON

PREFLIGHT BRIEFINGS AS SCHEDULED;

EARLY 0515

AFTERNOON 1315

LATE 2100

COVERS MUST BE WORN AT ALL TIMES. NON
MILITARY ISSUE TEE SHIRTS ARE NOT TO BE
WORN WITH UNIFORMS OR FLIGHT SUITS.
THERE WILL BE NO SKIPPING, REPEAT, NO
SKIPPING ON THE FLIGHT LINE.

BY ORDER

JOHN M. BREWSTER, LCDR, USNR
OFFICER IN CHARGE
DETACHMENT TANGO
DA NANG, REPUBLIC OF VIETNAM

Chapter 7

When Craig Nostrum first arrived in Da Nang it was 108 degrees and he was wearing the only set of combat fatigues he owned: they hung off him and sagged in the seat and bore another man's name over the left breast pocket; he had been given them at the last possible moment at Cubi Point, before his plane took off. Two months later, he was dressed in a gray flight suit he had bought black-market in Da Nang, jungle boots, an Aussie go-to-hell hat with the brims snapped to the sides of the crown, and he was already the senior tac/air man on Alpha crew.

Though the Vietnamese believed in the stars and fates with the same fervency that Calvinists attached to predestination, Craig thought his elevation to be a combination of his talent and hard work, as well as the capriciousness that he already associated with this place. One lingie had become ill, another gave up his clearance to marry a bargirl in Olongapo, and still another had received a hardship discharge due to a family illness. He walked down the worn path that led to the flight apron where they had their flight shack and the planes were parked in revetments. To the right he could see the barnlike structure that served as the terminal for the Fifteenth Aerial Port. He glanced at a line of new arrivals: newbies, FNGs—Fucking New Guys—that staggered from the surprise of the heat. He recalled what that moment had been like for himself and turned left over a dirt embankment.

Even after his thirty-fourth flight the planes still seemed too ungainly to actually fly at all, let alone fly ten-to twelve-hour missions off the coast of North Vietnam. They were Super Constellations, super connies, designated as EC-121M's by the navy. Once the flagship planes for TWA, the fuselages had been distended with huge radar domes on the tops and bellies. They were painted dark gray and white. He nodded good-morning to the ground crews; they grunted replies or ignored him and continued to gas up the planes and make minor repairs and adjustments. Everyone knew that these planes were kept flying by the ingenuity of the ground crews; that and a combination of spit, sweat, chewing gum, and baling wire.

Craig walked toward the dilapidated shanty called the flight shack where they held their preflight briefings and an occasional meeting. Like everything operated by Detachment Tango, it was in disrepair and an embarrassment. Touching the brass air-crew wings on his chest he felt a momentary bewilderment at being in Vietnam at all still. Take a right, and there you end up, ten thousand miles from home. He had been hauled into the maw of the navy, and now they sent him from one place to the next with sets of flimsy ammonia-scented orders that were now the engine to his life. He was just as surprised that he had already been promoted to petty officer second class, this time without the required exam. The tests were waived in the war zone. The promotions were sarcastically called Ho Chi Minhs. Other than these innocuous symbols of rank and air-crew status, he wore nothing that identified either his unit or himself. That had been a lesson taught early on: don't wear anything that will identify you as security group, as intelligence; the VC love to get intelligence people.

Across the field he watched Mai Linh, their house girl, walking toward the barracks with another Vietnamese woman.

Mai Linh smiled and exposed her black betelnut-stained teeth. Her age was impossible to determine. She stood at a halfway point with her friend Phuong and gossiped of things great and small: the peccadilloes of the Americans, which of the house girls were thought to be sleeping around, the portents of future events revealed in their tea leaves, her astrological charts. "These men are different," she said at last. She

smoked a Salem cigarette which she cupped in her right hand.
"Some of them speak Vietnamese with a Hanoi accent, I think
that they are spies."

They were, in fact, spies: but of a small and curious ilk.
Detachment Tango had been one of the first Naval Security
Group units in Vietnam. It was, for the most part, unheard of
by most of the men on the sprawling air base. When infre-
quent visitors arrived, and new men, someone from the det
always met them, otherwise they could not have found even
the compound, and certainly not the barracks.

Mai Linh continued, "They are crazy. I think that they have
great secrets and it is the secrets that make them crazy."

Craig Nostrum rubbed his cheekbones, but it did nothing to
relieve the dull ache of his sinuses. He was acutely aware of
his own fatigue. He was startled by the sudden scream of an
F4 taking off over the bay, a sharp screech amidst the normal
noises of war: the *thwup, thwup, thwup* of helicopter blades,
the grumble of artillery fire, the sputtering of endless machines that coughed to life.

"Morning glory."

Craig looked at Gerry Norton. "It's got to be a hundred
degrees already." He blotted his forehead on his sleeve. He
left a damp, oily smudge that bore tracks of the red clay dust
that was welded to his skin by sweat. "Does it always have to
be this hot?"

"No, we have two choices, hot and dry, or wet and cold, or
maybe sometimes hot and wet and dusty all at once." Gerry lit
a cigarette and smoked silently for a second. "That's what
gives this place all of its charm."

There was a crackle of small-arms fire but neither of the
two men bothered to look in the direction of shooting. "Probably a sniper," Craig said.

"Or some crazy-assed marines. I think half of the sniper
fire we take is from marines."

"Good morning, Viet-fucking-nam."

Craig was glad that when he finally got a crew, he had been
assigned with Gerry and Ted Trainer. Their shared past at language school, their friendship, seemed a bridge from his pre-
history to his present.

At last Craig nudged open the door and stepped inside, past
a sign that declared AUTHORIZED PERSONNEL ONLY—DE-
TACHMENT TANGO, DA NANG, REPUBLIC OF VIETNAM, HOME

OF THE BIG EYE SPOOKS. They had a logo, a ghost with bat wings on an orange field, but they hadn't found anyone to paint it on the door: it adorned coffee mugs and lighters and cloth patches that were mailed home or buried in the corners of their lockers.

Inside, they walked to the coffee urn and helped themselves to the freshly brewed coffee. Overhead, two old fans, left behind by the French, were set to *moins vite* and lazily stirred the air.

Craig filled his mug, the logo also lettered with his operator sign, Charlie November. "You want some?"

"Why not? I like to live dangerously. Besides, I like to look at the little rainbows in the oil slick."

Gerry's cup bore the name Giveme Nooky. It was not an authorized op sign, but he used it anyway.

Ted Trainer charged through the front door, whirled in a tight circle, and snapped his purple cape through the air. Tufts of curly black hair stuck out from beneath his leather World War One flying helmet.

"Nice entrance, Ted," Craig said, "Nice cape, too."

"It's the rage in the spying circles in Paris this year. I think MACV is going to adopt it for all of I Corps."

Gerry shook his head. "Someday they're going to bring in the butterfly nets and there you go."

"Spoken like a true troglodyte. Have you been taking lessons from Chief Masters and Chief Grady again?"

"No way, they miss you too much to even pay attention to me."

They sat down and listened to the preflight briefing with practiced inattention.

Lieutenant Commander John Brewster, the officer in charge, OIC, of the unit walked to the podium and leaned on the lecturn. "Okay, men, it's busy time again today. There will be Rolling Thunder strikes at oh eight hundred and ten hundred hours. Objectives will be southeast of Hanoi."

"Escalation! I love it!" Ted clapped his hands. "Go! Go! Go!"

"Settle down." Brewster's weariness was evident. "Some of you noticed that we had our sleep interrupted by an attack last night, and some of you may have noticed that a person or persons unknown took that opportunity to nail Lieutenant Ferris in the officer's outhouse. I ask you, was that a military thing to do?"

"Probably the VC," Craig offered.

"Nostrum, I have it on pretty good authority that the VC do not nail junior officers in the shitter."

"It's a new tactic. I'm thinking of writing a situation report on it."

"Don't bother, I'll wait for the *Reader's Digest* version, okay? Just lay off him for a while. That's an order not a request."

Ted shrugged. "I just want to know who let him out."

"Not me," Craig said. "I put two extra nails in it."

The air in the room was stifling despite the fans. Smoke roiled like a thick, city haze. Craig rolled his white, lucky stone between his fingers, his good-luck charm. He would, like the others, deny his superstitions, but like the others he held them as tightly as to a life raft.

"Settle down. If you would cooperate a little, and behave in the slightest manner as if you understood this was a military unit, it would make our long stay here seem just a little bit shorter." He waved his hands in dismissal. "Have a good flight."

Craig, Gerry, and Ted linked arms and began to skip across the runway toward the waiting plane.

"No skipping!" Brewster yelled.

"Would you rather we shot the moon?" Ted asked.

"Just go, and have a safe one." One more time, Brewster thought.

"You're cute when you're angry, Commander," Craig shouted, and clicked his heels in the air.

Brewster watched his men momentarily, feeling parental, thinking that there was some part of the ritual that he had forgotten, but unsure of what it was, he turned to the truck and the duty driver that waited for him. He saw Commander Lewis, one of their pilots, walking toward him, and jumped into the passenger's seat and told the driver to step on it. He knew he didn't need another lecture about military behavior this morning.

Alpha crew boarded the aircraft. Besides the four linguists, there were thirty other men. There were Morse code operators, an O-brancher who sent and received their classified messages in a tiny cubbyhole with a curtain that was supposed to represent a security wall for the secrets, a Korean linguist that handled the occasional North Korean pilots and spent most of his time plotting the tracking of the airplanes over

North Vietnam on a map, an officer who served as the evaluator—basically the OIC of the crew—and beyond the men from Det Tango lay the various personnel of *VQI* that served in capacities from pilot and navigator, to cook, to the banks of T-branchers who copied and interpreted the various radar signals that the North Vietnamese used.

The men filed onto the super conny without any order whatsoever.

Inside, even without the crew, the plane seemed crowded by the large banks of sophisticated electronics equipment. The equipment made the plane more than a ton overweight, and it required every inch of runway to become airborne. Craig had been on two flights when they did not make it off the ground. Once a careless pilot had sheared the tip off the wing by hitting a crane; the other time the plane just couldn't gather enough airspeed and had rolled from the end of the runway into a ditch. Both times they had had to get out of the bird hand-over-hand down a rope.

Craig took his position, number seven, the traditional seat for the senior tac/air man, and strapped himself into his seat. He clapped his earphones over his ears, tuned one of his radios to AFRTS, the Armed Forces Radio and Television Network and heard the disk jockey begin with his traditional greeting, "Gooood morning, Vietnam." While he listened to music he checked his equipment. He loaded a tape in each of his two recorders, set one earphone to each of his two radios, made sure the recording speed was set to fifteen inches per second. He spun the radio dials one at a time to make sure that his left ear was hooked to the radio and the right ear to the bottom. This was habit, and habits became important when things got busy: he knew this.

The plane made noises, settling sounds, odd squeaks. The sounds comforted Craig: he knew these planes intimately; he knew each creak, groan, and complaint.

Across the aisle, a radar intercept operator, a T-brancher, stared at the lifeless eye of his oscilloscope and finally smashed his hand against it. The screen blinked with an eerie green at once. "Part of our delicate training program."

Craig grinned back. "I want to use hammers next time."

The plane turned and lumbered down the runway.

Airborne, the smoking lamp lit, men scuttled and shoved their way past one another to get coffee, take a leak in the benjo, stretch, or just gossip for the twenty minutes they would fly before they reached their position "on track." "On track" was an elliptical pattern off the coast of North Vietnam where they circled for eight to ten hours on each flight. There were three planes normally operational and they usually flew three flights daily. Sometimes they had use of a specially configured jet called an A3D for their missions, and due to reduced fuel capacities the A3D flew only a four-hour mission.

Danny Baskins, flying as the junior tac/air man, was only on his fourth flight and he fretted over his equipment endlessly, reciting the rituals, naming each piece silently as he checked it. Since this was all still new, the switches and buttons and dials intimidated him.

Gerry and Ted were already in place with their cups of coffee, and arguing amiably about which of them was more essential to the success of their SAM team. Gerry copied the tracking channel, and Ted covered the chatter. Sometimes Ted had as many as eight or ten speakers. His ear was so practiced, so attuned, that no one ever second-guessed when he designated a different speaker's voice.

"You ready?" Craig stood over Danny's shoulder. "Everything checked out?"

"Got it," Danny said with no confidence whatsoever.

Knowing Danny from Monterey made this role of senior linguist hard on Craig, and he supposed that was the reason that Andy Jenkins had assigned them to the same crew. While Craig had to train and judge Danny, Andy was doing the same to Craig. Because of these positions there was a strain between Craig and Danny, and neither could breach it.

The first day of his arrival Craig and Danny had shared some beers and stories, but the moment that they were put on the same crew Craig established a distance between them, just as his peers had done to him when they were not yet sure that he could make it here. *Don't like a newie too much,* Andy had said, *they'll break your heart every time.* Craig was surprised at how often Andy's advice came back to him.

"On track," their pilot, Commander Baker intoned over the intercom system.

Craig adjusted the static in his ears until it was at a low, fine, irritating level. Anything higher and it might mask the voice signals for a few seconds while he adjusted, and it might make him listen less intently. More advice from Andy, he thought absently. He flipped on his intercom, recorded the preface message on each tape: his op sign, the date, the zulu time. He flicked on his intercom. "You concentrate on the odd frequencies, I'll pay special attention to 121.5 and 126.5 MHz," Craig told Danny. Those two frequencies were usually the busiest with actual tactical air operations. Each senior tac/air man considered them his own.

Craig's right knee jounced up and down like a piston, he rocked in his seat, he tapped his pencil on the fold-down desk in front of him. Twice he made sure he had a clean yellow legal tablet and six sharpened number-two pencils.

"Does he ever slow down?"

Barry Youmans, a ditty bopper, looked at Lieutenant Brooks Crenshaw, the evaluator and grinned sheepishly. "He makes me tired even when I see him asleep. He's like one of those old hounds that dreams he's chasing rabbits."

"I remember the first time I saw him," Brooks said. "I thought My God, he's just a baby." Brooks was surprised that he repeated this story, and that he had felt this way. He knew that Craig was not yet twenty-one, but Brooks himself was only twenty-six. Brooks had written his wife, Judi, about it, and she had written back that the command role was aging him before his time. *All of us*, he thought.

"But he takes to this shit like a duck to water, sir." Barry adjusted his own earphones and spun his dials listening for the distinctive dots and dashes that he listened to for a living. "He loves this place."

"I guess," Brooks said, and supposed each of them, or most of them, felt something here. "What do the others think of him?"

"He's different. He's like Dear Abby if you have a problem, he's a maniac if he thinks you fucked off and made a mistake on his specialty, he's a coach when he's training. He nags everybody that they ought to read more books. Busts your chops if you call the Vietnamese zips or gooks or anything at all. He's one weird piece of work and that's the truth, Lieutenant."

Brooks smiled. "You miss Alabama?"

"Every night, sir, and that's a fact."

"You glad you're tac/air, Craig?"

Craig puzzled over the question for a moment, wondered what had prompted it. "I love it, Danny. I wanted it from the first time I listened to a MiG pilot and ground controller. I told

Andy that the first time he sat down beside me to try to show
me which end was up."

"Why?"

"You're on your own, and you know if you're good or
not."

"That really matters?"

"Sometimes it's all that does."

Gerry turned to Ted Trainer. "When'd you do that?" He
looked at the purple mustache that had been drawn over Ted's
face with Magic Marker.

"When I went to get coffee."

"Why?"

"Commander Grady told me I looked like a Mexican bandit
the other day. I figured I might as well be a psychedelic one."

Craig glanced through his porthole window, the night cur-
tains pinned open, and watched an F4 sweep past in a deep
arc. He knew there would be another nearby. The Super Con-
stellation was unarmed, and two F4s accompanied each mission as protection: MiGCAP.

Oh eight hundred.

"Fansong radar active in Haiphong," a T-brancher yelled
out.

"We've already got him, asshole. My old friends at C6,"
Ted hollered back. There was always a friendly competition
between the radar operators and the SAM men over who could
catch a SAM activating faster.

Craig turned his dials, searching the frequencies for voice
traffic. "MiG up, Phuc Yen," he said over the intercom knowing that someone would tell Brooks Crenshaw. "MiG-21,"
Craig added as an afterthought.

During his first flights Craig had always worried that he
would forget the language, misunderstand the tonal symbols
and make a glaring error, but now he sensed the language as
much as he listened to it. *The cadences,* Andy had told him.
Listen for the cadences. Though by now he had copied a lot of
air traffic, he still felt that momentary anxiety before he fell
into familiarity once again.

Ted waved frantically in the aisle with his right hand and
logged traffic with his left until Brooks finally came to his
side. "Preparing to fire missiles, site C7, firing at an A4."

Brooks leaned close to Ted to catch the words. He was always surprised at the intensity of these men. Normally Ted screamed, and bellowed everything that he said, but copying traffic he seemed possessed and his voice whispered against Brooks's ear with a tickle.

This crew, the men on it, whether they were called Alpha or Delta, was Brooks's favorite. They were among the best of the men in all of their specialties, he was sure. He wouldn't give a nickel for all of the military behavior among them, but he knew that none of them would let down on the job.

The job.

Brooks wondered when he had picked up their habit of calling this the job, or the mission, using a tone that was usually saved for salvation on a Sunday morning evangelist's lips. He wandered up and down the aisle waiting for someone to motion to him. He felt the way he thought an expectant father must feel in the waiting room. No one chattered idly now, each was intent on his own tasks, and until needed Brooks was treated like a third wheel.

The job.

Craig logged down the conversation between the pilot and his ground controller in the shorthand he had been taught, some that he had created or modified. This was the easy part, just numbers, headings, speeds, fuel reports: that hard test was what came later if the MiG was vectored after an American pilot. Then the task was real. Then the job became reacting fast enough, with enough coordinated information to get a message to a SAR helicopter on one of the destroyers so that they could initiate a rescue if the U.S. pilot was shot down.

"What's happening?"

Craig slapped Brooks's hand free from his right earphone. "Don't ever touch my earphones again, sir."

"Sorry," Brooks apologized, and blushed. He knew better, but he was fighting off tedium.

"Something will happen, just not yet, Lieutenant," Craig said as an apology.

Brooks told Barry Youmans to keep a sharp listen, asked Ben Hodin, the Korean linguist, to plot the MiG carefully. He told them both the same thing; Craig had said something would happen and it would. He knew this by now. The best of them had a prescience, a sixth sense; in his three months here he had come to trust it.

Trust. Trust yourself. Trust your ear and your gut feel, that's where it happens. Andy again, Craig thought.

Take a chance, trust your instinct. Danny Baskins told himself this over and over, reminded himself how often Craig had told him this. He tried to settle the butterflies that ponged in his stomach. He felt more alone, more singular than he had ever felt in his life: deserted. Just me and the voices, he thought. The voices that were definitely doing something. He flicked on his recorder, read off the channel—115/MHz—and yelled for Craig to listen in. He colored when he heard Craig answer over the intercom, wondered why he had yelled instead of following the correct procedure, when he would ever feel right. "I think I've got a hot one."

"You either have one or you don't, you don't *think* you have a hot one."

"I've got a hot one."

"Okay, I'll take 115 and you keep a listen on 126.5 and let me know what's happening. Try to keep searching with your other radio and see if anything else pops up."

"Got it."

Craig spun both dials to 115 MHz and turned on the recorder to his top radio. He smacked his hand into the table. *"Bam sat."* Think you've got a hot one, he thought; you asshole, he's locking radar already. "Engagement coming," Craig yelled, ignoring the intercom, and began to copy it all down.

Brooks at his elbow, Craig said, "MiG-17 out of Kep airfield in Haiphong."

"You sure?"

"Does a wild bear shit in the woods? I think he's after a Thud."

"Sure?"

"Read my fucking lips, Lieutenant."

Craig scrawled the conversation on a clean tablet.

GROUND CONTROLLER: 312, do you see the pirate yet?
PILOT 312: Not yet.
GC: Ahead, to the right, fifteen degrees, 11 k.
312: Nghe gio. (Roger)

Craig had copied several engagements, but each one seemed like the first to him. He ignored a rivulet of sweat that dribbled across his right eye to his cheek.

GC: Ahead to the right, five degrees. Pay attention, be alert.
312: I see him. One pirate!
GC: 312, roger.
312: Firing missiles!
GC: Roger, 312.
312: Missed!
GC: 312, roger. Turn left, take heading 210.
312: Roger, 210.
GC: Increase altitude to 25.
312: Roger, altitude 25.
GC: 312, take heading 240.
312: Roger, 240.

Craig flipped back to his original channel and asked Danny to copy the rest of the landing. He turned to Brooks. "He missed this time. Send it out, engaged and missed."

"Shootdown!" Ted screamed. "Out of C7. They see the smoke and parachute, they say the plane is near the water. Get it out, Lieutenant!"

Brooks ran to the message center, pushed aside the curtain, and began reciting his message to the O-brancher at the telex console. Any engagement or shootdown required a spot report be sent immediately.

Craig noticed Danny was still scribbling furiously, and left his position to stand over his shoulder. "I told you I'd take the channel."

"It's a MiG after an F4 and I can handle it. Why don't you listen with one ear and just help out if I need you?"

Craig blinked, walked back to his position, and did as he was asked. He also barked over the intercom to get Brooks to position seven to see Danny Baskins.

Listening to the voices, even with one ear, Craig felt the phenomenon of his hearing becoming suddenly more acute. He barked over the intercom to Ben Hodin, the Korean linguist, that they should be southwest of Hanoi.

Youmans handed a sheet of tracking to Hodin, who plotted

it out, grinned. "Bingo! Wonder how he does that? He just senses where those fuckers are."

Craig tensed as the pace of the dialogue sped up with the increased intensity of the action. He got up again and stood over Danny's shoulder for a moment to see how the newer man was doing. Fuel readings, new headings, new readings on the location of the enemy plane; everything seemed in order. He jogged back to his own position and began taking light notes on a sheet of paper, capturing just the highlights to compare later. Craig knew this pilot's voice—Nguyen Van Bay. He was an NVNAF ace, Craig had read a story about him in *Nhan Dan* the North Vietnamese party newspaper.

GC: Ahead, to the right 7 kilometers.
403: Roger 7K. Continuing heading 320.
GC: Roger, 320, 03.
403: Roger.
GC: 03, Pay attention, be alert. *Chu Y canh gioi.*
403: Roger.
GC: Ahead to the left, 15 degrees . . .
403: I see him, radar locked on.
GC: Keep calm, 03.
403: Firing missiles.
403: Exploding! Shootdown! I see a parachute, two.
GC: Very good, turn right, heading 340.
403: Roger, 340.

Craig watched Brooks run down the aisle to the message center, and walked to Danny's position again. Over the newer man's shoulder Craig compared his notes to Danny's hand-logs. "Not bad."

"Thanks for letting me have it."

"No big deal." Craig sat down in his own seat again, dropped his headphones to his neck, and lit a cigarette. Too far inland, he thought, just too fucking far. They might send in a SAR helicopter team, but sometimes the pilots went down just too far inside the interior and the defenses were too dangerous to risk the rescue attempt. He sighed with a sudden gut-wrenching pain.

Gerry walked down the aisle to Craig's side. "How'd the newbie do?"

"He's a keeper, Gerry. Did good. We lost him anyway. He went down inland."

"Shit. Sorry."

We all are eventually, Craig thought. "That pilot will either be dead or on the way to the Hanoi Hilton within the hour." He thought about another conversation with Andy. Jenkins had told him that it scared him that sometimes he felt sorrier for himself, for not being able to save them, than he did for the pilots themselves. He amended, not sorrier really, but sorry in a different sense. Craig understood this now, but still could not name the feeling. Perhaps after you saved one you got this feeling of omnipotence, and that this reminder brutalized your ego.

"You can't save them all."

"Fuck," Craig said, and began to spin the radio dials again.

After the flight they stepped into a gray drizzle that was a welcome break from the heat. Craig waved off the duty driver and walked to the barracks, enjoying the rain, the chance to be alone. Wet and chilled, he stripped off his flight suit and hung it on the end rung of his bunk, turned his always-damp boots upside down and left them on the floor. He poured himself a scotch and water. He knew he would have to get out to the spaces to help write the day's reports within a few minutes, but for this moment he relaxed with his drink and tried to force himself to relax.

"Save me!" Craig was awakened by Gerry shaking him roughly. Craig blinked, shook his head from side to side. He knew that he had screamed, the dream was still vivid to him—a pilot was screaming at him, save me.

"You okay now?"

"Yeah. Sorry to wake you up."

"This place is just a slice of heaven, huh?"

"God, I hate losing them. On the map it's just a matter of inches, a thumb-length away, but in reality it's just too far. Too far to go." Craig rolled upright and reached for a bottle of scotch. He grabbed ice from the small refrigerator he had next to his cubicle, a shared investment with Ted and Gerry, purchased from the Hill 327 Exchange, and made himself a dark amber drink. "What time is it?"

"Three oh five."

"Looks like there's no attack tonight. At least the VC are showing some mercy." Craig knew that the war in Da Nang had once been a strictly nine-to-five war, but that was before his time. For months they had become inured to random attacks usually in the hours between two and six A.M.

"There had to be some good news."

"I know I can't save them all. We all know it and we say it, but every time I am up there, I think I can. I really believe that I can."

Gerry nodded, clinked his glass against Craig's. "To the ones we do save, bro, to the ones we do."

"Amen," Craig said. He started to lean back, reached for the bottle instead. "Maybe one more."

"Yeah," Gerry said. Not quite enough yet—he knew that feeling. Just one more.

Chapter 8

"Why me?" Lieutenant Commander Brewster looked at Andy Jenkins and shrugged his shoulders. Despite Jenkins's seniority and the fact he was only twenty-two, Brewster relied on him, not only as the senior analyst, but as a friend. He had been unimpressed when he first met the petty officer: Jenkins was short, had an elfin look including a pointed chin, had hair bleached white by the sun, and his only color came from his blue eyes. But, in time, Brewster had come to trust his instincts, to tolerate his madnesses, and to enjoy his company. Brewster, so often having to defend his unit against criticisms, also thought these were some of the most professional men on the job he had ever seen. "You know if you men weren't so good at what you do, you'd all be pounding rocks at Portsmouth. Sometimes that idea pleases me."

"Is there a problem?"

"Only if someone considers stealing a bike from an air force colonel to be trouble."

Andy grinned puckishly. "Was this particular bike stolen on the base?"

"No, it was taken in Da Nang, while the colonel attended a briefing."

"Is that what he calls visits to the Pink House?"

"You're saying that the bike was stolen at a skivvy house?"

97

"Hypothetically, of course."

"Considering that Da Nang is off-limits, I presume none of our men might have had anything to do with this then."

"Not on your life. But if they did, then what was the good colonel doing at a whorehouse that was off-limits anyhow?"

"Have any of you considered behaving like real people?"

"Once. We didn't like it."

"This is why I drink." Brewster reached into his desk drawer and retrieved a bottle of Dewar's scotch and poured them each a drink. "So you're saying that this colonel was busy at the Pink House, probably interviewing some of the lady experts on air warfare about the proper rules of engagement?"

"Sure seems true to me. Craig thinks so, too. Now, I wouldn't want to be him if this was known."

"Did it have to be that bike? There's a million bikes in Da Nang."

"What if . . ."

"I know, hypothetically, right?"

"Right, that a certain lingie had also been conducting some important intelligence matters at the same place and thought it prudent to leave?"

"Okay, just tell Nostrum not to do it again. I'll tell the colonel that maybe it would look bad. Maybe I can make him see the light."

"Or offer him some photographs. He doesn't know we don't have them."

"I've got to go over to a briefing by a minion at the puzzle palace. They're going to explain the objectives of the war again to me. It's a slow-learner's class."

"Don't let the bastards get you down."

"They always do. I ask for all of the things we need and they say no. It's getting predictable."

Andy thumbed through the day's reports and summaries that had clattered in over the telex. The crew list was hopeless. He stared at it and wondered how he could turn thirteen linguists into sixteen. Too few men, his chronic complaint. He wished that when they had decided to escalate the war that they had remembered it took a year to train a linguist. Four crews, sixteen lingies were ideal; he seldom had that luxury. He looked at the names, tried to decide which men could handle flying double flights, which were good enough, which would handle flying together. He knew he had helped to create the idea of prima donnas, and when he regretted it, he also knew that this competition was what made them excel. "There it is," he said, and logged the names on a sheet of paper.

Maybe the new man would work out as well as Danny Baskins. Even one more linguist was a chance for him to get some relief to the crews. He would know in a few days, a month at most. He glanced at his watch. Craig Nostrum should be picking up the new man any minute.

"Men go crazy in the heat, Ger," Craig said, and pulled on an olive-drab T-shirt with his fatigue pants.

"Where're you going?"

"Pick up the new man, Mitchell. Andy asked me to do him a favor. I wonder why I do these things and nobody ever cuts me a huss. You hear about the swabbie over at the new navy club?"

Gerry nodded. "Guess he turned the M16 to automatic and just opened fire in there. Six killed. *Chet roi*. The powers that be ordered the club closed indefinitely."

Craig looked at his feet, the pieces of pink flesh that peeled off, pulled on his socks and boots. "Guess that's a lesson to us not to shoot people when we drink. Have a couple of beers here for me."

"Don't bust his chops too bad, okay?"

"*Moi?* I'm a kindhearted soul deep down." Craig walked to the battered gray pickup and started it despite its tubercular cough.

Craig parked the truck and walked toward the terminal at the Fifteenth Aerial Port. He had sweated through his T-shirt already. He stood outside, in the sun, and watched a C130, a Caribou, taxi to the apron and stop. The back gate dropped down and men were expelled in an unsteady line looking confused, some angry, a few scared. From the distance it looked like a great bird expelling a string of khaki waste from its bowels.

Craig watched the men, newbies, cherry boys: the wobbly-legged column of endless arrivals. He had seen too many of them, he thought, had been one of them once. They all seemed to be the same one in that first moment. Their eyes were wide saucers that seemed shocked they were finally here, a place they had heard about, but had speculated their fates would not bring them.

"Yo, Mitchell!" Craig yelled.

Mark Mitchell raised a tentative hand. He had sandy hair and freckles, and Craig vaguely recalled seeing him in Monterey. "I'm Craig Nostrum."

"I know, I met you once in Monterey."

Craig shrugged, not remembering meeting him at all, but sure it probably occurred. The name on Mitchell's fatigues was Harmon, and Craig recalled Harmon had been a marine ditty bopper. It was the typical borrowed Det Tango uniform. "Drop your seabag and take your orders to that marine clerk. He'll get you stamped in all nice and proper."

"It always this hot?"

"You get used to it. You always hate it, but you do get used to it." Craig watched Mark Mitchell join the slow moving processional toward the check-in desk.

The men turned in line and chatted with one another, and Craig knew their conversations, they were always the same: Where are you from? What's your unit? This your first time? The hometowns are always the same place with a different name: a sweet shop, a kindly librarian, a Chevy dealer with a searchlight when the new models arrived, and sock hops on Saturday night. His home town was North Olmsted, Gerry's was Oneonta; Andy's was Kewanee; Danny's was the Bronx; Damon Arneault's was Calder. He thought that all of these were a litany, a responsive reading of the heartland of America. It's still the same town, and they are all still here and not there.

Welcome to Vietfuckingnam. He looked at the posters on the walls: ENJOY ENCHANTING VIETNAM, AN UNFOLDING VACATION SPOT, YOU'VE HEARD ABOUT IT, NOW SEE IT—VIETNAM. The posters were meant for the spate of civilian visitors that never seemed to arive.

"Nuts to butts," a marine sergeant yelled. "Close ranks!" The men pressed together like a sausage of olive drab: sailors, soldiers, marines, and airmen. They were a single stench and sound and swagger of sweat-damp children who had no dignity left at all.

"You waiting for a personal invitation?"

Craig turned to the burly marine sergeant. The sergeant, like Craig, was an E5 in rank. Craig ran a hand over his own collar, palmed a strip of silver. "I'm here to meet somebody, so back off, sarge."

"You getting smart with me, boy?"

"I wouldn't even attempt smart with you."

"You watch that mouth of yours or I can do some bad things to you. What's your unit?"

"Det Tango."

"Never heard of it."

Craig took away his hand, revealing an ensign's bar on his collar, and smiled. "We're in personnel, sarge. You know what that means? We can fuck up your paychecks for a lifetime and get you orders to some real awful places."

"I didn't mean anything by it, sir. I have to watch out for the malingerers."

"Well, you fucked up once too often."

The sergeant, his face flushed red, began to back away. "I didn't mean anything by it, sir."

Craig grinned, waved him off with a hand gesture. He knew that if the sergeant hadn't been worried about the ensign's bars he would have been worried over the word *personnel*. Everyone knew that it wasn't the generals that ran the war, but the clerks in personnel. They could screw up your life for a dozen lifetimes.

Craig lit a cigarette and felt an indolent success. He knew men in personnel, of course; he traded them favors. Everything in Vietnam was defined by a series of promises or favors owed to someone or another. Craig walked to the head to the line by Mark's side. "Is there some problem?"

"Don't push it, buddy," the corporal said without looking up from his orders.

"You call officers 'buddy' often, *boy*?"

The corporal glanced up. "Sorry, sir. Can I help you?"

"Why are these orders taking so long to process? This man is part of an essential intelligence unit here."

"We got to do things the right way."

"The right way can be a lot faster when you are *not* on report for insubordination, right?"

"He's all set, sir," the corporal answered, and stamped Mark's orders.

"Can't you get in some deep shit impersonating an officer?"

Mark had sounded so sincere, so concerned, that Craig was

silent for a second. "Nothing in the 'Nam is illegal, or immoral, except getting caught, or doing a bad fucking job at what we do. Remember that, newbie." He looked at the long line, wondered who would help them. "Get your seabag, FNG, and let's hit it."

Mark bent over, wedged his seabag between his neck and shoulder, and followed Craig to the truck.

Craig started the truck. Four months ago Andy had met him at the terminal and now he met Mark Mitchell. It was a continuum; like from one generation to the next.

Mark asked about each building he saw; he wanted an immediate familiarity with each sight. He tried to form this worry into words, but when he could not, he just asked what this was and what that was.

Craig understood, or thought he did: you needed to feel at home. But this wasn't home. He pointed out the sites with indifference. "The red mountains are the Marble Mountains. They make stone carvings there, you buy them by the roadsides."

"What are they of?"

"Buddha, dragons, who the hell knows?" There were also caves there that housed life-sized statuary. He wondered about these caverns. "The green one is Monkey Mountain, and yes there are monkeys there. That brown one with all of the barbed wire is Hill 327, Freedom Hill. It houses the base exchange and the prisoner-of-war camp." Like kudzu, the concertina wire looked like a weed grown amok along the short grasses of the hill.

"What's that smell?"

"That's how you know you're home. That is a poor dumb son of a bitch who got stuck with the job of burning barrels of human shit and piss. Loverly, huh?"

"Is it safe here?"

Craig laughed. "Just like being home, if you have VC lobbing mortars and rockets at your house." He hated Mark's question as much for its earnestness as for its naïveté. He lit a cigarette, fumbled under the seat, and yanked out a beer to drink. "Beyond 327 lies Happy Valley and that's home to the Vietcong. They own it, we take it, they own it again. It's the place the attacks come from most of the time."

"In the PI they say this is a secure area."

"Didn't your parents tell you about the tooth fairy?" Craig

sighed and sipped his beer. "Not six months ago the VC took some guy from the perimeter and nobody's heard from him since. Maybe he's in Oz. More likely he's in a VC prison camp."

"And somebody said I'd like it here."

"It has its moments." Craig stared at a signpost; it gave the distance in kilometers to Paris and Saigon and Vientiane and Bangkok: someone had tacked a cardboard arrow to it that read, *Real World . . . Ten Thousand Miles*. "The real world is even further away than Oz."

"Roger Tripp says you're a great lingie."

A great linguist. Craig had wanted that designation, yet when he heard it spoken he wore it as awkwardly as an ill-fitting suit. But he loved it. He nodded. "I am," he said at last. I have to be, he thought; if I'm not, then there are ten more men that would show him up. He thought about Roger Tripp, who had trained most of the men now here, and who was rumored now to be a faggot, a queer. When the rumors started to get too much attention, both Craig and Gerry had severed their ties to him. It was a sharp split: have your agent call my agent and maybe we can do lunch. He eased his guilt by making it obscure, forcing it away.

"You okay?"

"Always," Craig said suddenly. "Sometimes I'm great." He felt more distaste for himself and Gerry than he did Roger. Roger had never made an advance to him, never solicited him to go to bed, but the rumors had overcome any loyalty he felt, and any obligations to the man who had gotten him to where he was. The memory seemed like a noose. Hearing Roger praise him unnerved him. He eased the truck up a weedy hillock that separated two two-storied wood-framed structures and stopped. "This is home."

"You're kidding me."

"It's real."

"Shit."

"Aptly put, my friend, aptly put."

"What's next?"

"Grab your gear, find an empty bunk and locker, and move in. Then the duty driver will come back and take you to the rest of the spots on your check-in chart. If you don't plan to attend church, just scribble any initials you want in the chaplain's line. Nobody here knows his name anyway."

"Thanks."

"Just part of the free service." Craig watched Mark trudge across the dirt. One more. One more lonesome saint in the asylum. He backed out and drove to the well-guarded compound that held their offices—the spaces.

Detachment Tango had been created from refuse: borrowed shanties, mothballed planes, jury-rigged equipment. Beyond the compound was the tarpaper-shack village known as Dogpatch. Dogpatch was a sprawling city of its own, home to refugees and orphans and urchins and thieves and more than a few VC. It seemed to Craig to be symmetrical with Det Tango: another slum of the war.

Craig steered the truck onto the dried grass beside the six-foot chain-link fence that surrounded the compound. Barbed wire and concertina wire glinted from atop the fence. When the winds howled the wire moaned eerily.

Their single entrance had a small gateway and a guard shack manned by a marine guard. Off-limits signs were posted to either side of the gate.

At the far end, nearest the squalor of Dogpatch, was the small wooden structure that housed the Det T offices, and two low sandbagged bunkers. The smaller of the two bunkers had slots in the walls for firing weapons, and a placement for a machine gun that had long since been bartered away for more immediately important goods; Craig thought it might have been for their communal stereo and three cases of Chianti wine. At the other end was the hangarlike metal spaces of the Air Force Security Service. Midway was another small building, a snack bar, the geedunk, owned by the air force but built and patronized on a joint basis.

"Morning," Craig said, and waited for the guard to hand him his green foil badge. Already the face in the picture seemed too young to be him. He pinned it to his collar, and signed the log. "Is Jenkins inside?"

"Either that or some other short blond elf."

"Thanks."

"Godammit, Nostrum, you signed in as Mickey Mouse again."

"Testy, aren't we? The general been stepping on your pee pee again?"

"You better stop this shit."

"Think of this as Disneyland East, think of this as forever land."

"Asshole!"

Craig laughed. "Yo."

Det Tango's war was a tawdry, unimpressive one: most of the intelligence units were this way; unsung, understaffed, outside the normal supply and support chains.

The wind kicked red dust, the omnipresent enemy, and Craig rubbed a sleeve over his teeth leaving a dark stain. Grit rolled over his tongue like tiny pebbles. Da Nang dust, he thought; it's everywhere.

Craig looked at their shack without dismay; its squalor was familiar to him. Sometimes he thought it was the sheer depravity of their lives that allowed them to excel.

"Hey, Nostrum."

Craig stopped and glared at Chief Masters, still surprised to see him here. He had hoped once he left the PI that the chief would be left behind for good. He watched sweat puddle at the chief's jowls. Masters's eyes were red-rimmed and rheumy, and his nose was a series of broken veins. "What's up?"

"You need a haircut."

"Which one?" Craig touched his forehead, his sideburns, finally patted his chest.

"I mean now, sailor."

Craig shook his head. "You fly my flights and I'll get your haircuts." He started to walk past the other man.

"Someday your ass will be grass and I'll be the lawn mower."

"Don't make promises you can't keep, Chief. Unless you plan to learn Vietnamese. Of course, you might need a brain transplant first."

"Don't push me, boy."

Craig grabbed the chief's lapels in his fists, then smoothed them down. "You ever call me boy again and I'll kick your ass into next Tuesday and you'll need a proctologist to remove your head from your ass." He stepped away. "Have a good day, Chief."

Craig walked down the center aisle, past the wobbly tin partitions that separated the room into small offices. He walked to Andy Jenkins's desk, looked around, shouted hello, and finally bent down and looked under the desk. "Gotcha."

"Hi," Andy said.

"Any reason you're under there?"

"They won't give me a private office."

"Nice touch. Anything new?"

"Check the reading board."

"I was looking for a synopsis."

"You seen Masters?"

"Yeah, I just threatened to rip his heart out. He liked it."

"You're planning on making Portsmouth part of your travel itinerary, right?"

"C'est la fucking *vie."*

"Sir Genuine strikes again. You're a real fucking piece of work, Craig."

"I yam what I yam and that's all that I yam, I'm Nostrum the sailor man, toot, toot."

Andy crawled out and grabbed the hand Craig offered and pulled himself up. "New top-secret codeword today."

"Why? I just memorized the last one."

"Seems our esteemed secretary of state was carrying some classified information and let the nation's press photograph the document and the codeword."

"We did that we'd bust rocks, bet they made him write he wouldn't do it again fifty times on the White House walls."

"The new one is 'trine'."

"I was always partial to 'moron'. They'd never have to change it."

Andy picked up a clipboard with the daily intelligence summary for Vietnam on it. He ran his finger across it. "Lots of yellow." He used a yellow marker to indicate all of the places that Det T intelligence reports had been used.

"Nice. I like yellow. You get my stuff on the comms change?"

"Yeah, are you sure?"

"I'm not some nicky new guy, Andy. You want proof, then listen to it yourself."

"The tapes are blank."

"Fuck, fuck, fuck. Why can't we get any equipment that works?"

"It costs more than forty-three cents. I sent it out anyhow. Good work."

"Thanks."

* * *

Mai Linh hung the wind chimes and turned to Co Phuong for approval.

They nodded to one another.

Mai Linh said, "There are too many dead who could not be buried in their homes. Their ghosts haunt us here."

Phuong nodded.

"I am sometimes scared," Mai Linh said.

The afternoon flight had to be relieved on track by the next crew, which would mean another crew and plane would have to relieve them. The afternoon flight had had to feather two engines by the time they landed.

"This is bullshit," Andy said. "I can't even keep a crew rested and the fucking planes fall apart." He poured both himself and Craig a scotch and water in paper cups. "I hate this place sometimes."

"As someone I know once said, most times this place sucks, sometimes it is intolerable, and once in a great while you get a moment of sublime mediocrity."

"Don't repeat me back to myself."

"Uh, oh," Craig said.

"I hate 'uh-ohs,'" Andy answered.

"Fearless leader approaches at six o'clock and we have his scotch."

"Shit." Andy stashed the bottle in a desk drawer.

Brewster walked into his tin partitioned office, walked out again. "Anybody seen my scotch?"

"Scotch?" Craig asked.

"Chivas, to be exact," Brewster answered.

Andy pulled the bottle back out and poured three drinks this time. "I'll share mine with you."

"Why don't I believe you?" Lieutenant Commander Brewster accepted his drink and sighed. "I heard PR22 had to feather two engines and limp home. All souls safe?"

"Yes," Andy said. "So how was the meeting with the puzzle masters?"

"They did it with mirrors again. We're winning the war on the charts. Body counts, ratios of kills, everything is on our side. So I figure I have them in a good mood and I mention some of the things we need. You know what they say?" Brewster lit a cigar and puffed out blue smelly smoke. "They said,

we can help you. Just make the reports a little more positive.
Show some more excitement. Show how the gooks back off
and run rather than engage, maybe a shootdown or two."

Andy freshened their drinks.

"If this is your scotch, then why does it taste so much like
mine?"

"Probably fatigue."

"So I say we report what happens, and this jerk from NSA
says, you could do better. I know he means that we could lie,
and I explain my position on integrity of intelligence and he
said, one hand washes the other, and forty-five minutes later I
left."

"Bastards." Andy slammed his fist on the desk. "You want
to check and sign the reports?"

"Sign it yourself. You do my signature better than I do."

"They really want to spice things up, maybe I could write a
report on the cinnamon monopoly that is owned by a French
citizen and a Vietnamese general." Craig sipped his drink.
"What do you think?"

"That General Khanh would have us all shot."

Craig nodded. "What did you tell them?"

Brewster smiled. "That they could stick it where the sun
doesn't shine. They think I'm coming under the influence of
you renegades."

Ted Trainer stared at the wind chimes. "They're driving me
nuts."

Mai Linh looked at him. "Do not remove them, they keep
out evil spirits."

Chief Masters walked in with a *harrumph* and said he
wanted everyone in the spook mess, he had some changes to
announce.

Ted grinned at Mai Linh and Gerry. "Those chimes definitely do not work."

The spook mess, actually a lounge that separated the two
wings of the barracks, was the only air-conditioned room in
the two-story structure. They had acquired the air conditioner
through a process called cumshawing: a combination of illegal
barter and outright theft. It was the way anything of value was
acquired. Craig and Ted had filed off the serial number the
same night they installed it.

"We are going to make some changes. You are going to

begin acting like a military unit." Masters wriggled from one foot to the other as he spoke. "From now on everyone will be required to stand four-hour fire watches, just like in the real navy. You will relieve each other on time, follow the correct military protocols, and you will be awake and sober. I have brought a new notebook that will serve as the master-at-arms log. You will enter the information from your watch period in this log."

"Is this some sort of joke?" Ted asked.

"The watches will begin at 2000 hours, and run through 0800 hours, three shifts. One man per shift. I will post the schedule daily on the bulletin board beside the flight-crew schedules."

Gerry pointed to the wadded paper on the floor. "Flight-crew orders are posted there, Chief."

Masters bent over, swore, and smoothed the paper out and rehung it on the bulletin board. "I don't want to see any of these papers touched again. These are military orders."

The Chief turned for a moment and a dart sailed past and stuck in the center of the flight orders.

"All right, who did it?" he bellowed.

Everyone held up their hands in unison.

"That's enough!"

"This whole war is losing its charm and ambience, my friend," Gerry said to Ted.

"And you can have the first watch, Norton." Chief Masters grinned for the first time. "You men think you're excerpt from the rules, but you're not."

"That's exempt, Chief."

"I said you're not."

"Whatever, what's it like having English as a second language?" Gerry shook his head. "What do I write in your MAA log?"

"Date, time, your name, and make an entry an hour saying all is well, or logging unusual happenings. Breaches of military behavior should be logged, attacks, et cetera. If there is an attack, make sure that all men are present and accounted for, and if not list the ones who are missing."

"Yippee, skippee, fuck."

"You're on report, Norton."

"All in a day's work, Chief." He looked to the others. "Gosh, what do you think they'll do? Send me to Vietnam?"

* * *

Barry Youmans remarked of the linguists, "They're going to get all of our asses rosebud-deep in alligators someday." He fumbled with a cigarette paper and some marijuana. "But they do make this place fun. I think they are all just crazy-assed saints."

"That's against the rules, man, you are defiling the temple of your body and your body is owned by the United States Marine Corps."

He looked at Danny Morseth and grinned. "As they say, eat the apple, fuck the corps." He took a deep breath and let the smoke filter out slowly.

"You're as crazy as they are."

"But I'm a damned sight more personable."

To mirror Marks' discomfort at being at Detachment Tango he could not find a mosquito net for his bunk. He thought of this shortage as a portent, an omen. "So what now?" he asked Gerry.

"You steal one."

"Just like that?"

"It's what we do. You go down two barracks to the Screaming Eagles place and dodge inside, grab the first net you see, and bug out."

"Sounds swell. What if they see me?"

"Praying's good. Begging for mercy might work. Other than that just kiss your ass goners and we'll give them your bunk and locker in trade for a decent burial."

"How come I can't just ask for one?"

"You can, you just wouldn't get it. This is Det Tango, and when we fill out a request they send it to never-never land. You either steal, trade, buy, or offer a favor for anything that you want here."

"Gosh all fishhooks."

"Huh?"

"I try not to swear."

"Save me from newbies and naive farmers," Gerry said. "You run down and I'll try to cover for you."

"Thanks."

"All part of our free service."

"Are things always like this?"

"Nope," Gerry answered. Sometimes they're a lot worse,

he thought; it was this way and others, too. Nothing was ever just one way in Vietnam. Not ever.

There was a faint whistle and Craig awakened immediately and slapped his feet on the floor and snatched his flight suit from the end rung of his bunk. "Incoming!" he screamed.

The rocket was still little more than a ruffle on the air.

Most of the men were already running or walking down the aisles in various forms of undress and heading toward the bunker.

Craig slapped the side of Mark Mitchell's bunk with the palm of his hand and yelled to get up and move it.

Mark blinked sleepily. "What's up?"

"Uncle Ho's anniversary party. Come on, dumb ass, there's a fucking attack!"

"I'm in my underwear."

"Only God and us are going to see you. You rather be thought of for improper attire or as the late Mark Mitchell because a rocket bit your ass?" Craig grabbed the new man's elbow and dragged him along through the door.

The ammunition depot grumbled in successive explosions. Black coils of smoke curled through the sky.

Mark, still in his underwear, pushed away the hand that offered him a drag on the marijuana cigarette. "What the fuck is going on?" He paused. "I didn't mean to swear," he added.

Craig laughed. "Gosh, no. We're all virgin ears here. This is known as an attack. The VC found out you arrived and they wanted to say hey."

"You ever serious?"

"Not if I can help it." Craig accepted the marijuana, took a long draw, then reached for his beer.

"This sucks."

"Life in the fast lane, newbie."

A sharp keen of a siren screamed.

"What's that?" Mark asked.

"That's the warning siren. It usually sounds just after the third or fourth rocket hits. It's not much for alerting you, but makes a great alarm if you doze off." He crouched and moved to the other side of the bunker to take his place with Ted, Gerry, and Damon Arneault.

Craig glanced at Damon, grabbed another cold beer from

the trash can filled with ice and beer that was the first priority
to drag inside the bunker during attacks. He didn't understand
the other young man. Damon was dark, but had blue eyes,
and he stared icily around the confines of the bunker, ignoring
Craig's quiet offer of a beer, and finally reaching to get his
own. Craig and Damon were competitors, wary peers that
distrusted one another. In their frequent disputes over intelligence traffic Andy was the mediator. Craig thought Damon
was arrogant and aloof, Damon thought Craig had bought his
way into the fraternity of senior lingies accidentally.

Ted plunked the strings of his guitar, plucked out a common melody, "To the tune of 'Detroit City,'" he said.

Last night I went to sleep in Da Nang city,
I dreamed about those cotton fields back home.
I dreamed about my mother, my father, sister and brother,
Dreamed about the girl who's been waiting oh so long.

I want to go home, I want to go home,
Lord, how I want to go home.

Some folks think I'm big in Da Nang city,
From the letters I write home I'm doing swell.
By day I fight the wars, by night I chase the whores,
Living in my own kind of hell.

I want to go home, I want to go home,
Lord, how I want to go home—

Andy Jenkins drew himself into a knot against the sandbags as if it might comfort him. He didn't sing along. He'd
sung this song and all of the others too many times. No matter
how loud he sang, nothing ever changed.

Chapter 9

Mai Linh had helped Mark to decorate the cubicle he shared with Craig for Christmas. Bits of plastic ivy and red berries were stuck everywhere. Despite Mark's feelings that it was festive, Craig found it shabby and depressing.

Nothing amidst the decor was new; most of it had been unpacked from cartons Craig had used the previous Christmas; the artificial tree had come from his parents; the ornaments from his fiancée, Sheryl. The illusions that had sustained him a year ago now seemed forlorn and unforgiving. When he brushed against the paper leaves of the tree they rustled like the wings of the giant cockroaches that were everywhere.

Craig reached into the refrigerator, yanked out a cold beer, and took a long swallow. He tried to summon up some memory of cheerfulness, but instead felt a pervasive gloom. The decorations seemed as if they were just another indignity added to his life. He gave attention to the indignities he suffered with the same detail that the pious paid to the rosary.

Alone with the holly and the tree and the heat and the roaches, Craig felt hollowed. He remembered a radio program he had listened to as a child where the people were turned inside out, and the sound of this, a wet glove being pulled from a hand, made him shudder then and now. He rubbed a mildewed towel over his face, sipped his beer, and sat down on his bunk—the lower one. He wanted to take all of this down, but he knew it held meaning for Mark; the innocent always love the symbols, he thought archly.

"How's it going?" Gerry walked in and helped himself to a beer. "This place looks like discount night at Macy's."

The silence had been oppressive, but the interruption bothered Craig as well. He accepted a fresh beer from Gerry and crinkled the old can and banked it into the trash by bouncing it against Mark's locker and a good ricochet from the wall. "Yeah," he said at last, not sure what else was called for to say.

Gerry sat in the folding chair and propped his feet on the end rung of Craig's bunk. He flipped through the opening pages of *Good-bye, Wisconsin.* "Is this one any good?"

Craig nodded, "He was a friend of Hemingway's and Fitzgerald's, I think. I liked it." He finished half of the beer and changed to scotch and water. The water was gritty; dirt sank to the bottom like tiny stones or undulated like pale brown jellyfish.

"How the hell do you drink that water?"

"They don't even charge extra for the minerals, Ger."

"Gonna kill you someday, those look like boulders."

"Something will someday." Fake Christmas trees and plastic holly, he thought, but said nothing. He smoked in silence and took a long swallow from his drink. "You hear about Morseth?" Craig asked.

"No." Gerry thought about the marine ditty bopper who lived on the periphery of their lives like a small cloud. "What's up?"

"He got a Dear John letter."

Gerry shook his head. "Christmas brings out the best in the folks back home, huh? Packages, tinsel, and DJs, how's he handling it?"

"He talked to me for an hour about her, then he just walked off. I guess he'll do okay, everyone else who's gotten them has. Part of the charm here, right?"

"Yeah," Gerry said, paused, then spoke again with a chuckle. "Remember the one Jenkins got?"

Craig laughed, too. Andy's ex-girlfriend had written him that she had to change to the size of the sweater that she had been knitting him to fit her new husband. Craig burped and added some scotch to his drink.

"You and Damon still fighting?"

"We're not fighting. He's just pouting because I listened to some of his tapes. That and he thinks his shit doesn't stink."

"Thank God SAM ops aren't the prima donnas you tac/air men are."

"Cream will rise, as they say. Damon just can't handle that it's my cream."

Damon, of course, had a different point of view. He saw Craig as an interloper, a man who had not paid enough dues, and he knew that despite his attitude he wanted the job done correctly. Damon spent more time thinking of his future than his present. He knew he would be out of here one day, and he would make someone of himself. He would find the level of life that he deserved, and it would be good.

Damon Arneault beat his mosquito netting with a broom; motes of dust floated in the air. He brushed at his arms and face, smudged damp dirt on his forehead and cheeks and wanted to claw it off with his fingers. It would do no good, he knew. Dirt was omnipresent here. He settled onto his bunk with a sigh and opened a book. Just one more day, he thought, one more day that I hate.

Craig sat in his position on the plane and glanced at the luminous dial of his cheap Timex watch. Twenty-two hundred hours, ten P.M. in the real world language. He flipped on the record switch on his tape recorder. "This is Crunchy Nookie," he said. He touched the vinyl cover that he had snapped tight over his window. Inside the airplane everything was bathed in the pale green glow of the radar oscilliscopes. "Holy shit!" Craig slapped a hand to his forehead and noted the time on the recorder. "I've got a fucking MiG up!" He began to transcribe, and mumbled into the intercom, "Youmans, hey, you there?"

"Yo."

"I've got a MiG flyboy up, any tracking?"

"Quiet as a grave here, matey."

"Shit."

"You sure?"

"Who you think you're talking to, some nicky new guy?"

"Sorry, but I still don't have anything."

"Send the gerbil up, huh?"

"You mean Lieutenant Ferris?"

"You got another gerbil back there?"

"I read you five by five, sending up Sunny Jim."

Night flights were unusual, but not without precedent, and usually the ditty boppers had them as well. He copied the lazy conversation.

"You wanted me?" Ferris asked.

"Not in this lifetime," Craig said quickly, then shrugged. "I've got a MiG up."

"You sure it's not an ICC flight?"

Craig shrugged. "I'm not even sure I'm here. But I suspect you're dumb. Yes, I'm *fucking* sure. Check with the SAM guys, sometimes they double as tracking stations. They hate to shoot down their own planes."

"Watch the insolence."

"I'll make you a deal: you stop being stupid and I'll stop noticing it."

Gerry skirted around his position, bumped his shin, and cursed. "Hey, there is nothing up right now, but we did get a weird message. They said tomorrow Gia Binh would be active. What's that mean?"

"I'm a fucking lingie, not a mind reader."

"I hate it when I don't know what they're doing." Craig continued to copy the lazy dialogue of a ground-controlled approach, a routine GCA. "Hey, Lieutenant, check if we might have something up there now. Maybe this is a reaction."

"They'd tell us."

"They fucking sent a blackbird over the other day and never mentioned it. Just check, okay?"

"I'll check," Ferris said.

Craig slapped his left hand on his right knee to stop the jouncing.

"Nothing up," Ferris said, and grinned.

Craig knew that the lieutenant wanted to say I told you so, and he knew that if he did, he would hit him. "Who's flying the late flight tomorrow?"

"Brady's crew."

"I want it." Craig logged the last of the landing exercise. "Put me on it. Something is happening."

"The crews are carefully worked out. I can't just change them at your whim," Ferris said, his dark hair cropped close as fuzz. "I can't get you off of the early flight either."

"Don't. I'll take both."

"I don't have the authority."

"I do. I said I'll fly both and I will." Craig stood up. "Brady would give up his flight for a hangnail. Either you do it or I will."

"You don't have the authority, either."

"That's right, sir, I just have the talent." Craig pushed past the young lieutenant and asked Baker, the O-brancher, to send a message to Da Nang requesting that Craig fly both flights. Baker nodded and thought, This man is a real mess.

"You can't do that."

"I already did."

"This won't be the last, you hear?"

"You better hope not. My ear is what gets us by." Craig walked to the galley and got himself some coffee. Gerry was sitting in one of the forward seats taking a break. "Sunny Jim is the biggest asshole in the whole 'Nam."

"Probably."

"There's something happening, Ger. I have to know what it is."

"Don't let the gerbil bother you so much."

"I know."

Brooks Crenshaw stood beside Craig and watched the lingy spin the dials on the radios. Craig had long, thin fingers, a pianist's hands, Brooks thought. "I'm glad to have you along, but you're nuts for flying double flights when you don't have to."

"Sunny Jim graduated from Yale; if college makes you that fucking stupid, I don't want to go."

"You sure something's up?"

"We'll know in fifteen minutes. You developing some doubts?"

Brooks smiled. "No." He worried back the forelock of hair that drooped over his forehead. "But sometimes I worry that you're too intense."

"So do I, Lieutenant." Craig tested both recorders; they had failed too often in the past. Both spun tapes perfectly. "Ask the ditty boppers to see if they get anything, and the SAM ops."

"You're compulsive but cute, Craigers."

"I hate being called Craigers."

"Gerry said you loved it."

"Never trust anyone who has a permanent smile."

It was ten oh three before Craig picked up the signal on his radio. By the time the traffic had begun he had snapped two pencils in half and tossed them against the bulkhead. He flicked open the intercom. "Mark, see if you hear what I hear and for God's sake tape it."

Brooks hovered near Craig's elbow, read over his shoulder, but did not interrupt.

"Same old shit, he's just flying around." He listened to the MiG pilot get tentative landing instructions. The pilot answered the ground controller, *"Nghe tot, Gia Binh."*

Craig slapped his forehead with his palm. "Goddammit. I'm so fucking stupid I should be shot. Mark, get the fuck off my channel and hunt around, there's got to be another MiG."

Brooks clapped a hand on Craig's bouncing right knee. "What makes you think there's a second MiG?"

Mark Mitchell's voice came over the intercom, "Got it. One MiG and he's on GCA for landing."

"I should have caught it earlier, Brooks. They're ferrying some planes somewhere."

"What next?"

"When we land I listen to the tapes, plot out the headings, and figure what in the hell happened while I was sitting here with my thumb up my ass."

"We don't get down until midnight, and you fly the afternoon flight at four," Brooks Crenshaw said.

"Life's tough all over, huh?"

It was two-thirty in the morning. Craig stared at the ugly green clock on the wall and tossed a wad of paper at it. He stared at the map again, at the scars of erasures from his earlier attempts to plot the MiGs' path. He finally had it, and staring at the end product of his work the answer seemed obvious.

"This better be good." Andy Jenkins rubbed his eyes, and held his tattered green bathrobe together with his left hand. His hair stuck out in sleep-knotted tufts.

"It is," Craig said. "They reopened Nam Dinh."

Andy sighed. "I was dreaming of Mila Tabat. We were in at the Filipinas Hotel, and I was screwing my brains out. You sent Morseth to wake me up, to ruin my dream, to tell me

Nam Dinh is open? We bombed it to the Stone Age months ago." Andy staggered to the coffee urn and filled his cup.

"It's all right here," Craig said, and patted the map.

"A few false starts?" Andy looked at the new lines.

"I fucked up twice tonight. First I didn't notice that there were probably two MiGs up. Next, I assumed they were up out of Phuc Yen since we didn't have any tracking. Look at it."

Andy nodded, sipped his coffee and grimaced. "This coffee sucks."

"It's been sitting ten hours probably."

"Just aging." Andy studied the map, smiled. "So they came out of Haiphong, Kep Airfield. Sneaky little devils. Headings were due south for the most part?"

"Yeah," Craig answered. "That's part of what fucked me for a while. Once he headed south they reversed the headings, so I figured he was making a big circle. Instead, he was being vectored in for a landing. South end of the runway, no doubt."

"Shit. Good work."

"We need an overflight."

Andy sat down. "The air force already thinks we're a boil on their asses, or did you forget about the colonel's bicycle that you just had to steal?"

"If they have MiGs there, it opens a whole new attack route for them."

"Sometimes I wish you were more like Brady. He would have said it was two trainers landing in Hanoi and left it at that."

"Be glad it was me and not Damon. He'd not only wake you up, he'd make you listen to his tape and relive his plotting just to prove how brilliant he is."

Andy laughed. "You two are real works of art. I'll see what I can do." He lit a cigarette. "Have you noticed how much Morseth has changed lately?"

"No, but I haven't seen him that much. Probably still bummed out over that DJ letter."

"He's always been so strac, but his uniforms are beginning to look like yours. You used to be able to shave with the crease in his trousers."

"Maybe he's just getting as drifty as the rest of us."

"Maybe. I'll send out the message on Nam Dinh tonight if I can get Brewster to sign off on it."

"You could ask permission afterwards—those flyboys better know about this before they head in on Rolling Thunder tomorrow."

After his next flight, Lieutenant Commander Brewster met Craig at the flight line with a handshake. "Nice work. The drone confirmed that Nam Dinh is active again. Gerry and Ted reported some new SAM sites down there as well."

"How about sending some naked women as a reward?"

"How about a Wayne Newton record?"

"Torture is outlawed by the Geneva accords, sir."

Brewster laughed, looked at Andy, then Craig. "I have orders back to Atsugi for a while."

"Fuck a duck," Craig said. The whole business with temporary orders, the revolving door of personnel, bothered him, and of the officers in charge, Brewster was his favorite.

"Any idea on your replacement?" Andy asked earnestly.

"David Richland."

Andy's eyebrows raised; it accentuated his pointed chin. "Never heard of him, what happened to Hawkins?"

"He's Stateside. Got orders for the real world."

"You know this Richland?" Craig asked.

Brewster drummed the fingers of his right hand in his left palm. "I've known David a long time. I didn't like him when I met him and I still don't." He paused, stared at the ground, "You remember Gunny Harden?"

Both of them nodded; each remembered and liked the marine gunnery sergeant that had been the noncommissioned officer in charge for three months before Masters's arrival.

"Well, he knows Richland, too, and he told me that he wouldn't piss in Richland's ass if his guts were on fire."

The three of them laughed, each easily picturing Harden and his colorful language.

Craig smoked, and Andy asked the question for both of them, "Is he really that bad?"

"He's by the book and he's bucking for a promotion. He wants his captaincy as badly as an evangelist wants converts."

"So what do we do?" Craig asked.

"Keep a low profile and just keep doing your jobs. I'd watch the pranks and the jokes, though. He has no sense of humor at all."

Craig shrugged. "Things happen, sir, they really do."

* * *

It was two o'clock in the afternoon. Craig stumbled from the shower wrapped in a towel and stood in front of the cement piss tube outside to relieve himself. His urine splashed from the screen in bright arcs. Despite the deodorant cakes, the smell of urine was as thick as heat in the air. He wondered when they would really get urinals and flush toilets, a promise long dangled before them.

Mai Linh walked past and greeted him with a smile. She was unembarrassed by his activity.

Craig answered back and blushed. He knew he should be over the embarrassment; she and others had seen him taking a leak or naked in the showers too many times, but it still bothered him. Modesty was a civilian virtue, he thought, and walked naked across the field to the barracks.

Behind him Mai Linh spoke to Phuong and they both giggled.

"Good job on catching the Nam Dinh thing," Damon said softly.

"All part of our free service."

"What do you think is up?"

"No sorties yet, I'd presume it was being used for training and maybe some repairs. They know until they get after us that we won't send in any bombers on them, rules of engagement and all that shit. This gives them a breather to get things just right."

Damon slipped onto the bunk. "Shit hot. I think the boy has the right idea."

"Just figured it out a while ago."

"Tell anyone yet?"

"No. Andy wasn't around; besides, I didn't want to tell Masters because he'd give the old lecture about our job is to collect information and not to analyze it. He's got the IQ of a fucking grape."

"Not that high. Mind if I run it past Andy on the way to the flight?"

"Have at it. Up in the air, junior birdman."

"Maybe we can compare notes, have a drink or thirty when I get down from the afternoon."

"Sounds good, Kemo Sabe."

Craig sat down and began to write a letter to Sheryl. The thaw between him and Damon had come about so slowly that he did not notice it. They gradually eased their wariness, their flipness, and though they still competed, they had discovered they were friends.

From the back porch of the barracks, Craig watched the afternoon flight take off and curve over the bay.

One more time.

Chapter 10

When it was a sleepy fishing village under the French protectorate, Da Nang had been called Tourane. Now it had grown to be a city of more than a million as refugees swelled its population and drained its meager services. There were traces of the village still: small cafes, fish stalls, a monastery for Buddhist monks, a leisurely pace.

There were many Americans: USAID personnel, servicemen, CIA, consulate people, news correspondents, construction workers, missionaries, some whose only distinction was being white, but whose attachments to Vietnam were unknown. The town, so unsafe that it was declared off-limits for military liberty, was thick with civilians. Caucasian women in short skirts walked the same streets as delicate Vietnamese women dressed in traditional ao dais and walking under the shade of frilly parasols.

Twice it had been involved in active warfare with the central government in Saigon. The last time, South Vietnamese pilots under the control of Nguyen Cao Ky had bombed the city in U.S. warplanes. The strafing was halted when the American commander in Da Nang refused to let Ky's forces use the air base. Da Nang, like most of South Vietnam, had an uneasy relationship with Saigon: this was a country whose maxim was always that the emperor's power stopped at the village gates, and this Saigon government had become increasingly meddlesome. National police, dressed neatly in white, pristine against the decay of the city, against the backdrop of snaking concertina wire, directed the traffic with orchestral hand strokes. Their white gloves sliced the air with graceful movements. They were called "white mice" by most people. Da Nang was a city denied.

Craig nodded to the policeman on the dais as they drove past in their battered gray truck. Someone had painted over several of the dents with "ouch" or, in one case, flowers.

"Stop," Craig yelled to Ted, who was driving. He jumped out and bought some *cho gio*, spring rolls, from a street vendor and handed them out when he climbed into the back of the truck again.

"You want pictures? Very dirty, my sister. She cherry girl." The street urchin stood beside the truck and tugged at Craig's sleeve.

Craig waved the boy away, but handed him a bright MPC, military payment certificate, a quarter, anyhow. "We're going to the orphanage," he said for no reason.

"Is it true that you and Richland already had a fight?"

Craig looked at Will Ames, his current junior tac/air op on his crew. "Just a disagreement over what we need here. No big deal."

"Oh," Will said, and grinned.

The multistoried building enclosed by a fence, guarded by marines, belonged to the CIA, though everyone would deny this if asked. No matter what anyone knew of the city, they knew the CIA building. It was a landmark.

They saw China Beach—their first stop. The white sands glistened brightly; Craig shaded his eyes. The beach was dissected by rolling spools of wire: the barbed wire separated Vietnamese from American, officer from enlisted, men from women.

A day off, Craig thought, unsure when he had had his last one, and stretched out on a beach towel and slopped on a concoction of coconut oil and iodine he had purchased from Efram before he left the PI. Though he would, like all of the others, deny counting, he had flown eleven flights in the last seven days. Counting flights was anathema to them: it meant there was a finite number, which in turn meant there must be an end to them. The endings they envisioned were fiery and brutal.

A small Vietnamese boy, five or six, ran up to Craig, touched his chin, giggled, and ran off.

Craig laughed, rubbed his chin, wondered idly why his cleft seemed to fascinate the children in Asia.

"Another fan?" Will asked without opening his eyes.

"Probably a future cowboy." *"Cao boi."* They were the young ruffians that plagued the cities: they stole, they extorted, they broke their people's rules and morals and hearts. In Saigon they were endemic. "I wish women reacted to me that way."

Will grinned. "When women touch your face they just want proof that anyone can really be that ugly."

"Cut me a huss, huh? I need some ego strokes."

"So do we all. Heard that you're flying with Corey Lane as junior tomorrow. How come the change?"

Craig had expected the question, but dreaded it nearly as much as the new arrangements. Corey had flown with Damon already, and now it was his turn. Damon said the man just couldn't hack it. He was a hammer, he had a tin ear. Craig sipped a cold Coke and pressed the bottle against his forehead. "Evaluation time. We trade off juniors."

"Damon going to shitcan me just because he doesn't like you?"

"No way. We might be assholes, but we don't fuck with the job. You'll get your shot." More than that, he knew that Damon was happy to get a competent junior op, that he was glad to be rid of Lane. Craig closed his eyes and listened to the noise around him and the sound of the surf.

Craig was surprised that he dozed, but had to wake himself up to answer the question, "Football?"

"No football for me. I want a cold beer. I buy, you fly."

Ames nodded. "Show me money."

Craig handed over some crumpled MPC. "Make sure it's cold, okay?"

"Sun's going down," Gerry said. "Time to move on."

Craig nodded, eased himself up until he was standing. "I needed this. Orphanage?"

"Co chu," Ted said. "Certainly."

* * *

The Sacré-Cœur orphanage was a low pastel garrison built by the French, and the center courtyard was dominated by a single dwarf banyan tree. The walls had been whitewashed and the patio was kept swept clean. Craig and the others carried in their packages of food, clothes, and toys and left them outside the door of the mother superior's office.

Craig was not sure who had begun these visits, but they had become important to him; they tethered him to reality. He walked away from the others and sought out Sister Tsu Vien. He found her, as always, in the veranda filled with cribs of babies. "*Chao Chi em*," he said.

"*Chao Anh*," she replied. "Thank you for coming."

"How does Gunny Harden's adoption go?"

"They say there is more red tape."

Craig nodded. He pulled out some MPC for the orphanage, and some greenbacks for Gunny Harden. Sister Tsu Vien accepted them with downcast eyes and they disappeared into the folds of her habit. "Thank you."

"I wish I could do more."

He was glad he could scrape some money of his own together for the nuns, supposed they used it to buy black market medicines: but the purpose was good. He hated carrying Gunny Harden's cash since he knew it fed the graft and bribery of the South Vietnamese officials. He had started it when Gunny was on TDY to the Philippines, then because of his knowledge of Vietnamese, it seemed easier for him to do it: now it had become habit, a commitment, another mission.

"You do much, Craig Nostrum."

"There's so much left not done." He held one of the babies in his arms and cooed to him. He would not hold the girl that Harden wanted to adopt, he felt too vulnerable, as if by holding her he might not be able to handle it if something happened.

The other men played in the courtyard with the children and handed out candy. The children grinned and grabbed at them, shouting, *Keo, keo, keo*.

Craig walked to the opposite veranda to Duc Tho, the legless boy he had known since his first visit. "How are you, younger brother?"

"*Toi manh khoa, Bac Craig*."

Craig smiled at being called Uncle. He told Duc Tho the story of the pagoda of one pillar. Then he told about Uncle Remus and Brer Rabbit.

To the Vietnamese, time was no more than a chip from the face of the mountains, the change of a season; a continuum of time stretched relentlessly through their lives. When Craig walked to the mother superior to tell her of the packages, she thanked him quietly. He understood that in her view of life, it was better to be without excessive joy, and without excessive sorrow. She was a tiny woman whose hands moved gracefully like tiny poems.

"I wish I could do more."

"Thank you," she said. "Anything is more than we have."

Nearly everyone hated Richland, but no one really knew him. He, in turn, referred to his men as incorrigible, insubordinate, clownish, impudent. He kept to himself, except when he had duties to perform, or when he could associate with officers from the Naval Support Activity, or others removed from Det Tango.

"I don't understand why you're singling him out," Brooks said. "They're all about the same and they do a hell of a job here. He's one of the best."

Richland glared at Brooks Crenshaw; his dark eyes were set beneath great bushy brows. "You have to separate the leaders from the others. He's a leader. This Nostrum thinks that he runs the navy."

"He's gotten a basket full of medals. He's gotten us a half-dozen bravo zulus." Brooks thought about the commendations from the navy, BZs, and shrugged his shoulders. "What more can you want?"

"Military discipline. I want them to act like sailors."

Brooks chuckled, recalling the confrontation of the day before. Richland had told Craig that he expected him to behave more like a petty officer, and Craig had smiled back at him and said, "I like to think that I'm as petty as the next man, sir." Brooks sipped his coffee. "This unit has a great record."

"When it's strac, it's military, it will be even better."

"Yes, sir," Brooks answered, and walked out of the tin cubicle that served as the commander's office.

Andy Jenkins was folded into a lotus position on his desk, looked up at Brooks after a greeting, and mumbled hello.

"What mantra consists of saying the word fuck over and over again?"

"The one to the gods of crapola that sent us Richland."

"Fearless leader has you down, huh?"

"He's no part of Brewster and that's the truth."

Brooks picked up the daily report and flipped through the pages. He dragged his right forefinger over the page and stopped. "What's this?"

"Read my lips, forty-four minutes of GDRS." Andy stretched out, stood up again, "GDRS, Richland's baby."

"What the fuck is the GDRS?"

"General Directorate Rear Services. Part of the North Vietnamese Army. They send out these orders in five-digit numerical codes. The man says we will copy them on tape, write down these numbers, and send them off to the joint processing resource center in Japan. Now you and I both know that JPRC is so backed up they won't listen to a new tape for six months. The man is fucked, Lieutenant, I mean fucked."

"Someone else is copying it all?"

"Bingo. That's why we have to do it. He's afraid the air force will get all the credit for all these extra minutes of intercept. Let the zoomies have the credit for copying bullshit."

"He's got one hard-on for Craig, too."

"He's got a hard-on for anybody smarter than he is, and that leaves room for a lot of enemies. The man's so obsessed he doesn't know what this mission is all about."

"That's what I love about this place. It makes perfect nonsense."

"A slice of heaven," Andy said, and scrawled out notes for the new reports to be sent. "He wants me to spice up the reports, too. Guess he doesn't mind the silliness from the stone elephant as much as Brewster did. He says let's give them what they want, might get some better appropriations. Hell of a thing when the war effort is more worried about the funding than the end result."

"So what have you done?"

"Kept him entertained with new adjectives. I figure as long as I have a thesaurus I can keep him occupied. He really went crazy over *plethora* and *paucity*."

Brooks, startled with a sudden memory, laughed.

"It wasn't that funny, mon cowlickness," Andy said.

"I was thinking about the PI when they were looking for a new code name for some mission. I gave them 'merkin.' Nobody caught on for weeks. A merkin is a pubic-hair wig. Anyhow, I think it's all done, and the captain calls me and

asks me about it. Seems he does crossword puzzles and knew
the word. I told him, oh, shit, I said Merlin."

They laughed with shared conspiracies.

The plane groaned with takeoff and Craig ached with it.
The plane continued its laments as they banked over the bay
and turned north. Craig felt a spitwad hit his neck, turned to
Hensley, the T-brancher, and flipped up the middle finger of
his right hand.

"Your number of white parents, Nostrum?"

"Your IQ and sperm count, Hensley."

Old, tired jokes. Their familiarity was a comfort to them.

Craig looked over his shoulder at Corey Lane. "You check
everything out, Corey?"

"I have it under control."

Craig nodded, worked on his own equipment.

" 'If you hear well, don't answer'?" Craig slammed his fist on
the fold-down desk and glared at Corey Lane. "The phrase is
Nghe tot khong? Tra loi. 'Do you hear well? Answer.' It's the
same as INT QRK. For Chrissakes, you know better than this."

"It gets busy up here."

"You think I don't know?" Craig walked back to his position and tried to forget the sloppy handlogs he had seen. He
could not forget this, of course. He chewed the inside of his
lip and wished that he would get busy.

"You take it too hard," Damon said.

"I've known him since Monterey. We used to go drinking
together. Now I'm supposed to say he's a hammer and tell
them to dump him."

"If you can't stand the heat get out of the kitchen."

"He couldn't even get a comms check right."

"That's the same thing I saw when he flew with me."

"Don't you even feel bad?"

"It all depends; what would you feel like if you were a pilot
over North Vietnam?"

Craig, chastened, walked out to the spaces to talk to Andy
and to find a new junior linguist for his crew.

Craig's input: send Corey Lane to another detachment.

Gerry was ready when Craig returned to the barracks, "Did
you know that on this day in history—"

Craig turned away. "I'm not in the mood."

Ted continued, "Millard Fillmore got laid for the first time?"

"Oh, no," Damon shrieked. "A Fillmore party!"

The Millard Fillmore party had been the creation of Rick Stone, though no one could identify why Rick had spent so much time on the trivia of the president's life. The parties had started to celebrate his inauguration, then his birthday, and soon they became a party that was born from boredom, or anger, or joy, or for no reason. The party grew to whatever proportions the available time and booze allowed.

"Innkeeper, rum! I want rum for my mates!"

Craig handed Ted a beer in response.

"Thank you."

Danny Morseth ran past, doing frenetic handsprings and tumbling.

"He's sure feeling better," Gerry commented.

"I don't know. I think he's still acting strange," Craig answered.

Commander Richland returned from the officer's club in good spirits. He sat in the communal lounge in the officer's barracks with Brooks Crenshaw. He spread his arms expansively. "We're on our way."

"What?" Brooks wondered if he had not heard him correctly.

"We'll get some progress now. The people at the stone elephant understand me, and I understand them."

"Scary."

Richland looked up, startled. "Pardon me?"

"I said this place is scary sometimes. Attacks, you know."

"I know. Gets some of you down sometimes, these random attacks, but that's the way it is here. But we're winning, Brooks, we're winning this war." Richland rolled a cigar across the palm of his hand. "What's that racket out there?"

"Some of the men just letting off steam."

"I want it stopped."

"I'll see what I can do. They've been under a lot of pressure lately."

"I'll show them pressure. I want this stopped. This isn't some playground. This is a military unit." Richland glared at Brooks. "You order them to stop."

"I'll talk to them."

"Talk? Don't talk, order them. Don't let me down."

Brooks nodded and walked out of the barracks.

He jogged across the field and screamed their names as he ran, "Craig, Ted, Gerry, Damon, Andy!"

Ted sprayed beer from a can and doused an R-brancher. He looked at Brooks. "Have a drink, looey; this is as much fun as it gets."

"You guys have to stop this and hit the rack."

"You're nuts, we're on a roll now."

"Richland is bullshit and says it's a direct order."

"Tell him where to put his order, okay? I want it done sidewise."

Brooks shrugged and walked through the knots of drinking men until he found Gerry. "Listen up," he said, and repeated the same monologue as he had given to Ted.

"This is a fucking Fillmore party, Brooks, you don't stop until you drop."

"You seen Andy?"

"Not for a while. Maybe he's over by the beer bucket."

Brooks nodded and walked off. He passed Ted again, who was standing at one of the piss tubes, having just finished urinating, and there was a dart dangling from his left buttock. Brooks pulled it out. "You okay?"

"Indians, Brooks, they come out of nowhere."

"It looks like one of the darts from the spook mess."

"I threw it at some marine over in the MAAG-11 compound and this is what happens. Think I pissed him off?"

"Good chance," Brooks answered, and walked off again.

"Go back!" shouted Craig, but he lost interest when Brooks kept picking his way among them to find Andy Jenkins.

"Richland wants this stopped."

Andy nodded. "If any one of them stood still for half a minute, he'd pass out. They're tired, and half-drunk. They needed this."

"I know. But he's adamant."

"A little while. Once I get them all settled I might get drunk myself."

"You're sober."

"Someone has to manage the asylum. Give it a half hour, and I'll have most of them bedded down. You want to come back for some drinks, you're welcome."

"I might. I feel like an asshole telling them to shut it down when I know what they do, what they've done for this place."

"It sucks, but shit rolls downhill."

Brooks walked back to the officers' barracks, and by the time he began to talk to Richland the noise had begun to subside.

"Good man," Richland said. "I'm going to go to the O club for dinner, want to come along?"

"No thanks."

"You need to socialize more. Tomorrow I want all of the liquor confiscated, and all of the ration coupons seized. I'll advise Chief Masters, as well."

"Don't you think that's overreacting?"

"I want this unit straightened out. Do you understand?"

"Yes, sir."

"Call me Dave when we're here in the barracks. I'm a pretty easy guy to know, Brooks. Just do what I say." Richland lit a cigar and smiled. "This unit will be shaped up in sixty days. Take my word on that."

Craig was hung over; his head throbbed throughout the briefing. He swallowed three aspirin, drank them down with water, and poured himself his third cup of coffee. He still felt numbed and stupid.

"You look peaked, Craig," Gerry said.

"Speak softer. I could only feel better if I'd been dead for three years." He looked at his reflection in the coffee urn; the distorted image seemed better to him than he knew he looked. He had lost thirteen pounds from dysentery, an illness the doctor had said would last three weeks; it had already been seven weeks. But no drinking, he remembered the doctor cautioning him.

"You better slow down."

"You slow down here and you're on the shit heap. I won't be shit again."

"Relax, huh?"

"We fly soon," Craig responded.

They'd been on track for four hours. They flew circles in a black sky: it seemed interminable. The boredom seemed as tight as a vise to Craig. He sweltered in his own heat. "I have something up," he said, surprised at his own voice. "MiG, dammit," he said. He settled into the singsong pattern of their voices, ground controller and pilot, each part of the music. "MiG!"

"You want Baskins to copy it?"

Craig flipped the middle finger of his right hand. "If I wanted Danny Baskins to copy it, I'd ask him myself."

Brooks shrugged, embarrassed, not sure what he should do, unsure if others had seen the gesture. He sometimes thought he was the only awkward lieutenant in all of Asia.

Craig honed in on the voices of the pilot and ground controller and felt intimate and wise. He wanted to erase this moment, the ones before it, but he couldn't; now he felt alive. "He's going after the night planes after all. He's got a target."

"You sure you're okay? You've been sick as a dog even without the drinking."

"This fucker is mine," Craig said. He leaned forward to his desk, the earphones clamped tight over his ears, his hand moving steadily down the yellow sheets with the dialogue between the Vietnamese. His lethargy and his headache were gone, he drummed his right leg up and down. "He's after a Thud. Better check with tracking."

Danny Baskins listened to the GDRS and wrote down the numbers with a precision that frightened him. He wondered when this had become important to him. He had to blame someone, and so he blamed Craig Nostrum and cursed him. He had never felt such an exquisite anger before, and rather than puzzling over it, he swore some more. He was copying GDRS and Corey was being sent away. Both of these actions rested on Craig's shoulders. He cursed aloud and wrote some more.

"They backed off at the last moment. Guess he was afraid of a night engagement," Craig told Brooks. "But they won't be scared forever. I can remember when they wouldn't enter an engagement at all. They just need to get used to it."

"You sure you have it right?"

"I'm sure," Craig said. "If you doubt it, ask someone else to listen to it on the ground. The tape is all yours."

"How was it?"

Brooks, just down from his flight, tired and worried,

looked at Richland and shrugged. "Like most flights."

"You need to separate yourself more from those men. From the bad ones."

It's a matter of opinion, Brooks thought. "I know," he said in response, not knowing anything at all.

The men handed in about a third of their ration coupons, and half of the booze; the rest was hidden in the VAP-61 barracks with the permission of the VAP-61 squadron commander. Months before, after casting charges back and forth over who was stealing what from whom between the two units, Lieutenant Commander Howell and a Det T team consisting of Craig, Andy, and Ted had negotiated a delicate truce. Since that time they had both made efforts toward increased cooperation and shared resources.

Richland kept his ban in effect for two weeks before rescinding it in what he considered a gesture of magnanimity. The men, knowing the silliness of the ban and its lifting, took the new order with a smile and offered profuse thanks.

"I think I've begun to instill some pride in these men, they are shaping up," Richland said over a cup of coffee.

Brooks sighed and nodded. He wanted to say that these were men that had lost their pasts and were now like ghosts. They lived for this place. He said nothing and walked to talk to Andy Jenkins instead.

"Nothing too hot," he said to Andy. "Just some weather recces."

Andy knew the weather reconnaissance flights well: the pilot reported the type and height of clouds; the task of copying it down was boring and easy. "I figured as much," Andy said. "See how the fearless leader is gloating?"

"Yeah. He really thinks he's made some major improvement in this place. You guys are allowing him his delusions."

"For the moment. The merry pranksters are taking a breather, I suspect."

"Craig looks like hell. Can't someone get him to slow down?"

"Have a try, Kemo Sabe. He told me to mind my own fucking business."

"He's not over the dysentery even."

"I know," Andy said. "There it is." Down deep, he knew Craig needed attention; he also knew that it meant nothing until Craig wanted it to mean something. He rubbed his temples. "Brady's down sick again, so Craig's flying a double today."

"Brady bails off a flight crew for jock itch." Brooks shook his head. "Craig volunteered?"

"It was either that or Damon, and Craig thinks Damon is worse off than he is right now."

"Youmans told me once that Craig and the others were crazy-assed saints. Sometimes I think Barry's right. They're crazy-assed saints."

Craig Nostrum, one of those referred to as a crazy-assed saint, walked to the flight line trying to fight off his exhaustion through sheer willpower, and climbed aboard the willy victor.

One more time.

Chapter 11

Damon Arneault picked at the dust balls that clung to his sleeves and shrugged. He stared at his coffee, at the oily colors that whorled across the black surface, and said, "I hate this place," but no one listened. He picked up a week's worth of GDRS tapes as if they might be soiled diapers and dropped them back down. "Lots of minutes, huh?"

Andy Jenkins sat at his desk and stared at the centerfold from *Playboy*. "Makes a fella proud, doesn't it?" He carefully removed the picture, bending back the staples so as not to leave holes in her midriff. "Craig's almost finished his ceiling," he said enthusiastically. "Just two more, and Miss January here is one of them."

Damon shrugged. Craig's project to construct a ceiling for his cubicle had been a busy topic of discussion. He discovered that the beams were exactly one *Playboy* pinup apart, and proceeded to cadge and flimflam every one that he could manage. "I had some strange traffic the other day. I never did identify what kind of planes they were. Suspected they were IL-28s out of Gia Lam, but I couldn't really get a fix on it. Paradrops."

"I know, I sent it out. The NVN version of airborne, no doubt. I had Craig listen to the tape, too."

"You did what? Are you nuts? I had the fucking handlogs all done and done right."

"Keep your shirt on, I would have had you listen to his tapes if the situation were reversed."

"Andy, you ever pull that shit again, and I'll kick your ass from here to Phu Bai." Damon, incensed, slammed his right hand into the locker, swore, and stomped down the aisle to leave.

"Have a nice day," Andy mumbled.

Andy was relaxing, thinking he should review the latest summaries, when he heard Richland bellow for him. He rose slowly and sauntered to the OIC's office, "Yes, sir?"

"*Whoooo* did it?"

"Sir?"

"Drew a mustache on my wife's picture!"

"I don't know, I never really noticed her picture before, and if I did I probably would have just thought she had a mustache."

"Don't get smart with me, Jenkins."

"My Aunt Hilda's got one. Maybe it's glandular."

"I want the culprit. I want his name and his confession, do you hear?"

"I don't even know where to begin."

"You know as well as I do where to begin. Nostrum."

Andy shook his head. "He's on the early flight right now."

"Just because I noticed it now doesn't mean it was done just now. I don't stare at her picture, Jenkins, I just look once in a while."

"Sorry I can't help more," Andy said, and walked back to his desk, chewing the inside of his cheeks to keep from laughing. Had to be Craig, he thought, just had to be.

It was 1400 hours when the first rocket exploded near the runway, followed by quick explosions at the fuel depot and the ammo dump to the south. Confused, everyone ran in all directions. Craig finally ran to the bunker and stood outside the doorway and watched the flurry of activity.

"This is a new wrinkle," Damon said.

"I know. They never attack in the daytime. This is bullshit." Craig stared at a plume of smoke that curled from the fuel depot. The attack already seemed to be over.

"Maybe just getting their aims down pat. They scored a couple of pretty good hits."

Craig nodded, "Why don't we paint some big X's on the willies and see if they can max them?"

"No way, they'd probably hit them when I was either on one, or doing fucking wheelwells. Ever since that mustache incident it seems we get assigned wheelwells with increasing frequency," Damon said without either rancor or humor.

"I've washed every truck twice this week so far. The bean counter suspects I was behind it. Although, I have seen his wife and she does have a mustache."

Damon smiled, barely. "Just don't do it again. I don't care if the request comes from the puzzle palace itself."

Craig, knowing what the subject was, nodded. "I've copied a couple of them before, and Andy just wanted to know if this was the same as the others."

"Was it?"

"Yeah."

"Then don't do it again." Damon walked back to his cube with a broom in hand.

Craig listened to the siren's wail en route to the fire and lit a cigarette. Strange, he said to himself, and walked back into the barracks to pick up the book he was reading and a beer.

Mai Linh said hello twice to the young marine, but he didn't answer. He stared at the ground. She wondered what could make such a rich man sad. She did not know Danny Morseth well, he did not speak Vietnamese, and she finally just walked past him to fill her mop bucket. She told Phuong again how strange these men were.

Damon, down from the early flight, asked where Craig was, and when no one knew he walked down the street to the VAP-61 barracks. He walked into their lounge, a fancier version of the spook mess, and found Craig sitting at a table with a book, a drink, and occasionally glancing up at the blue movie that flickered in grainy black and white on a bedsheet hung on the wall. "Major comms change."

"Huh?" Suddenly alert, Craig shut his book. "When?"

"Today. I only got two of the new names. You have the early tomorrow, so I thought you might work on it."

"Thanks. How come?"

"Who knows? Maybe someone there broke security like our esteemed secretary of state did."

Craig chuckled. "You heard about the latest go-round between the bean counter and me?"

"No."

"Seems that we can no longer refer to the SR-71 as an SR-71. We're to call it a high-flying spy plane. I told him the Vietnamese call it an SR-71 in traffic, they used plain text to refer to it. I'm just writing down what they say. And he said, 'I gave an order, didn't you understand it?' And I said, 'Yes, sir.'"

"You're shitting me."

"I couldn't make up anything that stupid."

"He's making this place a joke."

"I know. Thanks for telling me. I'll keep alert tomorrow. Maybe we can piece it together by tomorrow night."

"I'll meet you at the spaces when you land."

"Only if you plan to buy the drinks later."

"You're on."

Despite Damon's insistence that he didn't need anyone else, that he wouldn't ever need anyone; they were becoming friends.

"So what's the movie about?" Damon asked.

"This guy on a motorcycle just pulls up in front of houses, walks inside, and fucks some girl. He never even takes off his helmet. I guess he's afraid his mother might see him."

The two of them ordered new drinks and watched the rest of the movie amidst the hoots and hollers of the other men.

"You did it, didn't you?"

Craig looked at Lieutenant Commander Richland with a blank stare. "What, sir? You mean did I get us a BZ on that comms change?"

"Drew the moustache on my wife. I haven't forgotten it."

"I wouldn't forget it if my wife had a moustache."

"My wife doesn't have a moustache. I'm going to keep up these work details until someone admits it."

Craig watched the other man roll a cigar in his hand, move it from one palm to the other.

"I like being out-of-doors anyhow. Excuse me, I have a truck to wash."

"You can't beat me. I'm a commander."

"Have a good one, sir," Craig said, and walked out.

* * *

"I joined the marines to fight, not jerk around here."

Barry Youmans looked at Danny Morseth and shrugged. "You're crazy if you want to get out there into the shit. This is a good place to be right now. Don't be pissing and moaning about it."

"I never killed a commie yet."

"Killing ain't everything, man, but dying sure the hell is."

The evening arrived in lavender that stretched pale until the night swallowed it completely. The bright crimson of the sunset was gone, and a red flare, as bright as a poppy, hung like its memory.

Craig looked at the bright red banner decorated with ideographs. It had been a gift from Mai Linh for the coming Tet celebration.

It was the Year of the Monkey. Those born this year would suit those born in the Year of the Boar, perhaps the Horse as well. Astrologers would advise them, just as they advised President Diem, and now President Thieu. Ba Mai Linh told Craig that this was a good time for him; she had heard this from Ong Tho who had cast the stones for her. She said this, and gave him bright pieces of paper and told him he should put these around his cube.

"Thank you," Craig said.

Mai Linh smiled and began to sweep.

Lunar New Year was the most important holiday in Vietnam. Craig recalled learning how to say Merry Christmas when he was in language school. The Vietnamese said *Toi chuc ong le giang xinh*, I wish you the birth of the moon (Christ). When his family and others asked him how to say it in Vietnamese he taught them to say, *Hang khong mau ham*— it meant aircraft carrier.

"Another comms change," Craig groused to Damon, wishing he understood what was happening. "They just changed two weeks ago."

"Two weeks and three days and fourteen hours," Damon said with his compelling sense of detail and order.

"Fine. Why again? We got hit at four-thirty yesterday afternoon with another rocket attack. The whole thing is one big cluster-fuck." Noticing Damon's silence, his preoccupation, Craig felt invisible. He smoked a cigarette, and tried to stop his right leg form bouncing up and down like a pump. He looked at his notes: Gia Dinh was the new code name for the controller at Phuc Yen, Ha Loi was now Haiphong, Binh Long was now Gia Lam. Gerry had told him that the SAM sites also had new designations. The GDRS traffic, boring still, increased daily and they shipped it off to JPRC where they heard it was stacked floor-to-ceiling and waiting for attention. He cleared his throat. "You still alive?"

"Why do you need to talk so much? You're like a constant barrage of dribbleshit."

Craig, stung by the rebuke, stood up. He didn't answer but walked outside and hitched a ride back to the barracks, grabbed some MPC from his locker and walked to the VAP-61 lounge to get a drink and watch the classic film *Ladies in Mating*.

Lieutenant Jim Ferris, Sunny Jim, was complaining to Richland that the men were serenading him at night and called him Sunny Jim, even to his face. Sometimes they even gave him a hymn.

Brooks Crenshaw, sitting between them at the card table, fought back a laugh. He'd heard the hymns. "Him, him, fuck him."

"Put them on report," Richland said.

"I don't know who they are."

"You know, or you can guess. The troublemakers are always the same ones."

"But I don't have proof."

"Believe me, I'll take your word over theirs any time."

Brooks finally chuckled, blushed when the others stared at him. "You have to admit that it's pretty harmless. At least they haven't nailed him in the shitter again."

Believing as they did in fate, the Vietnamese remained stoic. Craig thought that what was sometimes thought of as complicity with the enemy was really little more than their acceptance of destiny. Twice in the past two weeks the Vietnamese civilian employees had stayed away from work en masse, and each time nothing more happened than the inconvenience created when the PX could not open, and there were no barbers in the barber shop beside the spaces compound, and no cleaning was done, and laundry was delayed. Each time this happened the Americans predicted doom, the marine intelligence units predicted major attacks, but nothing happened beyond the stagnation of services that reminded each of them of home. When the Vietnamese returned after these incidents they said nothing and returned to their tasks as if nothing had happened. Marine intelligence continued to predict attacks, and Craig, like most of the men, thought these reports frivolous and repetitive. It seemed that if they predicted attacks daily, they would sometimes be right and then they could claim skills they did not possess.

Rumors of attacks had become as easily dismissed as the rumors of some dread venereal disease called Vietnam Rose. The rumors always said it was fatal and that men that contracted it were sent into exile on Polo Condore, an island prison in South Vietnam. They said the men always died in a delirium. This story persisted with such a diligence that even the skeptical sometimes worried; just as they were convinced that all military food included doses of saltpeter to reduce their sexual urges.

"Far out," Mark said and looked at the finally completed ceiling of the cube he shared with Craig. "How come you have two Miss Augusts?"

"That's all that was available. Besides, she has some nice tits, right?"

"Yeah. Too bad you had to cut off one of Miss November's tits to let the light bulb through."

"I christened her Miss Uniboob. Even with one tit she's great looking. Besides, I might paint a pink nipple on the light bulb and she'll be in three-D."

"Sure has been quiet this week."

"Tet's coming, and there's a truce."

"But they haven't even hit us for their normal two A.M. wake-ups."

"Be thankful for small favors," Craig said and opened a frayed copy of *Watchers at the Pond*. He settled into the folding chair and began to read. Beside him he kept a bottle of Chianti wine.

Baskins had been indifferent for more than a month, so when he asked for a transfer and came to say good-bye to Craig, Craig felt awkward and was unsure what to say. At last he said, "You would have made it here."

Andy, just back from his three days in the Philippines, shrugged his disappointment and walked away.

"I didn't want to. You never noticed that not all of us want to be like you and Andy and Damon. We don't love this place that much. We want to just get by and get out."

"That's what I want, too."

"No, you want to be Charlie November, super op. You want to soar here. I just want out. I don't care if I sit on a boat for the rest of the war. At least they don't have rocket attacks out there."

"I'll miss you." Craig wondered if he had said that to anyone else that left the det. He supposed not. Missing seemed too hard, leaving was too common.

"I don't hold it against you anymore, what you did to Corey. He's happy anyhow. I just can't be here. You're like a comet and you want all of us to burn out with you, and I can't do that. This is like four years of my life, but it's not my *life*. Understand? It's *not my life*!"

"Stay well, okay?"

"You, too. Try to find a way to sweat it less. You told me all about GAF. Live it."

"Catch you later," Craig said, and walked away. He couldn't talk anymore. The words were coming too hard for him, and he noticed a tremor in his hands. He smoked a cigarette and walked out to the spaces to review the tapes from the last three days. He didn't return until someone told him that Baskins had already boarded a plane for the Philippines.

"You take it too hard," Gerry said. "Damon's right about it, a little anyhow. It's like you just can't worry about someone going or coming, or whether the rocket might hit just right one time."

Craig took a swallow from his scotch and water. "I wasn't thinking about Baskins. I was thinking about how quiet it's been the last couple of days. It's like the truce started early."

"Just worried about you, bro."

"Worry over some other dumb son of a bitch. This fucked-up CT sailor is just fine."

"We're going to be welcoming the year of the monkey," Mark said, hoping Craig would break the stony silence that had lasted for two days.

"Do you think I drive people too hard, I push too much?"

Mark, startled by the question, hesitated.

"You do, don't you? Don't you understand that we have a job to do here? We're the best at it. We save pilots."

Mark recovered, nodded. "You don't push too hard. I want to do this and I want to do it well. I want to do it even better than you or Damon." Mark was embarrassed with the sincerity he felt when he spoke. He was not sure that he had known this was how he felt until he said it. Now he wished he could take the words back, wished he could feel differently.

"It's a real bitch, Mark, life's a bitch and then you die." Craig stood up and walked down the aisle to the spook mess. He turned back. "Come on, Mark, we got some ass to kick if you think you can handle some pinochle."

"You're on, Kemo Sabe."

There was too much to say, to explain, Craig decided, so he lost himself in the card game instead. Damon and Ted were partners against him and Mark; Gerry was at the VAP-61 club, someone said.

In the background, on the television Lucy Ricardo was trying to get into her husband Ricky's act at the Copa. Craig mused that this war was tied to *I Love Lucy*, and the war could never end until Lucy prevailed. Instead of saying this, he said did you hear the one about the man who walked into a bar with an alligator, and told a joke.

Damon felt an eerie worry, but said nothing since this had been his constant state lately. In the air he sensed dangers that were as constant and insignificant as the dust.

"I did a bad thing today," Ted said, and dropped his chin to his chest.

"What's that?" Craig asked, and offered his bid.

"I think I'm going to upset Chief Masters."

"Why?" Mark asked, and responded to Craig's bid, indicating his own double pinochle.

"Maybe not," Ted said. "Maybe he likes raw liver in his bunk." Ted grinned maliciously and threw down the ace of spades.

The whine of the rocket wakened them immediately. This sixth sense had become natural to them by now. Everyone scrambled for clothes and ran outside.

"There's a truce," Damon screamed angrily at the sky.

Craig put a hand on Damon's shoulder. "Things happen."

Chapter 12

No news was good news in the bunker.

The news that dribbled in was bad: the embassy in Saigon had been breached by sappers, Hue was under a state of siege, Da Nang was surrounded and the noose tightened by the hour.

Each day one color of flare was designated to indicate enemy contact: red, green, white; but now all three fell like blossoms and everyone knew there was contact everywhere. The artillery boomed and shuddered, the deadly warships called "Puff the Magic Dragon" streaked their red tongues of bullets across the ground all around the base perimeter. Behind the Det Tango bunker, F4s smoldered in their revetments, victims of slow response to the initial brutality of the attack.

"Shit, they got some of the F4s," Damon said. He spoke devoid of his usual sarcasm; he had seen two pilots die. He watched other men take photographs of the wreckage, of the men who had become pieces of bloody flesh. He recoiled from the memory and took a long swallow of marijuana smoke. The smoke fought back his nausea, but it did not lift his spirits. He wanted to be high, but it was elusive. He sucked the smoke deeper. Carry me, he thought, wondering when he had gotten desperate.

* * *

Gerry and Craig sat atop the small bunker in front of the barracks. The two of them had accepted M16s from Danny Morseth and sat over the gun emplacement that had been built for a machine gun they had long ago bartered away.

"They say there might be a human-wave attack from Dogpatch," Danny said.

"Who's they?" Craig asked.

"Everyone."

Craig smoked his cigarette, the rifle resting across his lap, the safety on. Craig nodded in response, aware of the wheels of the rumor mill, one of its cogs. "They won't."

"How do you know?"

Craig shrugged his answer. He didn't know. He wanted this to be true. He stared at the flares that drifted so gently amidst the warfare that they seemed anomalies.

"We need some volunteers." Brooks spoke softly, as if apologizing. The artillery, the rockets, the mortars, the explosions from any source roared and grumbled everywhere. The ground shuddered. "Richland wants us into the first phase of destruction. We have to get rid of the lowest level of classified documents and be ready in case the situation gets any worse."

"In case?" Craig screamed. "The situation is already worse. Maybe you didn't notice the fighting. They say there might be a human-wave attack from Dogpatch." Hearing his hysteria, Craig felt immediately silly, and ducked his head as if it were an apology. "I'm in," he said at last.

"Me, too," Gerry said.

Danny held his rifle resting on his right forearm. "You know I'm in."

"Come on, we have to walk. They don't want the headlights of the trucks to be targets."

Craig stuffed papers into the paper bags and Gerry dragged them outside where Danny set a match to them in the large barrel. The smoke seemed wispy and thin compared to the thicker funnels from the fires that raged across the base.

Craig heard the teletype machine clatter to life and wished there was an O-brancher present, but he stood before it and put his hands on the keys. He glanced at the code book to make sure that the wires had been properly set.

TO: DETT
DE: DETPB
ENTERING PHASE THREE DESTRUCTION. SITUATION SERIOUS.
HUE UNDER SIEGE. DESTROYING COMMS GEAR. MANNING
FIRE LINES AND BUNKERS. IT LOOKS THE WHOLE NORTH
VIETNAMESE ARMY IS MARCHING DOWN ROUTE ONE.

Craig tapped on the keys and asked who the speaker was.
BOYNTON HERE, came the response, WHO IS THIS?

Craig remembered Stan Boynton, a brash lingie with red
hair and blue eyes. They had met in Monterey.

DETT: GOT YOU 5 BY 5, THIS IS NOSTRUM.
DETPB: HOW ARE YOU DOING?
DETT: HANGING TOUGH, HERO. IS IT REALLY THAT BAD?
DETPB: EVEN WORSE THAN I SAY. THE WHOLE WORLD IS
    FUCKING COLLASPING UP HERE.
DETT: BE CAREFUL AND GOOD LUCK.
DETPB: LUCK IS GETTING IT QUICK. TAKE CARE.

Craig ripped the sheet from the telex and trashed it in a
paper bag. Kafka, he thought. He stuffed another burn bag
and handed it to Gerry.

There was no pretense of normalcy. The men grabbed what
they could to eat: C rations, cans of Bounty beef stew,
crackers and processed cheese.

Mark vomited beside the bunker and ran to the outhouse:
Da Nang shits. You got them when you were too tired, when
you had dysentery, or when you were just plain scared. They
burned and puckered your bowels. Craig wondered if anyone
in Vietnam had tight bowels right now.

"The bastards," Andy said.

Craig nodded agreement, not sure who Andy meant, but
sure they were all bastards. He wished he were still at the
spaces, at least he had been busy hauling trash. Here, he sat
dumb and worried and listened to the war.

"You remember the other time, not many do now," Andy
said.

Craig knew what Andy meant: the time the barracks had
been leveled by a rocket attack. The navy had built an ammo
dump right behind the barracks, and the VC had hit it. The
barracks had crumpled like matchsticks. The injuries were

mostly minor, except Andy. Shrapnel had danced up both of
his legs and left ugly red scars that looked like railroad tracks.
"This is worse," Craig said.

"I know."

"I sometimes wonder why I love it here."

Commander Richland read the message from the teletype,
surprised that he was the first. He tore it up and put it in a
burn bag. DO NOT BEGIN ANY DESTRUCTION. AWAIT ORDERS.
He picked up a pen and scribbled a note that he put in Crenshaw's personnel file. *He began destruction without waiting
for orders.* Richland smiled. This might all work out for the
best after all, he thought, and took his place in a bunker.

"That's the second one this morning." Craig stared at the
half-track truck that lolled with the green burlap body bags.
Sometimes you could tell the position of the dead man by the
way it rolled on the others. He shuddered. "Here's your letter
and here's your flag and here's your son in a plastic bag," he
recited softly.

Gerry nodded, looked at the ridge of scabrous mosquito
bites along his forearms. He picked at them gently, bright
blood flecks leaked under his fingers. "I used to laugh at those
jackets."

Craig nodded, knew what Gerry meant. They were black
silk and hand-sewn with a map of Vietnam and a dragon. The
words varied, but most of them said, *When I die I'll go to
Heaven because I spent my time in Hell.* He knew Ted had
bought several of them and sold them at a profit. He'd shot
holes in them with a forty-five and sold them as proof of
heroism to the rear-echelon men: REMFS, rear echelon
motherfuckers. Craig smoked and thought there were no
REMFs now. They were all in the thick of it.

Gerry remarked, "It's a fine mess you've gotten us into this
time, Ollie."

"Better to understand war, Stanley," Craig replied.

The bunker shook dust over them with every new explosion. The sandbags leaked. Craig brushed the dirt from his
arm, wondered if they would survive if the whole structure
collapsed. "Come on, Ted, let's sing."

"This is no time to sing," Mark said sullenly.

"This is the only time to sing," Craig said and led into a chorus of the Animals' "We Gotta Get Out of This Place." The song had become a theme of the war. He wondered how many times he had heard it sung, how many times he had sung it himself. Craig, made sullen by the lyrics, lit a cigarette and let the others finish the song.

The men cheered and laughed, clapped their hands. They drank warm beer because they were out of ice. When they had sent a man for ice, against orders to stay put, he was turned back by the marines.

Craig looked at Gerry. "You remember that time we all spent the night in Saigon?"

Gerry laughed and turned to Damon, who blushed and told them to shut up. "Damon's really testy about it, huh? Did something happen down there?"

Damon glared at them, lit a cigarette, and turned away.

Craig scratched his head, raised his eyebrows, and shrugged. "You must mean that bar episode."

"No one wants to hear it," Damon screamed angrily.

"Now wait, let's take a poll. If you want to hear it, raise your hands." Craig smiled as all of the hands but Damon's shot into the air. "As I recall Damon was telling us about the beautiful ladies of Saigon. It was his second trip there and he was taking us around. So we're in this bar and he hits on this pretty little lady right away. Gerry and I take our time and finally hook up with our own. Gerry's girl is the one that tells us what's going on."

Gerry grinned, "Yeah. Old Mimi is playing with my crotch and she says is your friend a *nguoi dan ong ua dang ong*? I say what the fuck is that? So she says that means a queer. I say no, why? She says, well, that girl that he's letting play with him is a man."

The laughter erupted immediately, and Damon stood up and walked outside. "Assholes!" he yelled.

Trovel yelled that he had a new song and began to sing.

Mrs. Brown, you've got a lovely body,
sons as dead as yours are hard to find,
Don't be sad, he doesn't smell too bad,
we did a real good job, we even found his head.

Walking along, even in a crowd,
you'd pick him out, he's the one,
did you proud.

Don't you know he didn't want to die here,
he came here 'cause you said you thought he should,
but don't feel bad, he had to fight your war,
He couldn't chicken out, he'd make his daddy proud.

"That sucks," Craig said, and stooped over so that he could walk outside the bunker. He slumped in the weeds next to Andy Jenkins. "You okay?"

"Seen Damon?"

"He's still sulking. You didn't have to tell that story."

"It broke the mood. Hell, it could have happened to any of us. Jenkins told me that Delcima's in Manila almost always has some transvestites working there, and how many of us ever checked their equipment out?"

"He'd have loved to tell the story on you, though." Andy giggled. "He'd have taken out fucking bulletin boards."

A series of explosions grumbled.

"This is a bitch, isn't it?" Craig lit a cigarette with shaky hands.

"Worse than that, this is Dante's vision come to reality."

In the bunker Gerry and Ted passed the guitar back and forth.

Ted said, "Gerry and I wrote this to honor all of the beggars."

The men clapped and hooted, joined in the singing.

Oh, it's shipping time again,
and I'm so happy,
I can add another hashmark to my sleeve,
I know that all my friends will respect me,
when I show to them my VRB.

Oh, it's crying time,
I got new orders,
The navy's going to send me overseas,
I'll go and ask the captain for new orders,
walk in his office proudly on my knees.

Oh, it's crying time again,
I failed the chief's test,
I do not know what will become of me,
I guess I'll have to go to Det Tango,
and get advancement automatically.

Craig turned to Andy. "That should be Henry's anthem." He was talking about the new first-class petty officer who had been assigned to the Det. Bill Henry had stated from the moment he arrived that he had asked for this duty for one reason, and one reason only, to get his Ho Chi Minh to Chief.

"Funny, when we get our Ho Chi Minhs, I think how much we deserve them; the beggars get one, and I think the whole system should be abolished."

"That's because we deserve them, and beggars should be abolished."

"What's it look like?" Brooks asked.

David Tyrrell shook his head. "Like shit, my man, like the worst shit imaginable."

Brooks nodded. He had known Dave for most of his tour in Vietnam. Tyrrell was an F4 pilot, a jet jockey. "Looks like we underestimated them this time."

"The word is that there are thousands dead in Hue and the fighting is street by street."

"Shit."

"You know what I want to do?" Dave asked.

"No."

"Bomb Vietnam back to the Stone Age, just like crazy Curtis LeMay said to do. He's right. These bastards just won't give up until they own this place."

Chief Masters barged through the door of the bunker. "Who did it?" His face was bright red and his breath came in sharp pants, like an overheated dog.

"What?" Craig asked.

"You know."

"Toi? Toi khong biet gi ca."

"Speak English, who put beef stew in my boots?"

The men applauded, whistled.

"This isn't funny," Masters said, though most of the men were laughing. "Who did it?"

Craig smiled. "VC sappers, no doubt."

"You'll pay for this. You understand? Every last one of you will pay for this."

"I've got a quarter I can spare," Craig answered.

The rumors continued, but little real news arrived. Someone said that the VC held the south end of the airfield, others that they had overrun Freedom Hill.

Fires still burned around the base. The wreckage of the aircraft lost in the January 31 attack were still there, the incoming rounds were too heavy to clear the rubble away. Det Tango's flights were canceled; no aircraft could get in or out.

"Okay, first break we can get in the fighting be ready to abandon Da Nang; we'll be flying our missions from Thailand." Brooks stood at the bunker entrance as he spoke. "Senior crews be ready. Pack some clothes, money, and make sure not to take any orange flight suits."

Craig sat in silence as Brooks read off the men's names who were to go. His was among the first. He knew about the orange flight suits already: In Thailand the monks wore orange and they considered it a holy color. Fly boys were not holy.

"Craig Nostrum, Ted Trainer, Gerry Norton, Damon Arneault, Barry Youmans..." Brooks rattled the names off quickly.

Craig smoked guiltily; if some were going, others would be left behind. He hated thinking of the men left back.

Later, after it was all over, they'd ask other men they met, Where were you when Tet came down? It would be a question that others would ask them as well. Strangers, warily meeting, would ask that question instead of your unit's name. The question and answer were always the same; a connective tissue between these men, these boys. We were here, they answered. We were here, too, others would respond. Right fucking here.

Where were you when the Year of the Monkey came screaming down in fire on us?

Here.

And something happened.

Chapter 13

Damon Arneault and Gerry Norton walked the main street of Korat, Thailand.

In Thailand pictures of the king hung everywhere: hotel lobbies, food stalls, taped in taxis, in the lobbies of massage parlors. The king looked frail and scholarly. Damon looked at the king's portrait in the window of a dress shop, finished gulping the last of his Singha beer and tossed the bottle into the gutter of the street. Brown glass shattered and scattered. Shards skipped over the curb. He had been one of the first men evacuated from Da Nang and now he wanted nothing more than to be drunk. He told himself that the others would all be okay; he repeated it over and over to himself.

A small boy dressed in a T-shirt and baggy short pants darted to Damon's side. "You want girl, numbah-one cherry girl, GI Joe?"

"No thanks."

"Numbah-one pot? Great smoke. You want Joe?"

"No."

"Numbah-one cherry boy? Me find cherry boy, too."

"Leave me the fuck alone."

"You numbah ten thou, GI. Numbah ten thou."

Damon slapped the child's hand away from his forearm and pushed past him. "Stupid little shit."

"They're all going to be okay," Gerry said.

Damon turned to Gerry. "I'm okay. No damage. That's all that matters. Just like I always said."

"Right."

"They should have gotten more crews out."

"The shelling was too bad."

"Nostrum's still there, so's Jenkins."

"They'll be okay."

"Hey, I don't care about them, just repeating a fact to you."

"Right."

"I want to get laid, Ger. Let's find some women."

"Women." Gerry squealed.

The two men broke loose like kites and sprinted across the street toward the harsh blinking of neon lights.

"I want the other planes here as soon as possible," Commander Richland said over the patchy telephone connection from Thailand. "I mean it."

Brooks Crenshaw listened to the phone, tried to ignore the cacophony of explosions outside the spaces. "As soon as they can get us out, they will. We're taking some heavy fire right now. The VC are holding the south end of the airfield."

"If one of those planes gets destroyed, it's all over for me. No promotions, nothing. I'd be a laughingstock."

"What about the men?"

"Bring some of them, too, of course. Get the senior men out first."

"What about the rest of them?"

"They'll be okay. We wouldn't let Da Nang fall, Lieutenant. Just make sure those fucking planes are okay."

"Yes, sir."

"Get those planes out, Crenshaw. Just get them out!"

Craig spread his legs out flat against the dirt floor of the bunker. The ground was rough, and his legs ached from being cramped for so long. He massaged his calves with both hands. Outside, he could hear the explosions. He had grown almost inured to the sound. The closeness of the bunker and its smells confounded him. He lit a cigarette and smoked it slowly. "I've had enough of this," he said. He stood up and walked to the shaft of light that spilled in the doorway.

"What are you doing?"

"Going for a walk, Mark. I'm getting crazy in here." He

looked to the north and watched as Puff, the dragonship, licked the earth with a crimson tongue of bullets.

"You're even crazier if you go out there. All hell's breaking loose out there."

"The best time to walk. Makes it seem like home. I'm from a big family."

"You think you're a fucking cowboy, don't you? You need to feel big. You're nuts!"

"Probably. I don't need to feel big walking around the war, though. I just need to get by myself." Craig picked up an M16 and walked away without turning around.

"Hey, GI, you want date?" Andy Jenkins jogged to Craig's side. "I'm tired of that hole, too."

"You should have been on that first flight."

"I missed it."

"I'd have gone in a minute."

"Maybe. They'll get the other two planes out tomorrow."

Andy settled into a leisurely stride beside Craig. The keen of sirens sending fire trucks off was almost constant.

Bullets kicked beside them.

Andy ran low and dove into a dried-out drainage ditch. Craig yelped, stumbled, and tumbled in after him.

Craig lay still. He held a hand to his right thigh, then pulled it back. The hand was sticky. He touched it to his tongue and tasted blood. "I pissed my pants." He said it softly, embarrassed, overwhelmed. He could feel the warm damp in the front of his trousers. "Getting shot at makes me pee."

"You okay?" Andy rolled close and touched Craig's thigh and looked at the blood. "Looks like it just grazed you. The bleeding's stopping."

"Wonderful. They'd hit me a clean heart shot and I wouldn't have cared at all."

"Purple Heart time."

"Bullshit. I don't want one. I was out playing. Save the medals for the guys who are trying to save our asses."

"Lots of men got them for less."

"I'm not lots of men, am I? I'm just one fucked-up CT sailor. They only have one plane, how the hell are they getting the job done? What about the pilots we should be saving?"

"Take it easy."

"Fuck!" Craig screamed it out, and closed his eyes.

* * *

The word came down at midmorning to be ready to run for the planes. "Take only what you can carry and run with. We hope to be gone only a couple of days." Brooks spoke quickly. "I'll read the names of the crews."

The bunker was silent as the names were read; even those whose names were called did not scream out with their joy. When the first crew had left, it seemed a lark still, and pandemonium had ensued. Now they listened as men do who are awaiting sentencing. Those reprieved restrained their excitement.

Craig touched Andy's shoulder. "What about the rest of those guys? What about Mark?"

"The next time they can get someone out they will."

"Take someone else."

"We need you there. You were worried about those pilots, huh? So get your ass in gear."

Craig nodded, followed Andy into the barracks, and jammed some clothes into a small suitcase. He crammed all of his money, MPC and greenbacks, into his pockets.

The horn from the truck bleated its signal, and the men chosen ran pell-mell for the truck and pressed inside the back.

Within twenty minutes they were airborne for Thailand.

"What's it like there, now?" Damon chewed his lower lip and did not look at Craig directly.

"Hell. Maybe worse. They're really blowing the shit out of the base."

"Heard you got wounded."

"No. One of those rumors."

"Andy told me. He was with you when it happened."

"Just rumor. Anything hot happening in the air war?"

"I lost one today. Went down by Bac Mai."

"Sorry."

"We all are. The sorriest bastards ever born."

Craig stripped off his shower towel and slipped into jeans and a T-shirt. "Who do I fly with?"

"Ted, Gerry, and me."

"No fucking way."

"Delta crew. They want the best up for the big strikes."

"Who flies junior?"

"Brooks said we'd both be equals. Whoever takes control gets the crew. Based on production."

"Shit, too." Craig shrugged. "Let's get laid and worry

about this shit later. I'm not going to lay down, Damon. No way I'm going to let you have that crew."

"I feel the same way, Craigers."

"I hate that fucking name."

"Touché."

Just beyond the gate of the air base they watched two elephants destroying an abandoned village. A small brown man poked at the beasts with a stick and barked orders in rapid Thai. The lead elephant crumpled a wooden fence like an accordian.

"Urban renewal," Craig said, glad to be outside the military base.

"Yeah."

"I could live like this forever, Damon. Just give me a nipa hut, a woman, and some mangoes, and beer."

"Give me New Jersey."

"I'd give you New Jersey just to be rid of you."

"Jealousy prevails."

"I just want a better companion."

The two of them reached the crossroads and separated. Damon walked toward the Chom Sarong Hotel, and Craig toward the New Asia Massage Parlor.

Craig scooted onto a bar stool in the lobby of the New Asia and ordered a Singha beer. He stared at a portrait of the king.

He looked at the ratty walls, the faded wallpaper, and finally to the glass partition that separated the bar from the room filled with lady masseuses that sat on long wooden benches. Each of the girls wore a number pinned to her tunic at their breasts.

"You like one?"

"I like all." Craig grinned at the proprietor. The man behind the bar grinned back, exposing two gold front teeth. "I just got here from Vietnam," Craig said.

"Vietnam very bad place now."

"So they say, Tonto." Craig slopped beer over his chin as he drank and blotted it with his forearm. "Number nineteen."

Craig slipped into the warm tub and let the small woman wash him. She lathered his head with shampoo and pressed his head back against the cool tile of the tub. He leaned back and felt days being washed from him. So easy, he thought, so easy, to come clean and whole.

He let her lead him to the massage table and allowed her to
help him steady himself as he rolled onto the upholstered surface. He felt limp and languid and fine. His skin stuck to the
material of the table and when he moved there was a sharp
squeak.

"You hurt."

He looked to the puckered skin that she touched with gentle fingers as if it were someone else's. There was no longer
any pain. He touched his fingers to hers.

"You are very kind," he said.

She smiled and touched the bridge of his nose. "You are a
good nose."

He laughed. "I am a good nose."

"Good nose."

He rolled onto his right side and traced his fingers over her
eyes and then her lips. "You're beautiful."

"No."

He propped himself up and kissed her. "Yes."

"No."

Craig blushed as he realized he had an erection. Think with
your brain and not your cock. He wondered who had told him
that. He stared at nineteen, thinking she was so tiny that she
did not quite seem real to him. He kissed her again. "Love
me, number nineteen."

"No understand."

"Love me. I need you." He lifted himself on one elbow and
enfolded her in his arms. He kissed her again and unfastened
her smock. The bright dress fluttered to the floor like petals.
"Love me."

She resisted for a moment, until she finally settled into his
arms on the narrow table. Their flesh was warm and soft as
they touched.

"We are the earth," Craig said. "We are the sky."

"Good nose," she said in reply.

He entered her gently. Their own scents mixed with those
of baby powder and stale air and bath water. I'm you, he
thought, I am you now. They made slow, tender sex. He
kissed her nipples, feasted on her flesh with his tongue. "I
love you, number nineteen." He said this in a voice more
tender than her name could have ever been.

Their juices spilled and spurted onto the table with the
baby powder and the sweat and the dust. He drove himself
into her as if she were a planet, as if she were salvation. He

exploded within her and shuddered with chills. He held her in his arms and buried his face between her breasts. "Love me, number nineteen."

"You are good nose," she said and giggled.

He laughed, kissed her, and found himself hardening again. "Save me," he whispered. "Save me."

"You look like shit."

Craig laughed. "Just the remnants of survival. Found a great lady."

"Hope you can handle the flight." Damon grinned. "I'd hate to win this by default."

"On track." The pilot announced.

Craig sat in the position that was usually considered junior and spun the dials of his radio. He thought about the woman called nineteen and suffered through the static.

Damon spun his own dials and thought of Da Nang. He thought of those hours, those days, the endlessness he had endured. He sweat with the recollection.

The hours—convoluted and timeless—seemed one changeless hour that was stuck forever. Craig flipped on the intercom, "Anybody hear anything new on Da Nang?"

"Still under heavy fire. We can't get anyone else out yet."

Craig felt doleful and cow-stupid, acutely and suddenly aware of his fatigue, of a mental numbness that was taking him over.

"I've got one," Damon said.

Craig nodded and continued to search. He listened to Damon's channel with one ear: a MiG-17 out of Kep was on a routine practice landing. He caught voices on a new channel and tuned the radio to it. He flipped on the recorder and began writing with a single fluid motion.

Flying missions from Thailand had increased the flights from eight hours to ten or twelve hours. The planes were always low on fuel by the time they returned to the air force base. Without relief crews the men were flying daily, sometimes having to take double flights.

"I've got a MiG-21 and he's being vectored toward a target," Craig shouted out.

Mark Mitchell stood at the edge of the compound, close to the base perimeter, and kept his M16 at port arms. The shantytown of Dogpatch was eerily quiet. It was the absence of barking dogs that disconcerted him the most. There were always dogs. He had not heard a dog bark since the battle began. "Pretty quiet out there."

The marine beside him nodded agreement. "There's still some rough shit out beyond the south end. The old pig farm is a battlefield now."

Mark scanned the street for signs of movement. "There's no human-wave movement yet."

"Won't be. This place has too much firepower. That's just one of those rumors somebody starts."

"You think we'll win?"

"Yeah. Can't lose."

A mortar *thwump*ed overhead, and the two men fell flat to the ground. Behind them came a sound of explosion, and the crackle of fire. Mark rolled over. "Holy shit. They hit the spaces." He stared at the shack, their headquarters, and watched the flames shatter the windows. "We have to make sure that no one's in there, come on."

They ran low to the ground, skittering from side to side. Mark kicked the front door open, jumped back from the heat. "Anybody in here?"

There was no answer. He crouched, and ran down the aisle. He came out, his face and hands blackened from the smoke. "Empty."

They stood there, transfixed, scared, and watched it burn to the ground.

Craig scrawled across the page. "He's firing. I think it's a shootdown."

"Of course it's a shootdown, asshole," Damon screamed out. "He said the plane exploded. What do you mean, 'you think'?"

"Get offa my channel."

Brooks hurried to the message room.

"How could you not hear that? It was plain as day."

"Fuck off." Craig rubbed his eyes. A mental lapse. He felt his own disappointment as sharply as he had felt the shrapnel.

"I've got another one," Damon yelled.

Craig nodded and continued to hunt.

The flight was busy, hectic. There were four SAM launches, one resulting in a shootdown, six MiG sorties, one resulting in the shootdown of an American, and another in the shootdown of a MiG-17 over Haiphong.

"I can't fly with him anymore, Brooks," Craig said. "We'll kill each other over this stupid rivalry."

"I know. Not much I can do about it yet. Richland tells me they're going to try to land in Da Nang and pick up a couple of more men this afternoon. If they do, I'll rotate crews again."

"It's as much my fault as his. I was half-asleep this morning, and he's right. When I listened to the tape again it was clear as hell."

"We'd have sent it out on a probable anyhow."

"It's not that, it's making the mistake. What happens if I make big ones next?" Craig stopped walking, stared at the luxury and permanence of the base buildings there. "You'd think they'd give us some of this high-class living, we're the ones in the real shit."

"Guess they don't want to build pretty buildings only to have them blown up."

"Boggles the mind, Brooks. Boggles the mind." He drifted off to the barracks to change and go to town.

Craig asked number nineteen where she was from.

"Thailand," she said.

He laughed softly, then loudly, until he was shaking with his laughter. He thought he might suddenly disassemble. She looked at him curiously, and began to massage his back.

"Love me, nineteen, love me." He felt desperate as suddenly as he had felt good. He wrapped his arms around her and pulled her down to him. "Make me live."

"How was it?"

Mark Mitchell smiled at Craig, pumped his hand. They maxed the spaces. Turned our fat resident rats into crispy critters. Kentucky fried rat."

"Shit. You're okay, huh?"

"Yeah. Scared, tired, but okay."

"Brooks is putting you on delta crew with me. Damon is taking over a new alpha crew."

"Good. Until Tet it never occurred to me any of us could die over here."

"I know," Craig said. He slapped his right hand to his knee to stop the tapping.

"Gerry's in the hospital."

Craig turned to Ted. "What the shit happened?"

"Some high fever and he passed out. Brooks and I got him to the hospital."

"What does the doctor say?"

"That he doesn't know anything. It's a fever of unknown origin. He's calling it 'flying fever.'" Ted ran a hand over his face, he hadn't shaved in three days. "This is the pits, man. I don't want to fly with anyone else. We're a team, we're tight."

"Who's coming to the crew?"

"Andy."

"At least it isn't that new asshole, Marshall. He's got the ear of a cabbage."

Craig walked into the hospital room. Gerry looked helpless to him. A bottle of intravenous fluid dripped into his left arm: dextrose, five percent. Gerry did not wake up, and his breathing was shallow and fast. He was slick with sweat.

"We think it's viral." The doctor had come in quietly, and Craig was startled by the voice.

"What's that mean?"

"That it's a virus, not a bacterial infection. We don't know what caused it. We don't know how it's transmitted. We haven't had anything like it before now. You guys fly too much."

"Take care of him, huh?"

"We'll do the best we can."

"Thank you, sir." Craig left the room with an unsteady walk. Forty minutes to flight time.

"I think I picked up a MiG-21 PFM today." Damon spoke quickly, his hands illustrating his language. "Wing-flap settings, the special takeoff procedures, the whole ball of wax."

"Did you listen to the tape?"

"The fucking recorder ate it."

"Shit. Forty-five degrees on wing flaps, right?"

"Yeah." Damon recited the other facts they know about the newer generation MiG. "You get something, let me know. Wake me up if you have to."

"Will do. Thanks for telling me."

"All part of the free service."

"Right on." Craig turned to walk toward his waiting flight.

"Craig? I'm sorry I was such an asshole the other day. You had it right anyhow."

"*De nada*," he said, and stepped onto the runway with a hop and skip.

"Brooks, send it out right now."

"You're sure?"

"I even got the tape. He took off out of Phuc Yen. Three extra steps on the takeoff procedure. I even got the order to warm engines."

"I'll send out a message that there are now PFMs in North Vietnam."

"The price of the war just went up, Brooks. It's high-stakes poker now."

Craig copied the traffic without thinking about it: it had become automatic to him, and it no longer surprised him to think in Vietnamese. He felt a hand on his shoulder. "Yeah?"

"Good work."

"Envious, Andy?"

"A little. Been a long time since I got to listen to something new."

"I almost wish Damon had gotten it."

"A crack in the competition?"

"I said almost." Craig searched the frequencies, immediately hitting on a second flight. "MiG-17 up," he barked.

Listening to the pilot and the ground controller gave Craig a sense of intimacy with them. They all felt this once they became proficient: The enemy seemed closer than their own men to them. A man at NSA had told him that it comes from eavesdropping. You feel connected.

GC: 302, what is happening?

302: He's after me.

GC: 302, take heading 220.

302: Taking evasive action.

GC: 302, stay calm, be alert.

302: I'm hit! Bailing out!

"MiG-17 down out of Gia Lam airfield in Hanoi."

Brooks rushed to send this report as well. With the American shootdowns the spot reports were to help initiate a rescue;

with the shootdown of the NVN plane they were fodder for press releases and briefings at the five o'clock follies.

Brooks settled into a chair in the galley and sipped his coffee once the message went out. He stared through the window. Far off, below them, he could see the slight color change from water to land: the coast of North Vietnam.

"Busy day." Craig joined Brooks in the chair next to his. "This keeps up, we're going to have to use packing crates to send off the reports."

"You look bushed."

"I am. Flying seven days straight, and doubles on two of those days, always puts me in a peevish mood."

"Can't understand why."

Craig laughed.

The plane groaned with the effort of crossing the mountains that separated Vietnam and Laos. There was a momentary quiet as if the engines stalled, and then the clatter of mechanical exertion. Craig's hands tightened around his cup, the knuckles white. No matter how many times he flew this route, this moment terrified him. His stomach sucked tight against his spine, and he finally sighed out the breath he had been holding. "Someday we're just not going to make it. There's just too much weight in these old birds to keep defying gravity like that."

"Let's hope it's long after we're back in the real world."

"At least it's good having Rowland back as a pilot. He's aces."

"Rumor has it he'll abort a mission for the slightest malfunction."

"He's also the gutsiest pilot we have. I was losing a signal once and he just turned into it and trolled close to the coast. We were close enough to get them to fire a SAM at us. Far enough it didn't hit."

"Is it true he once tried to land on an aircraft carrier?"

"Naw. Just pretended to. It was great. We're coming down out of a cloud bank, and the *Enterprise* is expecting to see an F4 and here we come. He said the controller was yelling his head off to pull up, and we could see all these deck apes just staring and then suddenly running, all assholes and elbows. Shit, I thought they were going to jump overboard."

Brooks joined in the laughter. "So what happened?"

"They chewed his ass out royally. He shrugged it off. He's the first one we heard use the line, 'What are you going to do, send me to Vietnam?' They would have grounded him as punishment, but what the hell punishment is that? Flying is the punishment." Craig reached into the left leg pocket of his flight suit and pulled out a copy of *The Razor's Edge*, and settled into reading until landing.

The plane bucked and plummeted toward the landing strip.

"On glide path." Rowland chuckled over the PA.

"My ass," Craig yelled back. "This is a glide path if you're on a roller coaster."

The plane touched down roughly.

"Hold up." Brooks stood in the aisle and waved the men of his crew to stand aside and wait while the others deplaned.

"This is probably the best crew that's ever flown. We've gotten two Bravo Zulus from the commander of the Seventh Fleet in the last three days. I'm proud to be associated with all of you, and we're going to celebrate."

Craig clapped his hands. "You going to come to town and get laid with us?"

Brooks grinned, worrying his cowlick with his right hand, "No. I'm taking you to dinner at the officers' club. Come on."

"You want to be seen with desperadoes?"

"I'll wear a mask."

The eleven men filed into the officers' club and signed in. Brooks spoke to the maitre d' in French. He introduced each man as his personal guest.

"Smorgasbord." Brooks stood aside and fell into the tail of the line behind Craig.

The room was redolent with food aromas: beef, potatoes, green beans, stewed tomatoes, ham. Craig held the plate in his hand. "It's real china."

"They have that for officers and gentlemen."

"But those are real potatoes, too."

"You guessed right."

"Wow."

The men settled for pushing three tables together and sat down to eat. The waiter filled their glasses with a French white wine.

"To the best," Brooks toasted.

"To you," said Craig. His heart hammered at his chest, and for a moment he thought he might cry.

"To the ones that go balls out," offered Andy with a wide grin.

"To Gerry," Craig said loudly, the others chorused his words, "to nineteen," he whispered to himself.

Commander Richland signed into the officers' club, walked into the dining room, and stopped. He glared across the room. Delta crew was sitting there eating, still dressed in ragged flight suits, clinking glasses of wine. He stomped past the other tables.

"What's the meaning of this, Crenshaw?"

"These men are signed in as my guests, Commander."

"Guests? They're enlisted men. Look at them. They smell."

"We're celebrating. They've gotten us two BZs this week. They deserve a break."

"This is an officers' club where we are being hosted as guests of the air force. What were you thinking? You weren't thinking at all, obviously. What do you think the air force thinks of this stunt? It's an insult."

"It's all legal."

"I don't care if God himself signed them in. You're going too far, Crenshaw." A blue vein throbbed in his forehead. He rolled his cigar faster and faster. "You men are trying to disgrace me. I won't settle for this. You're ruining this war."

Craig stood up, grinned. "Commander, I thought this war was pretty fucked up before I ever got here."

"Enough."

Ted joined Craig's side, his head cocked a little to the right, his grin twisted. "He's right, Craigers. This was a fine little war until you came along. I'm sorry, but it's true."

People at other tables were staring openly now. The maitre d' pranced nervously at the far end of the room, his hands weaving hopelessly in the air.

"Gee whizzeroo. Golly." Craig scuffed a toe into the floor.

"You're on report, Nostrum. The whole crew is on report. Get out of here."

Craig shrugged his shoulders, feigning nonchalance. "The place gives me gas anyhow." He tried to work out a fart and could not. "Must be the arrogance that does it." He led the others past Richland.

Richland stood motionless except for the cigar: it rolled

between his fingers as steadily as a metronome.

"You are an asshole, Commander."

Richland glared at Crenshaw. "You just pushed your luck once too often."

"I almost hope so. You're really crazy, sir. I mean that in the clinical sense. You don't understand reality at all."

"Get out! Get out! Out! Out! Out!"

Craig stopped behind the other men and stood on the lawn. He wondered how much had been spent to keep the grass manicured. He lit a cigarette and smoked in silence. He watched the other men walk to the street and stop. Friends, he thought, comrades perhaps; the closeness he felt to them sometimes scared him. He wondered what he would tell his son, when he had one, about what he did in the war. I laughed and drank and fucked and worried. I always sweated the small stuff.

"You waited, huh?"

Craig smiled at Brooks. "Umbilical cord just snapped me right back."

"Yeah."

"What a jerk. Stu-fucking-pendous jerk."

"A slice of heaven, Craig." Brooks watched as stars winked brightly into the night sky. "I would have pressed him to the wall on this one. I signed you all in as guests. He couldn't do anything."

"It wouldn't change anything, though." Craig lit a cigarette. "Curtis LeMay wants to nuke North Vietnam. I want to nuke Richland." Craig thought of Gerry and the IV that dripped life into him, of Gary Kraft who was suffering blood poisoning, of nineteen.

"This was the best crew ever."

"Yeah." Craig smiled. "Yeah."

Ted Trainer stood beside a cab and screamed to Craig, "You coming to town? We can't hold this cab forever."

"Go on. I'll catch you later."

Brooks put a hand on Craig's shoulder. "You going to see Gerry, huh?"

"Yeah."

"We're going to make it, Craigers. We are."

Craig smiled and shook Brooks's hand, and offered a proper salute.

Overhead, the moon bathed the club, the lawn, and the men in an embarrassed glow.

On the morning after their return to Da Nang, Brooks stood alone in the field that separated the enlisted men's and officers' barracks. He was whistling, almost happy to be back amid the chaos. The day before, he had had to bribe Ted's way out of a Thai jail. Now he wrinkled his nose to the odor of burning honey barrels. Human shit. This is the smell of Vietnam, he thought. There it is.

"You thinking or just vegetating?"

"Appreciating the smells of home. What's up, Ger?"

"Heard Gary Kraft got blood poisoning, too."

"Yeah." Brooks looked at a sign posted in the middle of the field: Da Nang Yard of the Month. It stood between two mortar craters. "He's pretty bad, I guess. Doctor wants him grounded. The kahuna says he's faking it."

"What caused it?"

"Doing wheelwells, I guess."

"Washing down planes with gasoline is such fun! Someone should have tossed a match."

"Then we'd be flying sopwith camels."

"Shit."

Danny Morseth grunted a greeting to them and walked toward the latrine. His uniform hung loosely from him, as if it were excess skin that he was trying to shed.

"He's lost a lot of weight, hasn't he?" Brooks asked.

"He's changing, just like the rest of the world. Won't be long before he starts letting his hair touch his ears." Gerry smiled. "At least when they maxed the spaces they let us move in with the air force."

"Flush toilets." Brooks said.

"Fun just to yank the handle and watch the water swirl down, huh?"

Andy Jenkins, a paper bag over his head, sat at his new desk and admired his sign. "Welcome to the Uncle Gene Show." Though no one knew why he had created the name, each of them fell into the habit of calling him "Uncle Gene." The paper bag had grotesque green eyebrows and a red stripe across it. He had cut holes for his eyes and mouth.

Andy set the reports aside. He worried over the reports and

he worried over the men. He stared at the typed summary and felt a sense of violation. He thought this was how a rape victim felt. He felt a cold, impotent rage. He scribbled marginal notes in Vietnamese. He cursed over the pages with helplessness.

This is what ambition does he thought: it teaches you to lie. There was no retaliation to make. He suffered the indignity and fell into a futility as resolute as the dust that settled everywhere.

To the Vietnamese, time meant little more than a stone, a chip from a mountain, the erosion of the rains. But time was on Damon's mind with increasing frequency. He thought about time's not passing at all, even as minutes were stolen from him, hours settled into his history. He didn't remember what happened the day he enlisted, or what happened the week before now. His past was slowly being chipped away from him.

Mark Mitchell settled onto the bunk beside Damon; the springs complained from the added weight. "You look down in the mouth, man."

"Just tired," Damon said, but what he thought about was the time, the fact they hadn't been attacked in days, that perhaps when the next attack came he might have lost his sixth sense. "I hate this place sometimes."

"We all do sometimes."

Damon nodded and he thought about the numbers, and how their sheer weight might crush him. Two hundred and thirty-eight flights. The numbers: the question of how many were enough, which one became too many, and that thought unsettled him. Recognizing the finiteness of the numbers meant recognizing mortality. "I'm going out to the geedunk and get some coffee and an egg burger."

"Mind if I tag along?"

"Help yourself."

Craig was telling a story to a new man. "So anyhow we're on the southern leg and turning for home. Suddenly Brooks runs up to me says one of our F4s says that they have visual contact with a MiG off our port side at eleven o'clock. Well, I'm spinning dials like mad and can't find a thing up. The ditty boppers can't get any tracking. The SAM guys have nothing. I tell Brooks there's not a MiG and he says, well, the F4s are about to engage. We're all shitting wooden nickels about this time. I recall an intelligence report on some new silent radar-controlled intercept procedure the Russians have and tell Brooks about it. It means they can attack without voice comms. So now the word comes that the F4s are firing missiles and we look out the portholes and we see an explosion and parachute." Craig glanced at the gecko lizard that sang on the screen and tossed a towel against the window. "So Brooks says this is bullshit and he is turning in his wings. I say I will, too. If we can't be sure we're safe up there, fuck it, right? So we walk into Commander Brewster's office and throw our wings on his desk."

Craig remembered the visit vividly.

"This is it," Brooks had said. "If we can't even hear them, we can't do shit to save anyone, even ourselves, John."

Commander Brewster stared at the two sets of wings, drummed his fingers on his desktop. "You saw this MiG?"

"Not actually," Brooks admitted. "But we saw the explosion and we sure as hell saw the parachute."

"That's right," Craig chimed in. "They should have the pilot by now."

Brewster rubbed his temples with his forefingers. "Do you know what an air force general sounds like when he's mad?"

"No war stories, John, we almost died."

"Brooks, this general used some words that I didn't even know. He told me that *my* trigger-happy henchmen had just shot down *his* drone. He said they shot it down so far out to sea that they couldn't even get the camera and film back."

"Drone? What in the hell does that have to do with us?"

"It gets better, Brooks. After the general, then the admiral calls me. He tells me that the general wants the navy to buy him a new drone. Now the admiral uses some words that I don't know and says he wants me to buy the air force a new drone. He also suggested that anyone connected with this misadventure be drawn and quartered. Looking at both of you, I am considering his advice."

Brooks picked up his own wings first, then handed the other pair to Craig. "Sorry."

"The admiral mentioned places like Adak and Greenland to me and asked if I knew what cold places did to a man with piles. Now what I would like is for you two to leave my office, and preferably stay out of my sight for the duration of the war plus ten years."

"Yes, sir," Craig said, and backed away.

"A drone?" Greg asked again in astonishment.

Craig laughed at the story, "So that's the way it was. Two weeks later it was in *Time* magazine."

The new man, Greg Kiner, said, "I read it."

"So did we. We tore it out and hung it on the bulletin board. We stamped it Top Secret. I had friends back home clip it out and mail it to Brewster. He was pissed."

"You miss him, don't you?"

"Yeah, I do. We used to kid him, call him Sergeant Brewster because he hated making decisions so much, but he stuck by us. He's a good man."

"You and Richland must hate each other."

"Staring contest. He looked away first. Guess when he flinched he thought it meant we tossed down the gauntlet."

Andy Jenkins walked into Richland's office with the report and set it on his desk.

"Yes?"

"Someone changed the reports. These things didn't happen. There were no engagements, particularly not with a MiG-21 PFM."

"I don't know anything about it."

"You know, sir."

"I won't tolerate being called a liar. Get out of this office."

"We have a reputation to keep up here, sir."

"You're dismissed."

"I'm not going to allow this, I'll go over your head all the way to NSA if I have to."

"Get out of here, or you're on report."

The four of them—Ted, Gerry, Mark, and Craig—sat around the table to play bridge. Craig and Mark were partners. "Three spades," Craig said, trying to remember the proper bid, the convention to go to slam.

Danny Morseth walked past rolling a large spool that left a black wire cable in its wake.

"Four hearts," Gerry said. "What's Danny doing?"

"Six spades," Mark said. "I don't know. Maybe he's just getting as weird as the rest of you."

Craig spread his hand down as the dummy, and got them each a beer from the spook mess refrigerator. "Hey, Danny, what are you doing?"

"Keeping out the snakes the communists are sending in here."

Craig looked at the young marine, noting how tired he looked, wan. "There's no snakes now, it's dry season."

"The commies turned them loose. I have to get this wire down," he said abruptly, and rolled the spool past again.

"He's going to sleep well tonight," Craig said, and watched Mark win the hand. "Nice going."

"Somebody has to pick up the slack for your bad playing."

"With you as a partner I don't need enemies, right?" Craig sat down and picked up the new hand that Ted dealt out.

Ted and Gerry took the bid at three no trump.

Sometime during the game the spool ran out of wire and Danny was gone again. Occasionally they glanced at the thirteen or fourteen strands of wire that ran through the barracks.

Gunfire is always sudden.

The men in the spook mess hit the deck, rolled under the card table, or the ping pong table, or behind the bar.

Willy Ames skidded into the room and squatted on his heels, Vietnamese fashion, by the card table. "It's Morseth, he's shooting up the front bay of the barracks."

Craig glanced at Willy, at the rancid wick that dangled from his right forearm. He grabbed Willy's wrist and pulled his arm closer to inspect it. "This needs to be changed again. What's the doc say?" Craig had already released Willy's arm and was standing up.

"To keep taking the pills and get the wick changed."

"I'll do it later."

"Thanks."

"De nada." He glanced at the closed door that separated the spook mess from the front bay, "How bad is it in there?"

"He's got an M16 and a full clip."

"Shit." Craig lit a cigarette and nodded to Gerry Norton. "You coming?"

"Whither thou goest."

"Did I marry you?"

"Marriage of convenience, matey; I hate to break the news, but I'm expecting."

Craig walked out of the barracks with Gerry. "I'll go in and try to talk him down. You wait awhile." Craig checked his watch. "Five minutes, huh? Then open the center door and check it out. Tell everyone else to get out of there and stay close to the jamb in case you have to dive for cover."

"You don't have to do this."

"Things happen, bro, they really do."

Craig walked through the dusty weeds past the bunker, stopped at the edge of the barracks when he heard Brooks call his name.

"What's going on?"

Craig repeated what he knew.

"I better get the SPs."

Craig nodded and started to walk off.

"What're you doing?"

"Going in to talk to him. Gerry's waiting for five minutes and then he's coming in the other end of the room through the spook mess. I'm kind of hoping he won't say, Hey, Danny, let's see how that baby works, shoot Craig."

"This isn't funny."

"Everything in the 'Nam is funny, Brooks. Everything."

"Guess you wouldn't listen even if I gave you a direct order?"

"Eh? Eh? Sorry, I have some trouble hearing."

Brooks handed Craig his .45. "Take this anyway."

"Thanks. Ask if they can send some sort of doctor over here, too. Danny's going to need some help. He's crazy."

"You're crazy, too."

"It's been said before."

"Why?"

"Because he's here, he's one of us." Craig walked across the dirt and opened the front door slowly. Danny fired a burst of rounds into the wall, fired again and shredded a wooden footlocker.

Craig eased forward, his feet scraping, whispering over the cement. He checked the safety on the .45 and put it in his waistband. "Can I have the gun, Danny?"

"Why?"

"I want to help."

"I can't. I've got to protect you. I'm a Marine."

Craig wanted to scream, perhaps cry, instead he nodded. "I know. Sometimes we have to help each other, though. We all need a break sometimes."

"Okay."

Craig accepted the M16.

"Over there. Shoot them!"

Craig wheeled and pulled the trigger. He sprayed bullets through the base of the far wall. The silence afterward seemed enormous to him. His ears rang.

"There!"

Craig whirled and fired again.

Gerry walked down the aisle whistling softly. The sound reassured Craig.

Danny was like clay in Craig's arms and Craig hated both Danny and himself at that moment.

"Good job," Gerry said. His voice cracked in the two-word speech.

Brooks walked into the barracks. "They wouldn't send a doc, but there's an MP coming. How is he?"

"Bastards." Craig looked at the rifle, Danny, and his own hands as if these were the trinity. Hail Mary, Mother of God, be with us now and at the hour of our deaths.

"You did everything you could," Brooks said suddenly.

"This is Vietfuckingnam, Brooks, nobody does everything they can unless there's a medal, a promotion, or some money in it."

"He's gone, man," Gerry said, his voice as soft as a slow leak.

"He'll be okay," Craig answered.

"He's fucked, Craigers."

Craig touched Danny's cheek with his forefinger. Danny did not flinch at all.

Damon stepped over the strands of cable and stood at Gerry's side. He looked at Morseth, then Craig. "It's the time. It sucks the soul out of you sooner or later. You and I don't even know the name of the place he is right now."

"We handle it," Craig replied.

"He didn't."

When the MPs arrived they took the rifle first, and then they led Danny away, one of them on each side of him. He looked small, childlike, as they led him off. One of Peter Pan's lost boys. Craig stood up, followed them outside, and watched until they disappeared in the night.

When the news came, almost three weeks after the incident with the snakes, life had settled into its normal routine for them. Craig had already begun his bean campaign: friends from home, men that had rotated out, sent beans—bags, cans, boxes of them—to Richland. Richland raged.

It was on such a day, when Richland had just received eight pounds of pinto beans, when the heat was oppressive, when red smoke ruffled from a hot landing zone south of the base and snipers had shot at the det truck when it crossed into the city for the mail run, that news came of Danny Morseth.

He had hanged himself with a bedsheet. He was already dead when someone found him swaying steadily from the window.

"It's the time," Damon said again in what seemed to be a litany for him now. He said this to everyone, but now as he stood with Craig he had nothing more to say. His words were gone.

Craig stared at the ground. "My cubemate in DC was killed on the *Liberty*. The Israelis said it was an accident. The chaplain and I packed up his belongings. Then a friend of both of ours hung himself. They were nineteen. Did you know Morseth was nineteen?"

"It's not your fault now, and it wasn't then."

"It never is. Things just fucking happen."

"You're drinking too much."

"I drink therefore I am," Craig mumbled. "He offered me an ashtray, a fucking ashtray."

"Snap out of this, who offered you an ashtray?"

"The chaplain. A souvenir, I guess. Remember your friend when you butt them out." Craig lay back on his bunk and stared at his ceiling of *Playboy* pinups. "It sucks."

"Cool down," Damon said at last, then clutched Craig's shoulder for a moment. "Good night," he whispered, then drew Craig's blanket over him like the close of a sentence.

Chapter 14

"You've been apprehended for driving a stolen vehicle."

Craig looked at the marine MP and smiled. "That can't be, sarge, some marines asked us to bring this jeep back to base and leave it near MAAG-11."

"Captain Carabetti reported it stolen four hours ago."

Craig scuffed his toe in the dirt and ducked his head. "Gosh, you mean those marines lied to me? They sure seemed like straight arrows to me. What'd you think?" He turned to Damon.

"They seemed honest to me, too. You sure this is a stolen jeep?"

The sergeant nodded. "Sure as I can be, and your squid asses are in big trouble."

Craig handed him the keys. "We were hitching back from China Beach and they asked us to take this back for them and they loaded into some beat-up gray pickup truck with a dent and a big canvas bag that said 'Classified Material' on it. I figured they must be doing something important."

"Holy shit," the marine said, and turned to his partner. "That's the truck that the Navy Security Group reported stolen."

"Shoot, now you're telling me they stole two vehicles?" Craig shook his head. "Not sure who you can trust anymore."

"Which way were they heading?"

"Toward the docks, I think."

"Thanks. You men hitch back. What's your name and unit?"

"Dirksen, Everett, attached to personnel."

"Thanks for your help."

Craig and Damon trudged along the road toward the base. At last Craig said, "Well, how did I do?"

"You do Oscar-Award-quality bumpkinness. Maybe it's your natural dumbness coming through, huh?"

"I got us out of that mess, Ollie."

"Well, Stanley, how do you plan to explain the missing truck?"

"Marines appear to be stealing everything with wheels from what that MP said. Shit, they traded us a stolen jeep, didn't they?"

"They ever catch our young asses and we can kiss old age good-bye."

"Hell, they'll probably trade it for a half-track before they get caught."

Giggling like schoolgirls, the two of them walked across the bridge to the base and didn't flinch at all when the marine guard opened fire on automatic to destroy some flotsam that bobbed down the river below them. This was a common practice. The VC sometimes sent booby traps that way, sometimes VC sappers held tight to the garbage and rode along.

Brooks Crenshaw stood in front of Craig at the spaces. His eyes showed evidence of his fatigue: dark circles beneath them, and tiny cracked wrinkles at the edges. "You don't know anything about the return of the stolen truck, do you?"

"*Toi? Quelle* shock. I'm pretty surprised you would even ask."

"Let me rephrase it: do you know anything about the truck getting stolen in the first place?"

"I'm really hurt, sir. You ask me about some stolen truck that I never heard of until you mentioned it and then you cast aspersions on my character."

"To have aspersions cast on your character, you must first have some character. You have never displayed any evidence of this at all."

"Beats the heck out of me."

"You didn't trade the truck for a jeep with some marines? You didn't perhaps make this deal while you were off-limits?"

"If they said that, then there was obviously a mistake. A lot of guys look like me."

Brooks grinned. "I just hope those marines don't find you and suffer another case of mistaken identity when they take you apart."

"I'll take that under advisement." Craig flipped through the reports, smiled. "No changes. You tie Richland's hands behind his back, steal his pencils and erasers?"

"Just doing damage control. Cookie made me a deal not to send them until I can compare them to Andy's reports. We leave some spicy words in, but take out anything erroneous."

"Good. Maybe the good guys can win the war after all."

"Yeah, helluva war we got ourselves here, isn't it?"

Craig smoked his cigarette. "I think Richland's whacko, Brooks. Not just funny, not just strict, I mean really unbalanced. He woke me up one night; I was dead asleep and he said, 'You won't win, boy.' He just said that and walked away."

"You sure you didn't dream it?"

"I didn't."

"He says some odd things to me sometimes, too. Just hang tough, huh? And don't steal any more trucks."

"Next time I go for an F4."

Gerry stood in the rutted field behind the barracks and stared at the listing bunker that was slowly collapsing in on itself. "We need sandbags."

Ted kicked a wall and watched it slip down further. "Supply says no sandbags. We're over our allotment. We have to wait our turn."

"Allotment, bullshit. We need sandbags and we need a bunker."

"The man said wait." Ted spit the words out angrily. "That fat fuck kept smiling like he was a laughing *hotai*. I wanted to knock his asshole up for a necklace."

"He wanted money, huh?"

"He just said that maybe things could be worked out, and grinned like a silly ape. Yeah, he wanted money. We have to buy our goddamned flight suits black-market already, I won't pay him for sandbags."

"So?"

"Get Craig and whoever else is around. We need to start a plan. Get the new duty driver, Devito, too. Anyone who can keep his trap shut. We are going to have a Millard Fillmore of a cumshaw party."

"Yes, sir." Gerry snapped his middle finger as a salute.

"You want to be in *this* thing when there's an attack?"

"Where do we meet?"

"Thirty minutes behind the VAP-61 latrine."

The men squatted on their heels, smoked, waited impatiently for Ted to say something.

"We need sandbags," Ted said, brushing past the other men. "We need a fucking bunker. I figure we can save about forty percent of what we have."

Barry Youmans yawned. "We shoring this one up?"

"Not in this life. We're building a new bunker. There." Ted pointed to the empty field beside the barracks.

"On this dirt I will build my church," Gerry intoned solemnly.

"Listen up, pilgrims," Ted said in his best John Wayne voice, "I already arranged to get some of those metal bomb crates. We fill them with sandbags, we put a good roof on it, and we pack it tight with sandbags on the outside. We have a list of materials we need." He handed a slip to Mark and asked him to read it and pass it along. "We need volunteers to get this stuff."

"Two-by-sixes?" Willy Ames beamed. "You know, they are using some of those very same items to build that new chow hall yonder. Now, if we appropriated that lumber we would delay the opening of that establishment, and possibly postpone ptomaine poisoning for hundreds of men. I would consider it a civic duty to head that detail."

"Oh, shit," Mark said. "This is where I came in. I don't want to crack rocks at Portsmouth for theft."

"Cumshawing is not theft. It is the appropriation of property that would be rightfully ours if anything worked right at all," Ted said. He marveled at Mark's retention of his innocence, his midwestern naïveté; of all of them, Mark seemed the least changed.

Craig, silent until now, snapped his fingers. "Sandbags are my talent. I might need some liquor-ration coupons, so everybody ante up anything we can spare. I also want two or three jugs of good booze, and a case of beer, and not that shitty Carlings either, something quality like Bud."

"Pass the hat and gather the coupons up," Ted said, and looked at Mark. "That won't offend you, will it?"

"I'll do it."

"Timing is of the essence. They predict attacks for tonight, but I don't feel it. I think we have until tomorrow. Anybody not flying is on the building detail. We need to get into some groups and organize our sorties."

Craig waved Mark, Willy, and Devito over to his side. "I'll have sandbags; you better have some lumber."

"Piece of cake."

"Rhymes with flake." Craig led the other men off to an open area in the field.

"This is a beautiful place," said Craig, and asked Devito to stop the truck. Craig was dog-tired from the night flight and no sleep, but his adrenaline was pumping and he finished off a cup of coffee from the geedunk. "See those marines over there, loading up sandbags?"

"Yeah."

"You are about to see the master at work." Craig hopped out of the truck and walked to the redheaded marine that seemed to be in charge. The man was stripped to his waist and sweating. "Hot as a mother," he said.

"Yep." The marine stopped digging sand and stepped back from the others. "You want something, or just like to look at half-naked grunts?"

"Name's Trainer," Craig said. "I might have a deal to work with you, if you're the man that can make it."

"Harrigan," the marine said, "and I am the man that makes the deals here."

"I need sandbags and you have sandbags."

"People in hell need ice water. You a squid?"

"Civilian, my folks just make me dress funny. I came here for summer camp because I won a senior trip."

Harrigan grinned. "God almighty, I thought I was the only by-God civilian in Vietnam."

"Semper Fi."

"So what's your deal?"

Craig walked to the truck and yanked out a bottle of Jack Daniel's, a bottle of Southern Comfort, a bottle of Ron Rico rum, and pointed to a case of beer packed in a trash can filled with ice. "We wanted some sandbags and they told us that we were over our limit. The man wanted some grease. I suggested we kill him, but the military gets pissy when you break their NCOs in little pieces."

"Wise move. I like a man who isn't too dumb."

Craig pulled out two cold beers and handed one to the marine. "We have unlimited ration coupons."

"We even offer a delivery service for the right price."

"That's a language I understand." Craig explained what they needed.

"We can do it, and do it by noon. Name the deal."

Craig flashed liquor-ration coupons and riffed them like a deck of cards. "Take your pick."

"Make it by ten-thirty. I think the boys and I might be getting a little thirsty."

"Maybe if we leave this cold beer, it will help keep the edge off."

"Why, it might at that, Trainer."

"Just call me Ted," Craig said, and walked back to the truck.

Ted had the lumber and the bomb casings stacked behind the old bunker, a crew of seabees with a backhoe had dug a pit that was the foundation, and some of the Det T men were already stacking the bomb casings as walls and filling them with the rotting sandbags of the abandoned bunker. "So how'd you do it?"

"Ration coupons and some booze. You better be sure the coupons are all here."

"They will be."

"I traded with some marines, and they think my name is Ted Trainer."

"You didn't."

"You think I'm crazy enough to use my own name?"

"You're a pisser. Keep things moving while I check on the coupons."

"There it is," Craig said, and jumped down in the hole to take his place in the assembly line.

"This is going to be the Taj Mahal of bunkers."

Craig looked at Ted and nodded. "Just hand another sandbag down, okay? We can admire our work when the rockets hit."

"Artists are never appreciated in their own time."

"Hand me another sandbag, if it won't break your arm to stop patting yourself on the back."

Ted threw a sandbag, and grabbed another to throw. "Let's get it done! When it's all over there's rum, rum for my friends!"

Brooks walked the perimeter of the bunker, ducked his head and walked inside, kicked the walls, tapped the inside of the wood-framed roof. "Impressive."

"Ted's baby all the way."

"Where'd you get the supplies? Wait, I don't want to know, do I?"

"No."

"There isn't anything in this caper that would make a mother cry is there?"

"Not unless they think that the navy should build new chow halls that serve their sons cardboard meatloaf with Day-Glo gravy."

"Don't tell me. Don't even tell me that when those SPs come by and ask about some missing lumber for the new chow hall . . . Am I now abetting a crime wave?"

"Probably just a moral oversight on your part."

Brooks worried back his forelock. "Only one problem that I see."

"Which is?"

"This is a great foundation, a nice deep hole, but what happens in the rainy season?"

Both of them laughed together as if on cue.

"I thought that this might be right up your alley, Nostrum," Richland said, and handed Craig a small tattered notebook. "I got this from a friend over at the stone elephant. I want it translated. He works with the Riverines sometimes."

Craig flipped through it quickly. "What is it?"

"Diary of a dead VC."

"The army, ASA, usually handles these, or maybe the ARVNs."

"It's a favor."

Craig riffed to a page and scanned it; the writing was

cramped but neat. Many of the tonal symbols were smeared from sweat or rain. "I'll take a look at it."

"Good," Richland said, and lit his cigar. "Very good."

Damon rested his head in his folded arms, and continued to spin the radio dials without looking up. He hated the fatigue almost as much as the boredom. He stopped turning the lower knob and sat up with a snap, fine-tuning the signal. "I've got something."

Lieutenant Ferris moved behind him and lifted the right earphone from Damon's head. "What is it?"

Damon slapped the officer's hand away and put his earphone tight to his ear again. "Touch my earphones again and you'll be wearing them in an uncomfortable place, sir."

"Well, what is it?"

"I don't know yet, why don't you check for tracking?"

Damon listened to the ground controller's voice and recognized him: Nam Dinh airfield. He scrawled the two words in large letters at the top of his handlog. "Tell them the aircraft should be out of Nam Dinh," he said. He listened to another exchange. "It's an IL-28."

"What's he doing?" Ferris asked.

"Flying southwesterly. Planes do that."

"I'm not looking for insolence."

"Then don't find it." Damon looked at his watch, the flight was slow and lazy, gentle arcing turns.

GC: You should see the landing lights soon.
617: Roger.

Damon looked up. "Are you sure there's no tracking?"

"The R-beats don't have anything at all."

He glanced over the headings, the gentle turns. "The plane is landing south of Nam Dinh. He never went back."

"Near Hanoi?"

Damon snapped his pencil in two. "Hanoi is north of Nam Dinh." He wondered what the penalty for killing a lieutenant, junior grade, would be. "He's south of Nam Dinh which means he is at Vinh. So why don't you send out a SPOT report and say that there is now an IL-28 light bomber in Vinh."

"Are you sure?"

"Lieutenant, there is a bomber in Vinh which is about one cunt hair from the DMZ, so send it!"

"I better send this out, they might be planning something."

"Do that, sir," Damon answered. "I wish I had thought of that."

Damon stumbled into the barracks, slammed the door behind him without thinking, and paused as if this would still the noise he made. The barracks remained silent. It was not yet three A.M.

Footsteps. The door. Craig listened to the sounds—faint noises, Mark's rhythmic breathing—thinking, wishing he could fall to sleep. He sat up and lit a cigarette, swung his legs over the side of the bunk until he could stretch to the refrigerator and snatch a cold beer.

"What are you doing up? You fly in three hours."

"Thanks, Mom," Craig said, and handed a beer to Damon. "Besides you could have wakened the dead with all your noise." He looked at Miss November who hung on the ceiling to the right of the light bulb. He thought she might be his favorite now. Mosquitoes hummed within and without his mosquito net, and he swatted one flat on his forearm into a dull blot of blood.

"Something wrong, Craig?"

"Here in Wonderland?"

"I just had to put up with Sunny Jim Ferris, and I still might kill him. How does anyone get that stupid?"

"Just get orders to Det T and it comes naturally." Craig smiled. "So you come in like a herd of bull elephants."

"I'm sorry. You sure you're okay?"

"Just leave me alone, okay? I just need some rest."

"Yeah, g'night."

Craig nodded. "Yeah, don't let the bellybugs bite." He stretched out in his chair reached under his pillow and pulled out the diary. He opened to a page randomly. He read the words, *I am lonely here in the south, and there is so much that is strange to me. I miss you and think of you even when I am working with the cadres to bring on the enlightenment of the people. How can any war be this long and hard on all of us?*

Craig closed the notebook again and stumbled to his bed. He kept his eyes closed tight until he fell into a restless sleep.

* * *

Craig sat at his position and scanned the reports from the previous day's flights. He knew that the reports should have been left at the spaces, but he hadn't had time to read them; sometimes security became a battle of procedure over convenience. He tucked them back into the leg pocket of his flight suit. He noted the IL-28 landing at Vinh with a vague feeling of unease, was glad that Damon had gotten the intercept.

The weather was dreary and wet; Rolling Thunder missions had been canceled, and Craig listened to the static with a bored attention. Twice he got a phantom voice that blew into the microphone and gave a quick count of four, *mot, hai, ba, bon*, and a repeat of it, *mot, hai, ba, bon*, and yet another. He laughed quietly. He and the other linguists had dubbed this voice the Phuc Yen janitor. They thought of him as someone who swept out the control tower and seeing a vacant microphone could not resist the temptation.

"You look like hell."

Craig glanced at Brooks and shrugged. "You want Steve McQueen, you have to pay more."

"Want to talk?"

"Not at all." Craig got up and walked to the galley to get a fresh cup of coffee. He reached into another pocket and yanked out a letter from Sheryl and reread it. She talked about walking in the rain, about the way she felt about him, how soon could he be home to her. He read it and lost himself from everything around him.

The flight had been uneventful, and Craig jotted his notes reporting the same. NSA. No significant activity. The fact that the abbreviation was the same as the initials for the National Security Agency brought a smile to him; as always, he wondered which man had thought it up. No one claimed authorship. Craig walked down the aisle and into Commander Richland's office. The tin partitions waggled as he breezed into the small room.

"Did you finish the translation?"

"Yeah. I finished."

"And?" Richland stared at Craig Nostrum; he drummed his fingers on his desktop.

"It's a letter to his girlfriend. He just writes about what he feels."

"No place names, places where they cache arms or anything?"

"Nothing like that."

Richland frowned, closed his eyes, opened them again, and fished his right hand into his desk drawer and withdrew a thin sheaf of papers. "I have some names here, places where they were, places where they probably stashed some rice or arms."

"He doesn't talk about anything military at all, except that he questions the war sometimes. Like all of us."

"But he might have. You know the syntax. You could go ahead and enter a few of these, sprinkle them around, make it a great report. Maybe put in something about how many rifles they left or how much rice."

"There's nothing like that," Craig said again, and suddenly aware of what Richland was suggesting, he shook his head. "You're asking me to lie."

"Do it as a favor. Favors get repaid."

"The kid was only seventeen years old!"

"He was a communist!"

"Fuck off."

"What? What did you say?" Richland scrambled around the table with a speed that surprised Craig.

"I won't do it, sir."

"You're being silly. This would help someone else, and they would help us."

"You, they'd help you," Craig said, and walked toward the doorway.

"Get out! Give me my notebook back."

"I destroyed it."

"What?"

"Stuff it, sir!"

Mark, concerned, touched Craig's forearm.

Craig seemed surprised by the way he jerked his head up, and he nearly spilled his drink. "You startled me," he said. "How old are you, Mark?"

"Nineteen."

Craig nodded, surprised that only a year separated them, he felt older. "Two more years."

"I'll be twenty-one."

"If you were him, you would have been dead for four years by then."

"You've got to get out of this mood, man. Who're you talking about?"

"Nobody."

"You're not making any sense. You want to hit the air force club with me? We haven't busted that place up in weeks."

"No. Just leave me alone, okay?" Craig said this mildly, his mind on Long, the dead VC boy. He added more scotch to his glass and took a swallow.

"So what do you think is going on?" Damon ran a damp towel over the metal rungs of his bunk, shook out his mosquito net, and watched the motes of dust shimmer like tiny insects in the air.

Gerry shrugged, drank from his beer. "I don't know. Craig just won't talk to me this time. I can't even get a rise out of him by calling him Craigers. He just sits and drinks when he's not flying, and he drinks alone."

"Has to do with Richland, you can bet the farm on that."

"Yeah, Richland's a dumb asshole overall, but Craig's taking whatever this is too personally. You have to GAF over some of this shit."

"There it is."

Craig struggled into his bunk, wrestled his way through the mosquito net angrily. He closed his eyes until he could barely see specks of light, until they reminded him of sunshine dancing on the edge of a knife blade, and at last he cried.

"What I'm curious about," Brooks remarked to Bill Patterson, a new lieutenant, "is how they stayed sane this long with all the shit we catch. You're not going to love it here, Bill, but you will see some major shit. You'll also work with the best men you've ever known. Come on, we have a briefing to attend."

One more time.

Chapter 15

There are two types of monsoon rains: a quick, brutal squall, and the constant rain that pummels like tiny fists and looks like steel. Silver steel. In the last twenty-four hours they had had the squalls, rains that, if you watched carefully and ran fast enough, you could outrun to shelter. Now the rain came in gun-metal-gray sheets, in walls of dull heavy water. Beyond the shield of the rain nothing was truly visible.

The oyster glow of dawn brought only a fulgence to the downpour, an iridescence: the sound a constant hum, a roar. "Let's give Sunny Jim a hymn," Craig yelled, drenched but happy.

Inside the officer's barracks, the BOQ, Lieutenant Ferris tried to blot out the yells of the enlisted men that were louder even than the rain.

"Him, him, fuck him. Him, him, fuck Sunny Jim."

"Don't they ever give up?" Ferris asked of Brooks Crenshaw.

Brooks shrugged, stifled a grin. He hated the whine in the other man's voice. Sometimes he thought that it was the whiny quality, even more than his pompous attitude, his rich-boy braggadocio, that the men hated. "You treat them like they had scurvy."

"They're enlisted. We're not supposed to be buddy-buddy, but you wouldn't know that."

"They do a great job for us."

"Don't you see the way they dress, the way they act? Yesterday Craig had on a T-shirt under his flight suit that was like some hippy would wear."

"You see T-shirts, I see results."

"I want them to show proper respect."

They probably do, Brooks thought, but said, "We all do," and walked off to be alone in the officer's lounge.

Cooksey, a tall redhead, was an A-brancher in charge of the administrative duties at the detachment. He was affable, bright, and kept everyone at an arm's length. He had learned early on that taking sides was dangerous to your career: he never volunteered and he never argued. When the gall got to him he would go on a silent, lonely drunk. He told the others that he was Switzerland: an isolationist, neutral country between the battling sides of Richland and the linguists. Now, as he sat over the telex machine and typed the message, he wanted to blame his fingers and not himself for the betrayal he saw on the page. Stay out of this, he told himself. It's not your problem. But when he finished and the message was acknowledged from the main station in the Philippines, he rose, and walked back to the barracks to find Craig Nostrum.

Dusk approached, an eerie silence that worried Craig each time it fell. The days he marked off on his short-timer's calendar seemed endless to him, as if they stretched to infinity or beyond. He thought about Danny Morseth, and the nature of time, and the sinking feeling that he was never going home again, that he was somehow getting old without aging. He stared into the canal, watched the trash and litter bob in the water, and tossed in his cigarette butt.

"You got a minute?"

"Hey, Cookie, how's things on the safe borders."

"I want to talk to you."

"So talk."

"Sometimes you can be a real asshole." Jim Cooksey turned on his heels and walked away.

"Wait! Hey, I'm sorry. I was sitting here moping and feeling like shit, I didn't mean to take it out on you."

"You're going to be sorrier," Aaron Cooksey said, and walked to Craig's side.

"Why?"

"I sent a message to the Philippines today. It was a request for an investigation of the drug dealers here. Your name was first on the list. Nine lingies were named." Cooksey handed over a copy, something he had never done before, and felt dirty with this act.

"The stupid bastard."

"They'll pass this along to NIS."

Naval Investigative Service, the new name for the Office of Naval Intelligence. Craig nodded. The rain had stopped, but Craig sensed more than knew it would return soon. He wiped a hand over his forehead and lit a cigarette. He burned a leech from his right calf. "Fucking leeches," he said at last.

"It's not true, is it?"

"No, Cookie, it's not true."

"I didn't think so. I just thought you should know. Can you get the word to the other guys without telling them where you got the information?"

"Can do," Craig answered. "Why'd you do it? I mean, I know how much you want to stay neutral."

"You ever play paper, scissors, rock?"

"Huh?"

"It's about choices, it came up scissors."

"Yeah."

"There it is."

"Thanks," Craig said, and stood up. "Things do happen, my friend." Craig let Cooksey walk off before he walked to the barracks and removed the marijuana cigarettes from his locker and hid them in the refrigerator in an empty carton of orange juice.

"Things are going well, but we need more pizzazz," Richland said, his cigar ashes falling on the floor of the officer's lounge. "Make them spice things up."

"They won't lie for me any more than they would for you," Brooks replied, wishing he could just leave, pack up and head for the real world.

"Just make things better, no lying, really. Just make us more noticeable."

Brooks nodded. "We might add some analysis."

"That's the ticket, Lieutenant."

"Yes, sir."

Richland smiled as Brooks left his office. He wondered how that left-wing lieutenant had ever commanded the men's respect. He picked up a tablet and scrawled his notes. *Today I noticed that Lieutenant Crenshaw was losing his control, perhaps his senses. He suggested we doctor reports to make them more exciting. He seems dislocated. I am watching him closely, but fear for the results.*

"So how come Marshall's still here?" Ted slapped his hand on Andy Jenkins's desktop. "Come on, answer me! This is fucking Alice in Wonderland bullshit. The man has the linguistic capabilities of a rutabaga."

"Richland said to give him more time," Andy answered abruptly.

"Where's His Highness?"

"Probably safe at the O club."

"The man's the shits, Andy, the ever-loving shits."

"This may surprise you, but I am not in charge here. I have orders to follow. Why don't you step on someone else's pecker?"

Ted walked to Richland's office and kicked over the trash can, playing soccer with the wadded papers. "He has my message."

Turnip. That was Craig's word, Andy thought. Craig assigned almost everyone he disliked to a vegetable category. Richland was collard greens, Ferris was a turnip, Masters was a beet.

"I'm history," Ted said.

"Take care," Andy said, and stooped to gather up the trash. Just call me the janitor, he whispered.

Craig listened to the rain and read from Glenway Westcott. The rain soothed him; the sound was reassuring. He flipped the next page of his book.

"Card game," Ted yelled, though he was beside him.

"Maybe you yell because your ears are so small," Craig replied, and continued to read.

"Thought you were at the spaces."

"Couldn't you just talk at a normal decibel level once? The navy said we might lose some hearing because of the static, they never said I'd go deaf because of you."

"So get some beer and join the party. You and Willy Ames against Gerry and I. Pinochle."

"What if I want to read?"

"Bring the book, it might keep you entertained as you're losing."

"Shit, too, leather lungs."

Andy finished cleaning up the scattered trash: Angry men, he thought, there were too many of them here. He touched his chin and rubbed the blond stubble of a three-day beard. He was glad it was Ted and not Craig that had caused the scene. Craig would have taken the trash to Richland's bunk and dumped it over him. He grinned with the thought.

The spook mess was crowded: men in groups, or pairs, or alone. Outside, the heavy rain continued.

Ping-pong balls popped in sharp cracks, quick as small-arms fire. Two R-beats played against two I-beats. Craig rooted for the I-beats, the lingies, from camaraderie, though he wanted Barry Youmans to win in his heart. He liked the southern boy who had slowly become one of them. He laid down his double pinochle and grinned. "Meld anyone?" he asked.

Damon had replaced Gerry, who wanted to see a movie at VAP-61. As in any of their competitions, Damon could not be happy if Craig won. While he did not puzzle over the competition between them, he sometimes wished it would stop. He knew he could not let Nostrum best him in anything, or it would soon get around that he bested him in all things.

Craig held his cards, gritty and flimsy, and led off with a spade.

Steve Marshall won the second ping-pong game series, which led Ted to say, "I don't care if he wins Miss America, he's a shit and a hammer and he needs to be chipping paint over the side of a ship."

"Is it kind, is it true, would you want it said of you?" Willy Ames said, and trumped the trick Ted thought he had won.

"Even if he was a good lingie, I wouldn't like him."

"Why not?" Craig asked, and led his ace of hearts.

"I just don't trust him. Besides, if Richland likes him nobody else could."

"I'll buy off on that," Craig said, and gathered in his trick.

"We made it easy, even with the handicap of having Willy as a partner."

Steve Marshall edged to the card table and stared over Gerry's shoulder, until Ted gave him a black look and he moved off to watch *I Love Lucy*.

"We're worse than a bunch of old ladies sometimes: hunches, feelings, twitches. They shouldn't call this place Det Tango, it should be Madame Baba's Tea-leaf Parlor." Andy said as he sat down. "How about a change to poker?"

Ted grinned, "New blood! New money! Booze! Innkeeper, rum, I want rum for my friends!"

"Sobriety has no redeeming qualities whatsoever," Andy said, and shuffled the cards. "Five-card stud."

Craig, down from the early flight, drenched with rain, stood in his cubicle and stripped off his clothes. He hung the flight suit over the end rung of the bunk to dry. He knew that the jungle boots with green canvas panels would never dry out. He took off his socks, and pieces of pulpy flesh came off as well.

"You hear the news?"

Craig looked at Ted. "We just landed ten minutes ago, how would I have heard the news? For that matter, how did you hear any news?"

"Devito told me."

"Told you what?"

"The news. Guess he didn't want to be the one to break it to you."

"Read my lips, Ted, what fucking news?"

"The commanding general of I Corps came for a surprise visit and he found our quarters to be lacking. He decided that the pinups are bad for morale and he ordered them down."

"Take a flying fuck."

"Hey, it's all true. Richland said yes so fast his tongue got a cramp in it."

"He would." Craig wrapped himself in a towel and flopped onto his bunk. "I guess it's time for the bean shipments to start again. You in?"

"I'll give you twenty."

"Good. Maybe pinto beans this time, the real tiny ones, loose in a package so when he opens it they fall all over the floor."

"You're going to piss him off."

"Gosh, why didn't I think of that?"

It was midnight, though through the rains it was difficult to tell the difference between night and day. Craig was glad to be airborne, though he felt rancor that Brady had claimed illness again. His ambivalence toward Brady had turned sour. He begrudged Brady's attitude, his lack of the same fervor that drove him and Damon and Andy and the others. Where all of them shared the GAF attitude toward the military, each was committed to his job with an intensity that sometimes seemed like religious zealotry.

"You okay?" Barry asked.

"A little tired, and I can't believe that I lucked out and got the one flight a month that Chief Masters makes to earn his flyboy pay. See what he did on the work chart?"

Youmans grinned. "I saw. You have to empty the benjo."

"Enjoy it while you can, my friend, wait until next flight when I'm making up the list again."

Benjo duty involved taking the portable toilet and carrying it from the plane to the barrels to be emptied and burned, the worst of the postflight chores and usually reserved for the newer men.

"You're a legend in your own mind, Craigers."

"Bug off, boy, don't hassle a star." Craig flipped on his tape recorder. "Got something up, night GCAs probably, tell Sunny Jim on your way to the back, huh?"

"At your command, O wondrous one."

Lieutenant Ferris, his glasses perched near the tip of his nose, leaned over Craig's shoulder. His breath was warm and sour.

"Practice takeoff and landings," Craig said and scribbled *TOLs* on the dust jacket of the tape.

"Anything I should send out?"

"Only if they miss the runway."

Craig looked out the porthole window, saw thin trails of smoke, watched the blades sputter and quit on engine three. Feathering number three, he said softly. He'd heard the words so often before. They flew on three engines routinely; he had finished one mission with only two engines functioning. The pilot told him they could even make it with one if they had to.

Craig logged six periods of *TOLs*, and the volume of the

traffic surprised and worried him. Night practices were rare enough as it was. He made a point to bring it to Andy's attention when he went to the spaces to write the postflight report.

"So what do you think it is?"

"Not sure. New pilots, new planes, something. We might see if the zoomies have anything on it, maybe some ideas."

"You're taking them down."

"That's what I like about you, Mark, your keen grasp of the obvious." Craig folded the girls one into the other accordian style, a daisy chain of pinups. He pressed each one flat with his fingers, smoothing them carefully.

"I'll miss them."

"Yeah," Craig replied. He took Miss April, his latest favorite, and held her for a moment before folding her with the others. He glanced at Mark, who had come to seem like a younger brother as much a friend, and shrugged his shoulders. "You seen Gerry?"

"He's down at the slop chute, watching the movie."

"We finally get a new one?"

"Nope. Still *Tarzan and the City of Gold*."

"I even know Cheetah's lines by heart now." Like so many other things, new movies never quite made it as far as Det Tango. The slop chute, a shanty that sold beer and snacks, endlessly showed whatever movie they had, projecting it against the outside wall of the latrine. The men sat on the dirt hillocks of the field.

"We fly in forty-five minutes. I'm filling in for the new guy, Freeman. Seems he has an abscessed tooth. He's across the base getting it fixed."

"Flying junior again? How are you going to handle it, Mark?"

"By showing you up."

"Not on your life." Craig thought about Gerry, could easily picture him sitting patiently and watching the movie again without any sense of anger. Gerry seemed to be perpetually renewed, an innocent who remained untouched, unsoiled by the shabbiness of their lives. Craig set the pinups on a locker shelf and covered them with a T-shirt. "Bad for morale . . . bullshit. You know what's bad for morale? Rocket attacks, and snipers, and military beggar assholes!" Craig kicked the locker. The barren beams seemed forlorn and depressing to him. He smashed the locker again.

"Wrecking our humble home isn't going to fix anything."

"Shut up." Craig shook his fist, rubbed his knuckles knowing that if he didn't do something, he might cry.

"We better head for the flight."

Craig nodded, relieved to have something divert him from his mood, his anger, to lessen his sense of impotence and violation.

He grabbed his Aussie go-to-hell hat and slapped it on his head. "You know the pleasant side of the monsoon season?"

"No."

"There it is."

They walked outside. The clouds were thickly crusted behind the hills, like sky mountains, the rain splashed over them with big slow drops.

The flight, like many, was uneventful.

Craig stepped onto the ladder to climb down from the Willy Victor, hit the fourth step, felt it give, but could do nothing but flail his arms uselessly as he fell to the pavement on his back.

"Holy shit, you okay?" Mark bounded to Craig's side, and helped ease him to a sitting position.

"My back hurts like hell," Craig whispered, still having trouble catching his breath. He stared at the broken step that dangled from the ladder. "Bastards! Somebody should have fixed that sucker before now."

"Maybe you better stay here and we'll call for a truck."

"Just help me up." Craig gripped Mark's forearms and slowly rose to his feet. He leaned against Mark's side, draped his left arm over the other man's shoulders. "Go slow, huh?"

Back from the dispensary, Craig repeated the doctor's comments to the men in the spook mess, 'nothing broken, probably some deep bruises, maybe a disc out,' "but they couldn't find it on x-rays, so he gave me some muscle relaxants and Darvon for the pain."

"So how do you feel?"

"Even the Darvon doesn't take all the pain away," Craig answered.

"Sure are graceful—that's what I love most about you, Craig—is that wonderful ballet-dancer quality you have."

"Fuck you very much, Ted. How about a drink? Can someone be a good sport and get me a fucking drink?"

"Should you drink when you're taking all those pills?" Mark received a stony stare in response. "I'll get you a drink."

A night without rockets, a day without rain, welcome portents that caused Craig to remark, "Things are looking up," and almost immediately regret it. But within an hour his expansive mood had vanished.

"That was an order, Nostrum." Chief Masters stood nose to nose with him, his breath sweet with a Lavoris scent.

"I said, no way." Craig stared into the chief's eyes until Masters finally looked away. "You take that fucking order and shove it sideways."

"Richland issued the order on behalf of the general, you are not going to ignore it."

"Watch me." Craig walked off, wishing that instead of crankcase oil he had filled the chief's boots with napalm.

"Come back here!"

"Or what, Chief? What're you going to do? Send me to Vietnam?" Craig kept walking.

It was sunny and the ground steamed with the humidity and the pools of rain that spread like ponds. Mosquitoes bred, spent their life-cycles, bled the men, and died between the bogs and the barracks. Craig swatted a plump one, fresh with his blood, on his right forearm. He winced with the sudden movement that jarred his back, and swallowed a Darvon, dry. He mixed himself a scotch and water in his cube, and farted.

The order. Two men had been found dead in Da Nang. They had been visiting a skivvy house, had been beheaded by the Vietcong. They put the bodies on display at the morgue and ordered the men to view them: a lesson in immorality.

Craig sipped his drink, looked at his Timex watch. Two o'clock. He opened a can of Bounty beef stew with the small John Wayne can opener and ate it cold.

After he finished, he tossed the can in the trash, added more scotch to his drink, and walked outside. He sat down on the bottom step of the outside stairway that led to the second story of the barracks and smoked a cigarette. A dozen men played a slow volleyball game, slopping through the puddles and mud. Craig knew he should be used to the indignities of this place, the relentlessness of the heat or the rain, the absurd orders; the knowledge did nothing to lessen his aches.

"Brooding alone, or can anyone join the fun?"

"You seen the chief, Gerry?"

"Yeah. I told him to take a flying leap, preferably from a Willy Victor in flight."

"Me, too."

"I know; he's already talking about a court-martial. I volunteered to be on the firing squad."

"Thanks."

"Anything for a buddy." Gerry popped the top of his beer and took a long swallow.

"The general's as fucked up as Richland. He thinks pinups are bad for morale, and dead bodies are good for it."

Gerry stuck his thumbs in his ears and waggled his fingers.

"Life is brisk at the asylum," Craig noted.

"Richland got some beans this morning. Cookie told me he was raging like a maniac. Said that he'd find a way to prove you were behind it."

"He's demented."

"You say that about all the beggars."

"Yeah. They all need knee pads, they're so used to kissing ass."

"You're hurting again." Gerry regarded his friend. "You been back to the doc?"

"Nothing new. I started getting some Darvon from the corpsman." Craig swallowed some more scotch. *"C'est la vie."*

By the time Craig finally settled into his bunk and fell to sleep he was drunk and the pain receded. When he dreamed he saw two headless boys, and they were more hideous and helpless in his dream than they could have been if he had actually viewed them.

Chapter 16

The attack shocked them. It had been peaceful for thirteen days and the men had fallen into the comfort of repetition and safety. Now they huddled in the bunker, quiet as rabbits. They leaned against one another and the bunker walls. Dust sifted down on them from the bags overhead. Four inches of water soaked their feet and cuffs, and their legs cramped from squatting. The rats had skittered out as they charged in: the rats, fat and bold, squealed complaints at being dispossessed.

"Bastards!" Andy Jenkins screamed. He stood in the doorway, framed by the stark gray of the sky, and shook his fist at the unseen enemy.

"Come on, sit down." Craig took Andy by the elbow and urged him inside, until they squatted side by side. He felt Andy trembling beside him from the damp, the cold, fear—a combination of the three, probably.

"I'm short, Craig, fourteen and a wake-up."

"So short you can't start a long conversation."

"Sometimes it scares me. I keep thinking that the day my freedom bird takes off I'll be stuck here in the bunker."

"It'll be okay."

"Yeah," Andy said hopefully.

Craig was looking at Andy, and in the half light he seemed to shrink. Fourteen and a wake-up, Craig mused; already he had begun to miss Andy. The problem with the revolving door, of men who passed in and out of his life, was that you began missing them too soon or too late. He settled into a crouch. He could smell the sweet smoke of marijuana from the other end of the bunker, was sure that it was Damon and Gerry smoking.

The explosions were muted by the rain: flares danced brightly, then died in the distance.

"They make us crazy this way. You never know when they're going to attack. Goddamn, I hate this." Damon spoke softly, more to himself than anyone else, and took another long swallow of smoke. He held it until his chest burned and let it out in a long slow exhalation.

Gary Devito stumbled through the doorway. He was soaked and muddy. "They caught two sappers inside the base, they had satchel charges."

Craig nodded. "Talked to Hennings up in Phu Bai the other day, and he said they caught one of their housegirls poisoning the food at the chow hall. What a way to go. I mean, it's bad enough the food sucks."

As suddenly as it began, the attack was over. The all-clear whistle sounded shrilly. The rain gave it an eerie edge, like some prehistoric creature crying for its mate.

Damon Arneault was flying the late mission, and surprised that he was glad to be airborne. The unit had already telexed the plane that they had come under attack again. He was glad to be on the willy instead of cramped inside the bunker.

"Got something up," he said. "Do the ditty boppers have any tracking?"

"That's a negative," a Morse operator named Bruce Swansburg answered.

Fred Stone, flying as junior tac/air man, was startled by the clarity of the voices on the radio, but the language confused him momentarily. "Hey, Damon, I've got some Chinese up."

Damon turned around. "Tape it, we can get someone to listen to it on the ground. Keep searching the other channels."

Lieutenant Hermann, a new evaluator just in from Japan, walked to Damon's side. "They have some tracking now. We can't grid it so far; seems unusual, Bruce said."

Damon mulled this over as he copied the traffic onto his handlog: night flight, Chinese, odd tracks. He grinned.

"Check north, above Yen Bay, these are probably ferry flights from China. They sound like MiG-19s."

"A guess?"

Damon's eyes were canny and alert. "You can bank on it."

"Where are they landing?"

"Phuc Yen."

"Want me to send it out?"

"Sure, new planes always make a big splash. Gives Johnson all the more reason to perform escalation on the North Vietnamese."

Hermann grinned. Despite his newness, a wariness that existed, he liked the men. He walked to the cubbyhole with the telex and had the O-brancher send out the message.

It was hot and dry, a rare interruption to the cycle of rain. Craig sat near the banks of the drainage ditch which had become his own spot, his resource and refuge. He watched a snake swim lazily past. At this distance, safe, he thought it looked noble and graceful. The sheer pleasure of the weather and the quiet made him thoughtful. With a light breeze carrying the scents of salt and sea and fish, he could almost imagine himself in San Diego, on his first liberty from boot camp. He did all the normal things that day: he went to the zoo, drank a few beers, went to the burlesque show. Rites. Just as being promoted to senior lingie was a rite of passage, each act had led him toward this place, until it was inevitable. He lit a cigarette and watched an A4 split the sky in two and disappear into the steeped bank of white clouds.

Nine and a wake-up. The thought came as rudely and suddenly as an attack. On the tenth morning Andy Jenkins would be gone. Home. The Real World. The world that seemed remote to him now, a complicated puzzle that he could neither fathom nor see. It existed in the rumors from the newspapers, in letters, but its shape was vague to him.

He dozed, then woke, startled by a jet going to afterburners. In that moment of wakening he felt disoriented and confused: This world he had come to know so intimately was a strange and fearsome place. He lit a cigarette and calmed himself. He pulled Sheryl's letter from his pocket and read it again. It had been four days since he had gotten any mail, so he read this letter over and over, as if each time it was new. She said things were fine back home. Yes, there were protes-

tors, but they were a small minority. He shook his head and
looked back at the brackish water.

"Hey, Craig!"

Mark jogged down the hill toward him and skidded to a
stop at his side. He cast a long shadow over the water and
Craig watched debris float into the shadow, then reappear in
the sunlight. "What's up, Mark?"

"Drug inspection in twenty minutes."

"How'd you hear about it?"

"I have my sources, too."

"I don't even have a stick of marijuana. No sweat."

Mark smiled smugly. "Rumor also has it that there was
some planted in your locker."

"Shit." Craig stretched out flat and stared at the sky.

"You better come."

"Why? I find it, they just find another way to fuck with
me. Why not just let the whole thing get over with."

"Because this place needs you, and you need it. Besides,
I'd have to break in a new bridge partner."

"You ever just been too tired to want to fight?"

"Yeah, but you can't let him win. He's still in rage over the
beans. Sending them to his wife was a nice touch, too. She
says she's the laughingstock of the officers' wives club."

"Come on, Tonto, lead the way."

They jogged back to the barracks, side by side, their
shadows congealed into a single amorphous form.

Craig dug through the haphazardness of his locker. He
pulled out clothes, books, papers: the flotsam and jetsam of
his life. His hands burrowed in the nest of confusion with
practiced skill, rummaged and foraged into the corners of the
drawers. He pulled out a small newspaper-wrapped package.
He opened it slowly, revealing the twenty sticks of marijuana.
"You warn the others?"

"Yeah, Ted had a package too."

"Shit on a stick." Craig buried the marijuana in a trash can,
and walked back to his cube to get a drink and wait.

Commander Richland led a lieutenant from the Naval Investigative Service into the squad bay, announced an inspection, and ordered the men to stand at attention at the end of
their racks.

Craig leaned against his bunk and crossed his legs.

The progress was slow. The two men stood at the opening

to each cubicle while Chief Masters and another man actually did the searching. Drawers were emptied onto bunks, bedding stripped from the bunks.

Craig did not come to attention as they approached, but squared his shoulders a little. He stared at Richland, then looked across the aisle to Ted Trainer and winked. The inspection revealed nothing.

Richland swore, asked Masters to check everything in Craig's locker again.

"Clean, sir."

"As a baby's bottom," Craig said with a grin. "Maybe you should be checking the BOQ instead."

Richland fussed, blustered, and finally called a halt to the investigation entirely. He strode out of the barracks and slammed the door behind him.

Within two hours of the invasion, Craig, Gerry, and Mark were discussing the outline of a plan. They met in the stale dampness of the bunker, breathing the mildewed air as they plotted the return of the pinups. Since Craig was the aggrieved party, he was leading the discussion. In their sub-rosa hierarchy, leadership was bestowed by common consent. Craig whispered his plan.

"When?"

"Today," Craig said. "What the hell?"

The three of them grinned, slapped their hands together, clapped, and went about their individual errands.

"What makes you think this will work?" Mark asked.

"Things like this always work. Besides, I conceived of the plan, and I know how to plan payback."

They sat on the porch stoop and the sky was the lavender haze of twilight. When Mark didn't speak again, Craig said, "He'll cave in. Just like he always looks away when I stare him down." With that said he stood up and walked into his cube again. He looked at the ceiling: the beams were now papered with pictures of wrestlers, each of the magazine pictures signed in Magic Marker—*"Love, Brucie," "Love, Mark," "Love, Gorgeous George."* Craig lay down and fell asleep with the faces smiling down at him with muted benediction.

* * *

"You think everything is funny, don't you, Nostrum?"

"I try to maintain a sense of humor."

"I don't consider this travesty very amusing at all." Richland twirled an unlit cigar in his left hand. A blue vein had popped out bright against his left temple. "I want them down."

"As soon as my ladies go back up."

"You can't blackmail me."

"And you can't make me take them down. It's a trade, really."

"Anybody that walked in here would think this was a barracks filled with homos."

"Probably think we had a faggot for a commander, too."

Richland broke his cigar in half. "Put the women back up, but this isn't the end of it."

"Thank you, sir. I appreciate a supportive senior officer."

Richland made a tight, ugly sound, then dropped the cigar on Craig's floor and stomped off.

Damon stood in the empty field smoking a Pall Mall. He watched the C-130 make a slow arc over the blue basin of Da Nang Bay, and turn on a southerly heading. Chu Lai, then Saigon, then Clark Air Base in the Philippines. He imagined that he was on the plane, and it broke his bitter mood for a moment. He had not gone to the terminal to see Andy off, and now as he watched the airplane disappear it was still hard to imagine that Jenkins was really gone. He ground out his cigarette butt under his heel. He walked into the barracks to get his first beer of the day. It was oh nine hundred hours.

Craig did not consider the tears that leaked from his eyes to be crying. He stared at Andy's locker, at the single gray flight suit that hung there with a note pinned to it. He finally removed the note and opened it.

Craig—hate to say goodbyes. You know all the stuff I would say to you, about friends, keeping in touch, keeping the faith, hanging tough. The cliches mean something, I guess, old buddy. I am going to miss you, and I am glad to be going home, too. The flight suit has been a lucky one for me, it's yours now.

Keep clear of the numbers, don't count flights, get one

for the gipper, and if you don't keep in touch I'll come
back and kick your ass into next year.
hallucinations and hogbellies,
your friend always,
uncle gene

Craig touched the sleeve of the flight suit, finally took it
down from the peg, and walked to his own cube to hang it up.

Barry Youmans walked with such a steady stride that he
seemed purposeful even when he was dawdling. Since he was
one of the few spooks who ever used the base gymnasium to
lift weights or visited the doughnut dollies at the Red Cross or
crossed to the new navy chow hall to eat military meals, he
served as a bridge for the others. He carried news of other
units, general information, and delivered precise messages
from one to the other of the men. His voice was syrupy with
his southern accent, and even when he brought snide messages
they were received calmly. It was seven in the morning and
amid the din and chatter of the barracks he was walking
slowly, cube by cube, and asking for a hacksaw.

"I think Damon has it," Gerry said, though he was not sure
when Damon had actually had the hacksaw—it could have
been yesterday or three months ago. The fact that Damon had
had it at one time seemed a near certainty to him, though.

"Not me. The last I saw of it, Devito had it."

Barry shook his head; the whole procedure made him feel
like a rumor that was being carelessly passed along.

"Why do you want it?" Craig asked.

"I don't, Chief Masters does."

"Why?"

"Someone put wood putty in the padlock to his locker."

Craig laughed. "Really?"

"He says it was you."

"Probably the same VC sappers who short-sheeted his
bunk last week."

"Do you have it?"

"What?"

"The hacksaw."

"No. Ted had it once, though. He was trying to saw the
legs off Murphy's bunk to make him think he was shrinking."

Ted had the hacksaw, but by the time Barry had found it
and taken it to the chief, Masters had kicked a dent in the door

of his locker and was swearing a steady string of blue language. "What took you so long?"

"It wasn't easy to find."

"Nothing ever is in this place." The chief wheezed and began to cut the lock off with a furious jerk.

It was oh six hundred and Craig stood in front of the flight shack and watched the early crew walk to the plane. He had given the briefing and he stood awkwardly in pain, wondering if he should take another Darvon.

The crew was Baker crew, and Mark was the senior tac/air man. Craig would be getting yet another newbie that afternoon. He looked at the crewmen as they walked, and though not a man was over twenty-two, they had the mincing shuffle of old men. Too many days without rest, too many flights, too many attacks, low-grade fevers, dysentery—too many of any and all of the various indignities that were heaped on them and they shrunk under the weight. He hated looking at them, but like rubbernecking at an accident on the highway, he was transfixed. He felt paternal, the way Andy had said it would be, but the emotion still puzzled him. While a new man had taken over as analyst since Andy's departure, Andy's mantle of leadership had passed to Craig. He smoked silently, having already forgotten the subject of the briefing that he had given, and walked back inside for some coffee and a chance to use a flush toilet instead of a four-hole outhouse.

"You see how they look?"

Brooks Crenshaw nodded. His own face showed the wear of the days. The days were intimate, unlimited in their capacity to drain them. Brooks coughed tubercularly, a hollow, dry cough that had been with him for a month. "What's to do?"

"We could get a couple of lingies from the ships and send some newies out there, and give some of these guys a huss."

"I asked Richland about it. He just stared at me. He said he wasn't about to mollycoddle some wimps."

"Fuck him." Craig walked into the bathroom and slammed the door behind him. The walls were paper-thin. He knew as he sat down and grunted with the roiling of his bowels that any pretense of privacy was a ruse.

Brooks walked to the map of North Vietnam and noted the locations of the tactical airfields from memory. He knew the names by heart: Phuc Yen, Bac Mai, Gia Lam, Yen Bay, Nam

Dinh, Kep, Vinh. He turned as Craig walked out. "Feeling better?"

"Than what?"

"Good point; reality is even worse when you have something to compare it to. You going to the spaces?"

"Yeah, I want to look over last night"s reports, see what's come in from other sources, maybe drop by the zoomies' office and see what they have."

"You have the afternoon flight?"

"That's a roger. The crash-and-burn special on old *PR21*."

"Uh, oh," Craig said, and lowered himself in the seat until just the top of his head was visible.

Beside him, driving the truck, Brooks turned. "What's up?"

"Drive around the block and let me think, okay?"

Brooks glanced at the Green Beret captain who was standing across the street from the main gate. "That special forces captain make you nervous for some reason?"

"A couple of them, actually."

"Such as?"

"He told me to salute him and get a haircut, and I flipped him the bird and ran inside the spaces. I think I said *nyah, nyah, nyah* to him and wiggled my fingers in my ears and stuck out my tongue. Maybe. The marine guard wouldn't give him my name."

"Looks like he could eat you for breakfast."

"Don't remind me."

"I drive much further, and we'll be in Dogpatch and probably be shot as deserters."

"At least it would be quick," Craig said. He looked in the rearview mirror. The captain's patience worried him. The man didn't move at all. "Doesn't he have a job to do?"

"Probably."

"Shit. Okay, here's the plan. I'm going to get on the roof of the cab and then jump to the top of the fence and drop inside the compound."

"Good idea. First you'll get ripped to shreds on the concertina wire, then the marine's going to shoot you. His orders are to shoot first and ask questions later."

Craig wriggled in the seat, his right leg bouncing up and down at full speed. He reached for his Aussie go-to-hell hat and drew it down over his forehead. "Just slow down and I'm making a run for it."

"It's a bad idea, but have at it. Should I yell for him to shoot you?"

"Not funny, Brooks. Not at all funny."

Craig ducked low and ran through the gate, signing the log and grabbing his badge in a single deft move before skidding around the corner and out of sight.

"Stop that man!" the Green Beret yelled. He walked up to Brooks Crenshaw. "Do you know that man?"

"Just a hitchhiker I picked up."

"You going in there?"

"Yeah."

"Find out his name and unit for me."

"I'll try," Brooks said, and walked inside the compound.

Cooksey, just recently returned from his five days in the Philippines, was tanned and genial.

"Catch anything?" Craig asked.

Cookie clapped his hands twice.

Craig laughed. "Ah, the old drip, drip, huh? You're no-where near the record, though. Frenchy had it seventeen times."

"It's not a record I want to break."

"So what's shaking back at San Magoo?"

"Rumors flying fast and furious. They had one that you'd reenlisted and wanted to be assigned full-time as Richland's orderly."

"Fuck you very much."

"They're investigating Roger Tripp."

Craig knew without asking what the charges would be. The rumors about Roger had been around so long that he thought they had finally died out. For a time the rumors had touched on him and Gerry as well: they had been called his fair-haired boys. Craig backed away from Cookie and the conversation as if it might be contagious. Craig felt guilty: Roger had trained him and looked out for him; he felt he had betrayed the confidence Roger had shown in him.

"We keep dancing around it, but we have to face up to it, somebody in this place is a fink. Somebody planted the pot, somebody keeps Richland aware of what we do, somebody is snitching on us at every turn." Ted bellowed this out, punctuating it with his hands. "We have to find out who."

Craig shrank back a little, sure that Ted was right, but unwilling to believe it. "Who?"

"I don't know," Gerry said, "but not an I-beat, and that's for sure. Got to be a ditty bopper or maybe an O-beat, maybe one of those T-branchers, you know they don't ever fit in."

Damon nodded agreement, thinking it had to be a marine, one who thought the unit was not strac enough.

"What about Hegarty?" Gerry asked.

"No way," Craig said. "He likes things military, but he's a good guy." Craig watched Ted's face. "You have somebody in mind, don't you?"

"Who's always sucking up to us, hanging around like a fucking black cloud? Who should be out chipping paint but somehow survives?" Ted demanded.

"You don't have to shout," Damon said.

"That's his normal volume," Gerry said. "Comes from listening to the Mothers of Invention albums over and over again. He's getting deaf. Besides, look how tiny his ears are."

Ted blushed, touched his ears, and brought his hands back again with a jerk. "Marshall," he said at last.

"There's no proof," Craig replied.

"Then we keep an eye out, we plant some stories and see what happens. He'll trip himself up."

"Payback is a motherfucker," Gerry said.

"You look like hell, Ger. You sure you don't want to head for sick bay?"

Gerry shook his head. "You're a fine one to talk, or do you like walking stooped over?"

"The pills will kick in soon, and I'll be okay. You're running a fever and you have the shakes."

"Just need some rest. Maybe tomorrow."

Craig sat beside his friend's bunk confounded by his helplessness. He poured Gerry a glass of water and handed him two antibiotic capsules he had cadged from the corpsman for a bottle of Jim Beam. He sat patiently until Gerry fell asleep. Gerry's breathing rattled. Craig drew a blanket over him and walked away.

"How is he?" Ted asked.

"Sleeping."

"They med-evaced Tim McElroy out today. They're calling it flying fever, just like when you and Gerry had it in Korat."

"Isn't medicine wonderful?"

"A bitch man, this place is a bitch."

Craig woke angry, took a cold shower since there was no hot water again, and walked to the spaces. He thought of the red peeling flesh on his feet, the severe back pain that only abated when he mixed pills and booze, the angers that vexed him as certainly as plague. He collected his ID card and walked into the spaces.

"Morning," an airman said.

"Fuck off, zoomie." Craig walked into Richland's office and stood in front of his desk. "We need some relief. We need some time off. We need some time to heal." He paused. "Get Foreman and Castle in from the ships to help out, and rotate the crews so that the sick men get two or three days' rest in a row."

"You can't barge in here and give orders."

"You do this. Just like I outlined."

"I don't have to do anything, Nostrum. You want to get put on report, maybe lose your stripes?"

Craig's fatigue had settled so deeply that it overcame both fear and reticence. He stood silently for a moment, and when he spoke his voice was quiet, and firm. "Because if you don't, then I'm going to do two things. First off, I'm going to the base chaplain and the chief medical officer and tell them about the shape we're in. Next, I'll toss in my wings, and so will the other senior lingies. You want minutes, you'll have to learn Vietnamese and tape them yourself."

"You can't do it." Richland's breath was uneven; he glared at Craig.

"Consider it a promise." Craig unpinned his wings, held them in the palm of his hand.

"That would be mutiny."

"Flying is voluntary duty, we can turn these in any time we want. DOD rules, navy regulations. Don't push me on this."

"You wouldn't do it."

"In a minute, sir, in a fucking minute."

Brooks walked into the office, sheepish for eavesdropping, unsure what to say.

"You're in on this, too?" Richland asked numbly.

"Lieutenant Crenshaw had nothing to do with it. He didn't know about it until now."

Brooks brushed the comment away with a hand. "He's

right, Dave. They need rest and they need help."

Richland nodded slowly. "I'll issue the orders and get some men as soon as possible. But I won't forget this, not from either of you."

"Thank you, sir." Craig said softly, and walked out, Brooks at his heels.

"You're going to be a hero in the barracks tonight."

"Don't say anything to anybody. I didn't do this to be a hero. Just let it be."

"You'd have done just what you said."

"I hope so. At least he thought I would."

Richland pulled out the personnel chart he had been carefully keeping for weeks. He wrote several entries that showed that Brooks was not only drinking too much, but had begun to suffer delusions. *Chronic lying, possibly pathological,* he wrote in bold letters.

He closed the file and smiled.

One more time.

Chapter 17

The Sacré-Coeur orphanage was built by the French during their "*mission civilitrice*" on the outskirts of Tourane: unlike the city, the orphanage's name had never changed.

Sister Tsu Vien, her habit freshly pressed, was the first to greet them. Her voice bore traces of a French accent, though she was ethnic Vietnamese: she had been educated in France. She called out cheery welcomes to Craig and the others. She pointed to a porch and watched as they unloaded cartons of clothes, food, and dried milk.

The mother superior, who seemed so old that her papery skin might at any moment turn to dust, leaned on her thick cane and limped toward the men. "*Merci beaucoups, messieurs*," she said. "Thank you. *Cam on cac anh*."

Craig followed Tsu Vien to the veranda where the babies slept in cribs and bassinets and empty crates. Craig reached into a bassinet and touched a baby girl's face with his finger until she cooed and smiled. This was the baby that Gunny was adopting, still trying to adopt. The bribes were depressing. The baby was Amerasian, like many of the children, and without Gunny she would have no life at all. To the Vietnamese the half-breeds were anathema: on the streets they would be turned to prostitution, thievery, or slavery. He turned to the next crib and looked at a baby that was listless with fever, scabrous with sores. He looked away, nauseated and ashamed.

"She will not live long. She was left at the gate last night."

He nodded, feeling numbed and stupid. He dug in his pockets and pulled out two envelopes of greenbacks: one held the new bribes for the gunny, the other his own cash to help buy medicine for the babies. She accepted them and the envelopes disappeared within the folds of her skirt.

Each embarrassed by the transaction, they did not speak for a moment and finally Craig excused himself and walked into the courtyard.

Butterfly, a small girl of seven or eight, ran from one man to the other and begged candy with a gap-toothed smile. "*Keo, keo,*" she said, and hugged and kissed her benefactors. Craig took his place, hugged her tight, swung her up, and handed her a bag of M&Ms. "*Toi yeu co,*" he said.

"I love you, too," she answered.

Craig handed her to Ted and walked across the courtyard to the bed where the legless boy, Duc Tho, lay on a cot. He sat down and patted the boy's head, then told him stories. It was a ritual, a habit; Craig sometimes thought this was his moment of redemption.

"Long ago there was a mighty king who lived in a great castle. He was emperor of Vietnam. He was a good and moderate man and he always kept his altar, and visited the graves of his ancestors. The mantle of heaven rested easily on his shoulders."

Duc Tho listened intently, though he had heard this story many times. When he'd had parents, his mother had told it to him. It was the story of the pagoda with one pillar.

Craig, hurried by the bleat of the truck's horn, finished his story with a rush. He patted Duc Tho's head, hugged him, and left him candy and two American dollars.

"How do you like kids, Ted?" Mark asked.

"Fried or parboiled."

Craig smiled, he knew Ted's deceptions as well as he knew his own. He settled into the back of the truck and lit a cigarette. He accepted the cold beer Gerry handed him.

"I feel so good when I'm there, and so shitty when we leave and nothing is really any better."

"Remember the first time we stole a truck?" Ted asked. "You know, the bombing range . . ."

The three of them, Craig, Gerry, and Ted, laughed with the

recollection. They had stolen an army jeep, and had taken a wrong turn and ended up on the practice bombing range. Overhead the first Vietnamese plane broke the horizon and dropped a bomb and they drove like maniacs to get back to the main road.

Craig fiddled with the dials on the tape recorder at the spaces and listened to the beginning of the tape. He stopped it and took off his earphones. "Another one, hot shot."

Terry Denver, the new man, shorter than Craig, his sandy hair feathered over his forehead, said, "You think you're going to stump me? I am probably the best lingie that you've ever seen."

"The mouthiest one for sure." Craig walked off to check the reading board and left Denver to transcribe yet another tape. Another newbie, he thought, but this FNG was good, better than good. He wished Andy were there. *This one might be the best we've seen, Uncle Gene.* He poured himself a cup of coffee.

"Here it is, teach—lousy tape, though."

Craig accepted the handlog. "Lots of days are like that, newbie." He scanned the pages and located a section of XGs representing an unknown number of garbled words. "Let's make a try at this part together." He walked back to the recorder, plugged in both sets of earphones.

"You think you can catch me?"

"Won't know until we listen," Craig said, knowing that he had to do it. This was the critical time. Knock out some of the cockiness without breaking the spirit. Andy's words again.

They sat beside one another, the tape turning. "Right here," Craig said. He stopped it and replayed it three times. "Got it?"

"Still XG to me."

"He's saying he's jettisoning his auxiliary fuel tanks."

"You sure?"

"Listen to the cadence as much as the words. *Vut tung ro phu.* Hear it?" He played it again.

"You're right," Terry said with surprise.

"Trust me," Craig said.

They went through two more tapes together. Craig was buoyed with the effort. Next to flying, he enjoyed training the new men the best. The good ones, anyway. Just the good ones.

Gunny Hardin, looking embarrassed, asked Craig about the adoption.

"I gave more money, more red tape. I'm sorry."

"I appreciate you doing it for me. My wife and I weren't sure at first, then we wanted her so badly. Now I'm afraid to go and see her week after week, month after month, I'm afraid I'll get to love her too much. That if something happened, I couldn't handle it."

"She really is beautiful, Gunny. She really is."

"I know. Thanks. I mean it."

"De nada."

"Do you really think that they'd have thrown in their wings with you?"

Craig paused. "I don't know, Brooks. Probably some of them. If only four of us had done it, they would have had to shut this place down. I thought I asked you to keep it quiet."

"I didn't say anything to anyone."

"Everybody sure knows."

"It's extended your mythology."

Craig shrugged. "You notice how burned out Damon's been lately?"

Brooks nodded. "He's asked to go back to the P.I. as an instructor. He knows Roger can't keep us with all of the new men they're going to be pushing through."

"He'll get over it."

"I don't think so. I'm not sure I blame him."

"You'd miss us too much, Brooks."

"I'd be with Judi, and the only noise over there is fire-crackers."

Craig handed Damon a beer and sat down beside him on the steps of the stairway. Around them the night was quiet, a lull in the fighting.

"So you really want to leave?"

Damon nodded. "Look, there's contact just east of Marble Mountain." He pointed to the red and green flares that spread like blossoms.

"I was in Baltimore when I was at NSA. I saw Blaze Starr strip."

Damon shrugged. "I'm tired of flying, tired of the war, tired of the myths."

"You belong here, like the rest of us old guys. We *are* this det."

"I don't belong here. I want to be in the PI drinking beer, fucking, laying on the sand, and getting tan."

"You're really going."

"As soon as they let me."

"Oh."

"You're wrong, you know. I don't belong here. Andy did, you do, but not me. Not now, not ever. When I walk out of this place, I'm going to degauss the memories like they were an old tape." Damon stood up and walked back into the barracks.

Craig sat alone in the night and drank.

"I'm Chief Ogden. I don't expect much of you men at all, just you follow a few rules and remember that I make the rules."

The new Chief, Masters' temporary replacement, was tall and angular, with a jutting jaw and iron-gray hair. "I'm sure we'll all get along just fine."

"Swell," Craig said.

"Now the first thing we need to understand is, I don't like silly shit happening, and most of all happening to me."

"Things are going better than usual," Craig remarked to Gerry, and accepted a cup of coffee.

But men, like prophets, can sometimes speak too soon. It is not always possible to be both optimistic, and correct.

"Craig, you better get your ass moving. You, too, Ger." Mark shook his head.

"What's up?"

"Come on outside. You have to see it to believe it."

The three of them jogged down the aisle and burst through the back door. Mark pointed at the new barracks being built behind them, and they could hear the steady beat of a hammer.

"So what? They're working on the barracks again."

"That's not the seabees, asshole, that's Ted. He's tearing the barracks down. He says it blocks his view of the runway."

"No way."

"Want to bet? That's Ted's hammer of freedom ringing out right now. He's using a sledgehammer on the struts."

"Wow." Gerry whistled a low long note. "Ted's right, it does block our view."

"Somehow I don't think the navy is going to agree with that philosophy." Mark shook his head again and grabbed Craig by the elbow. "So what're you going to do?"

"Me? Hey, Kemo Sabe, I'm not involved at all."

"How about you, Ger?"

"My momma didn't raise no fools, Mark. Ted can handle this all by himself."

"Well, somebody better do something."

Barry Youmans, sitting on the steps, listening to the three of them with casual interest, felt the steps sag and looked up. Chief Ogden was walking down with a hacksaw in his right hand. "You're not going to help him, are you, Chief?"

Ogden rolled his eyes. "Youmans, you ever think at all before you talk? Who gave him the hammer? I took the saw off him an hour ago."

Brady, walking back from the latrine, looked at all of them, "Better do something before Richland finds out."

"Fuck you," Craig said, and walked across the field.

"I am King Montefuckingzuma, and this is my scepter. You want to be knighted?" Ted slammed the hammer into another of the uprights; dust sifted and timbers groaned. "I don't plan to have my view blocked one minute longer. We are a subjugated people and have the right to revolt. I claim these rights in the name of my subjects."

"Your Highness, somebody's going to get real pissed if you tear down their barracks."

"Fuck 'em if they can't take a joke." Ted hammered away with a steady swing.

"Come on, Ted, give me the hammer."

"You try to take it and I hammer you," he said drunkenly.

"Give me the hammer."

"Suck eggs, douchebag."

Craig met Gerry at midfield.

"Well, how'd it go?"

"It didn't. He offered to crack my head open with his scepter if I kept bugging him. What about Ogden?"

"He's not a bad guy. He's laughing his ass off and saying if it were him he'd have swiped a stick of dynamite and blown the fucker up. He also says Ted's ass is grass if Richland gets wind of this."

Youmans straggled over to join them. "Boy, you all never were wrapped too tight. How long is that drifty dude going to keep this up?"

Craig heard a loud crack, watched as one of the stanchions collapsed. "Oh, shit. I mean, oh, shit."

"I'll get a blanket," Gerry said.

"Better a tranquilizer gun." Craig answered, and waited for his friend to return.

"I'll throw it over his head, you help me tackle him, hold him down, and, Barry, you get that damned hammer and run like hell."

"You think I'm nuts? I don't interfere in no crazy I-beat trouble."

"On the count of three," Craig barked.

"Y'all owe me one," Barry said softly, explaining that he'd hid the hammer at the slop chute. "Where's Ted now?"

"Passed out," Gerry said. "Just where he belongs."

"You're really leaving tomorrow?"

"All packed up. Not a trace left behind, except maybe the dirt." Damon hefted his suitcase to the bunk. His seabag lay on the floor.

"I'm going to miss you."

"You miss everybody, Craig. You should be more like me, just forget the whole thing." Damon sipped his beer and sat down, straddled the seabag. "You really are hooked on this dump, aren't you?"

"Yeah."

"You get Ted out of the mess he was in?"

"Passed out like a babe. Ogden's being a decent guy about the whole thing. I think he might be okay. A lifer rather than a beggar."

"You know why you need this place so much? Because it's the first time in your life you were worth a shit. Here you can live on the myths about you, you're king of the hill. The indestructible Charlie November who lives with pain and disdains the glory. The perfect fucking op. That's you."

"That's enough."

"Enough? You and your Dear Abby gosh-I-can-help-you

smile and nose into everything and everybody's business, and you want me to stay because you want some more people to validate you, to prove you're as good as you think. Well, you're nuts. You're not as good as you think, and I don't give a rat's ass what happens to you or this det."

Craig, stunned, stepped back, stood a brief second, and then walked off to his bunk and a drink.

In September, three weeks after Damon's return to the PI, Gerry, just back from his three days at San Miguel, came to Craig with the first real news of what was happening back there. "He's taken over all of Roger's classes. Roger's confined to quarters for the rest of the investigation."

"House arrest? Don't they know what he's done for this place? He flew two hundred and fifty missions before he took over teaching that class. Rumors take a long time, but they do come true, right?" Craig emptied the last of the scotch bottle into his glass and threw the bottle into the trash can. "What's going on with Damon? He okay?"

"Yeah. They're yanking people back for the investigation. He said to tell you he was sorry. He said he didn't mean it, but he didn't say what it was about. You want to talk about it?"

"No. They going to pull us in?"

Gerry said, "I don't know." Trying to be gentle with both of them he added, "I doubt it." Though he was sure they would be questioned.

Craig accepted his friend's lie as it was intended and opened a fresh bottle of scotch.

Commander Brewster, returned only for a month while Richland was in Japan, was ebullient when he called Craig into his office, "Well, it looks like you've won a round at least."

"How's that?"

"It seems that the puzzle palace was talking about this great op Charlie November and they were talking to Captain Darby in the Philippines and asked him why they had never given you a letter of commendation, and then Darby asked Richland and Richland said he was just getting one ready."

"No shit? Sorry, sir, I mean really?"

"No shit, Craig. He has got his tit in a wringer this time and he has to write a letter. He's going to present it to you himself in the P.I. in three weeks, as well as give you a four-day pass."

"The Lord and navy work in mysterious ways, sir."

"That they do. How's Richland been doing lately?"

Craig shrugged. "Okay. Better maybe, he's not changing the reports now. His quiet worries me more than the open warfare." The middle-of-the-night visits, the times when Richland seemed totally irrational, he kept to himself.

"God, I miss this place sometimes. Japan is nothing but hidebound rear-echelon mammas who don't have the first idea of what's really going on."

In the silence, thinking that there should be more to say, wanting to find the words, Craig heard the faint whine that he knew so well. "Hit the deck!" he yelled, and fell to the floor beside Brewster.

"Quite a welcome home," Brewster said, hoping it sounded wry or sarcastic instead of fearful. He thought of his wife, his promise that this would be the last trip. Ever.

"Let's move to the bunker."

Outside, flares flashing like strobes, the two of them ran for the bunker, flak jackets on, helmets on their heads, each holding an M16.

The night grew quiet except for some distant artillery, but flames crackled from the spaces they had vacated. A direct hit. Craig and John Brewster stood in the doorway of the bunker and watched.

Brewster smiled, said, "Just like urban renewal."

But too close.

Much too close.

Chapter 18

A river separated the Philippine city of Olongapo from the naval base at Subic Bay. The river reeked of refuse and garbage and night soil. Children perched on canoes and begged for coins, and when Americans threw them from the bridge the boys dived into the brackish waters to retrieve them. Craig paused, tossed a handful of quarters, careful to send them into the canoe itself. Beside him, another sailor, a fleetie from one of the ships in port, tossed a handful of coins into the water and laughed.

Craig walked across the bridge and onto the main street. He looked at the brightly colored kiosks that existed illegally but were tolerated. They exchanged pesos for greenbacks at the black-market rates. The Philippine constabulary strutted amid the crowds, ignoring most of what they saw.

From the first doorway, extending the length of the street, stretched food stalls, prostitutes, pimps, thieves, and the ever-present black market. Craig stopped at a kiosk, haggled, and got twenty-four pesos for the dollar.

There were six thousand bars, hundreds of seedy hotels, and more than ten thousand bargirls in Olongapo. Some men called Olongapo the dirtiest, most crime-laden city in Asia: the place where spies pried loose more secrets than anywhere else. With a cautious canniness that had protected his wallet, his watch, and his life, Craig walked on the curb and occasionally changed sides of the street. He warily eyed each stranger who passed him.

There was a mist, but it was not yet rain. Craig walked along Magsaysay Boulevard and wondered how the Philippine hero and ex-president would regard the street that bore his name. It didn't matter, of course, it was just a street: a street Craig loved and loathed. He felt comfortable on that street, in that city.

He shooed away the street urchins and the pimps, the sellers of watches and sex and drugs, and finally climbed the stairs to the second story of a restaurant called Papagayo's.

"Comasta kau, kaibegan?"

"Mabuti," Craig answered. He followed the head waiter to his table and sat down. The band played "Danny Boy," the song they had chosen as his signature on his first visit, and he grinned stupidly and clapped. Different friends had different songs.

He accepted a J&B and water, on the house, and listened to the music. He ate bean soup, a salad, lasagna, and bread sticks, his traditional order. The people at Papagayo's, as infrequently as he was there, remembered him, in fact seemed to remember every customer.

Craig ate at a leisurely pace, ordered a Galliano for after dinner, and drank fresh black coffee. In Vietnam he would have had *cafe sua*, a coffee with rich, thick milk and sugar. It always reminded him more of dessert than a beverage.

"Everything was okay?" the maitre d' asked.

Craig answered that as always everything was excellent. He smoked a cigarette and paid his check.

"Come again soon, Craig."

"When I can," Craig said. "When I can."

Craig saw Jack Brady on the street, and unable to duck into a doorway without being obvious, he walked over to him and extended his hand. "How's it going, Jack?"

"Trying to enjoy my R&R, but everything's so expensive, and I won't stand there and buy drinks for a dozen guys I don't even know."

Whining. Craig hated the nasal whine that Jack used so often over so many things: the weather, his peers, the prices —everything was an equal vexation for him. He thought that being with Jack for any length of time must be like being in a bad marriage. "Other than that how was the play, Mrs. Lincoln?"

"Huh? Hey, I hear Richland is giving you a BZ letter."

"Shit rolls downhill."

"Doesn't it ever? After all I've done for that place, you'd think I'd have one."

"Yeah, no justice, huh?" Craig lit a cigarette.

"You heard about McElroy, right?"

"Yeah, he's in Japan. Probably strapping his ass off right now with those girls on the Ginza."

"He's dead."

"You're crazy."

"Thought you knew. They don't know why. He had meningitis and he died. Weird, huh?"

Not a rocket, not a sniper, not the crash-and-burn flight that every one of them expected, but a disease. A fucking disease. Craig sagged against the building corner. "I don't believe it."

"Hey, everybody knows. Maybe you were en route here when it happened. Guess a couple of the guys were really broken up."

Craig rubbed his eyes. "I have to get going. Theresa's waiting for me. You know how she gets."

"Sure, afraid you'll butterfly around on her. She probably has her paruparu knife sharpened and ready."

"McElroy's dead," Craig said again.

"Yeah, guess something has to kill us all."

Craig shook his head and walked off without saying another word. He wondered why he didn't punch Jack.

Craig walked into the Sphinx Club and stood in the foyer and looked over the crowded tables. At one, a sailor was buying her drinks, watered tea really, priced at twice a normal drink. He winked at her and walked to a table alone and ordered a scotch and water. He swallowed a Darvon with his drink. He wondered if the back pain would ever stop without help.

"You no make trouble?"

Craig looked at the proprietor, generically called Papasan, and shook his head. "She'll be leaving with me, though."

"Other sailor already pay."

"Then give him his money, or get him drunk. She wants to come with me."

"You no tell me how to do business here, Joe. I call PC ziggy now."

"You ziggy and I tell them what I know about this place and you won't be open for an hour. I thought we were *kaibegans*, Papasan."

"You right, we friends. Have other girl for drunk sailor from ship. Fleeties not as good as CT sailors."

"You got that right," Craig said, and smiled. He handed over twice the going rate.

Craig sat at a corner table and a Filipino band imitating the Beatles poorly sang a medley of their songs.

"He was silly sailor," Theresa said brightly.

"They all are." We all are, he thought. McElroy had had a crooked smile that always cheered Craig. McElroy had always had a good word for everybody. He hugged Theresa to his side and kissed her.

"*Ikau guapo,*" she said.

"*Ikau maganda.*"

"But you have good nose."

Suddenly Craig was angry; he was tired of hearing about his high nose, tired of their inferiority complexes, and their saying they loved him no shit, and the thousand lies that they engendered every time they met. He kissed her again, roughly, and stood up holding her hand. "Let's go."

In the room, the tiny pattern on the wallpaper was faded and the roaches quivered like tiny moving flowers. Craig stripped to his underpants, then undressed her one piece of clothing at a time. Naked she looked vulnerable, young, too innocent to be there, and Craig touched her tenderly with his mouth and hands.

They made love quickly, athletically, and Craig could not hold himself back. For these moments, he felt that this woman with her witchery was the only tether he had to earth.

Here sex was playful and sinless: he thought this, but there was no one to whom he could say it. Theresa would never understand the meaning he meant, and his friends would not care about the satori he felt. They would understand though: sex here was without promise or expectation and the lies were so easily accepted that they seemed like truths. He breathed in their odors, the smell of sperm and vaginal juices and sweat and cheap perfume and Christmas-present English Leather aftershave lotion. Here sex was a self-fulfilling prophecy. The pungent aromas made it real to him.

"I love you, no shit," Theresa said. She giggled and ran her fingers over his chest and his scrotum and his face. She teased his nipples with her lips.

He lay back and let her bring him to arousal again. It would be the twenty-sixth time he had made love to her, but he didn't count them, really.

He had made love to forty-one women; he didn't count them either, but the numbers were easily recalled.

He drove himself into her again, slowly.

Making love he felt connected, real, and he squealed pig-gishly with his pleasure.

Save me, he had said once. Save us, he had said the next time. He rode this sex like a promise of immortality.

A cock crowed beneath the window and he stirred, and wriggled free of Theresa's arms. He inched himself loose and walked to the window. The air was already fattened with hu-midity, and his breath came uneasily. People, market bound, scurried like ants. A pig squealed as it broke loose from its keeper and darted behind old crates.

He kissed Theresa awake.

Theresa touched his nose, the cleft in his chin, wondered when she would find the one who would take her from this place to America. There she knew everyone was rich and beautiful and had dimples and clefts and credit cards that allowed them to buy everything they wanted. I will, she had told her mother when she left her barrio, I will marry an American.

They made love again. Craig thought, I could be happy here. We could thrive here, but never in Ohio. He drove him-self deep into her.

It was the way here, he thought.

"I've got to go," Craig said at last.

"Come back soon. I love you no shit, GI Joe."

"Me, too," he said without knowing what he felt. He kissed her quickly and walked outside to catch the bus back to San Miguel.

The bus was filled with mostly servicemen, some of them he recognized vaguely, but he knew none well. He sat alone in the back seat, the worst for the kidneys, and closed his eyes. He didn't want to know anyone more than he knew.

Ten-thirty in the morning. Craig glanced at his watch, then draped himself over a chaise lounge at the base pool. He wig-gled a San Miquel beer.

"I heard you were back."

Craig opened his eyes, nodded to Roger Tripp, and closed his eyes again. "Hi."

"I guess you heard that Damon's replaced me."

"Yeah." Craig didn't know what to say, kept his eyes closed.

"You been to the big shindig yet? Spies questioning spies. Bizarre."

"I haven't been yet."

"I hear it's fun." Roger spoke without bitterness, but sounded tired. "You'll be going, everyone will sooner or later."

"I guess."

"I got a postcard from Andy."

"Really?" Craig leaned forward and looked at Roger for the first time. "God I miss him. When did you hear?"

"A week ago. He's thumbing his way across the country right now. He wrote me from Miami. He said he'd seen Boston and New York and D.C. already."

"I'm glad. He deserves it. He busted his nuts over there. Maybe he'll get some roundeye ass."

"How's Gerry?"

"Fine," he said.

"It's funny what happens to friendships here, huh?" Roger smiled, shrugged his thin shoulders. "Heard you're having some trouble with the commander who wrote you the citation letter."

"Only because he's mad as a hatter and believes that intelligence reports are based on Creative Writing 101."

"Right up your alley."

Craig shook his head, unsure whether Roger was being sarcastic or not. "I saw Phil Parker the other day. He's as antsy as ever to get to Da Nang. I told him to stay here. I don't think he's right for the place. He writes too well, he thinks too much; I think the place would kill him with the insanities."

"I would have said the same thing about you, except you went nuts here. Funny, isn't it? You have a nuts commander who wants a promotion, and I travel with SP guards."

"And I rage on about my problems, huh? Sorry."

"Sir Genuine in search of the holy grail. Remember the e. e. cummings poem that Steve sent you?"

Craig nodded. "Rosebugs, I do. . . ."

"The grail is like a well, there's nothing but dead things down there. Be careful."

"See you around."

Roger shrugged again, looking helpless, small. "Not likely. I'm under house arrest. Hang tough, hero."

"You, too."

"You never asked me if the charges were true."

"No reason to," Craig said awkwardly. He looked at the pool, the elastic ripple of waves caused by the breeze.

"Fears are a funny thing, Craig. You have to face truths about someone else and you might find yourself there, too." Roger stared at the swimming pool for a moment, then walked away toward the two SPs waiting for him at the gate. "It's hell growing up, isn't it?"

The corridor at the headquarters offices was deserted except for Craig. He knew only one man at a time was being allowed to wait for the interview, they didn't want any collaboration. When it was his turn he was called inside by a thin lieutenant with glasses and red hair that had begun to thin from his forehead.

Craig was motioned to a chair, sat down. The back of his shirt stuck to the naugahyde of the seat.

"Do you have any knowledge of Roger Tripp's alleged homosexual behavior?"

"None."

"I understand that you know Roger Tripp very well, that you spent a lot of time with him."

"He was my instructor before I went to Det Tango."

"You also socialized with him here and later when he was in Da Nang TDY."

"I did." A lot of time, Craig thought, wondered how to define the time. Hours and hours of drinking and talking. Days and days on end. Discussions of Plato and Sartre and Schwarz-Bart; talk of writing and reading, and moments of their lives.

"What did you do?"

Craig repeated his thoughts aloud.

"Do you mean to tell me that two enlisted men would spend hours discussing the intricacies of philosophy?"

"That's right."

"I find that hard to believe."

Craig wondered why he felt guilty, worried. "You asked me a question and I answered."

"Now tell me the truth."

Craig leaned forward. "I did, sir."

"You expect me to believe—"

"I don't expect anything of you at all," Craig said. "I don't even happen to give a rat's ass."

"You're dangerously close to insubordination."

"You're dangerously close to stupidity."

"You're on report."

"Fine." Craig walked to the door and took the handle in his hand. "What are you going to do, send me to Vietnam?"

"I'm not through."

"Inconvenient, I am." Craig walked out the door, ignoring the threats that followed him like an echo.

The NIS lieutenant was explaining that he wanted Nostrum up on charges, a captain's mast for insubordination. "He was rude, he walked out on *me*."

"You're talking about a man with six air medals, a man who's back here to get a letter of commendation for excellence and for setting an example. How do you think it would look to write him up?"

"You can't let him get away with it."

"He's heading back for Da Nang soon, anyhow. We might bust him, but then what happens? He doesn't fly. Do you know how many linguists we have? Too few, that's how many."

"He was insubordinate."

"He's needed. Besides, you can't be a hero and a faggot at the same time."

"Expedient morality here."

"We have missions to man, Lieutenant. You tell me how to do it and hang the men who do it at the same time and I'll back you a hundred percent. There isn't one of them we couldn't file some charge on."

"He never even finished the interview."

"He did. He's not there anymore, is he? He'll be back in Da Nang soon; just forget the whole thing and clear up this other mess as soon as possible."

"Yes, sir."

The commander smiled tolerantly, the way one does when indulging children. He was tired of the unmilitary behavior as well, but he also looked at the rosters from Det Tango and the other detachments and knew he had to bend. He had been told that serving as executive officer at San Miguel would be knock duty. He wondered when it began. Right now, it all seemed like punishment.

The club's air-conditioning hummed; but the rooms were still too hot. Craig sipped a rum collins. Pale pieces of lime floated in the glass; it reminded him of a glass paperweight that when you turned upside down showed snow falling on a tiny Vermont village. Craig turned from the drink to Damon. "How'd you hear about it already? It just happened an hour ago."

"Word gets around fast here."

"So the XO bailed my ass out, huh?"

"So the rumor mill says."

"I might even salute him the next time I see him."

Damon chuckled. "Walked out on him. I like it. Pretty cool."

"Things happen, my friend, things happen."

The investigation had created a disquiet, a tenseness so real that it seemed palpable.

"You heard three squids got busted for black market, didn't you? One was Loper, the guy who was running the supply shack for us."

Craig nodded to Damon. "They should bust those guys. Better they should bust the ones in Da Nang who are selling us our own goods or peddling it in downtown Da Nang where we have to buy it from the Vietnamese." He rubbed his hands over his freshly pressed uniform, wiped a tissue over his brass belt buckle. "I hate getting up there in front of everybody."

"Don't sweat the small stuff, you look fine, hero."

"They could have mailed it to me," Craig said, and sat down beside Damon in the front row of the bleacher-type seats.

When they called his name, Craig stood and walked up the steps to the dais and took his place at Commander Richland's left side. He slipped on the second step, but caught himself before he fell. "Graceful," he whispered, and colored red.

Richland read the letter quickly, his lips barely moving as he spoke.

Craig, pleased with Richland's discomfort more than the letter itself, grinned foolishly.

"Petty Officer Nostrum is a credit to the naval service, and I take pleasure in presenting him with this letter of commendation."

Craig accepted the letter, saluted, and flashed a thumbs-up sign to Damon as he left the stage to take his seat again.

Two air medals were awarded to R-branchers. A letter of commendation for a T-brancher from the radar station. Next, two SPs accompanied Roger Tripp to the stage.

Craig nudged Damon. "What's this about?"

Richland presented Roger Tripp with his fifth air medal with the thanks of a grateful nation.

Roger shook his head, took the medal, and walked to the edge of the dais and down the steps. He dropped the medal to the dirt as soon as he stepped onto the ground. One of the SPs handed it back to him, and he dropped it again. A Filipino darted over and picked it up. He regarded it for a second, then stuffed it in his pocket and ran off again to tend the golf-course grass.

"Three more days," Craig remarked, and sipped on his cold beer. He sat on a chaise lounge on the polished bamboo balcony of Damon's nipa hut. He watched the bold red and orange of the sunset behind the Capone Islands. "Richland went back tonight. Those poor bastards over there are going to wake up to find Brewster deposed again. What a shitty deal that is."

Damon grinned. "At least he's out of here."

Craig looked down at Tessie's Sari-Sari store. Two women squatted in the dirt street and were picking lice from each other's heads and biting them in two. He stretched in his chair. "How about another beer?" He started to rise, but Gina, Damon's *menamahal*, had already brought two new ones. "Thank you," he said.

"Saklamit po." Gina walked back to the kitchen.

"They're gossiping like crazy in there," Damon whispered. "Probably about us."

Craig laughed. "Gina and Theresa have plenty to gossip about. Probably the new movie magazines."

"Or how Gina bought some charm from the local witch and she's convinced that's why I came back to stay. She thinks it was magic. Probably telling Theresa where to get one."

"Theresa would have the whole Seventh Fleet here if she said bring back my lover."

"How can you say that?"

"It's true. That's one of the things I like most. She has this intense jealousy if I even look at another girl, and she thinks because hers is a business that it doesn't matter."

"You know that time I lit into you about you needing Da Nang because you never could make it anywhere else?"

Craig blushed as he recalled it, his feelings freshly tender from the memory of the rebuke. "I'd forgotten it."

"I'm sorry. I didn't mean it."

"It's true. That's what pissed me off so badly. I need that place more than it ever needed me. It's all that I can do well. That's me. Charlie November."

"You can do anything if you want to. That place is an aberration. You're good at it, but it isn't the end all for the world."

"But, I'm the big man on campus there now. I like it."

"You could stay here."

"What?"

"Teach with me. They're pushing more and more lingies out all the time. They know they need to get some help here. You and Theresa could stay with Gina and me until you found a place. There's a nipa hut right down the way that's up for rent, and they even let you pick and keep the mangoes."

"No way. This is nice, Damon, but I belong there. It's my place. Weird, huh?"

"You're crazy. You could live like a king here."

"Probably. Even Andy used to tell me that I was too obsessive. Compulsive Craigers, he said."

Damon sniffed the air, the aroma of lumpia and pork adobo cooking in the kitchen. "Dinner's almost ready."

"Good, I'm starved."

"Think about it, okay? Promise me you'll at least consider it."

"Maybe."

The afternoon was oppressive with the heat, and Craig met Damon at the Starlight Club for lunch.

"Air-conditioning crapped out at the spaces so we canceled class."

"Lucky break," Craig answered, and ordered a round of rum collinses.

"You give it any thought? You leave tomorrow; there's still time to make a change. I know I can get Lieutenant Freund to go along with it."

"I have to go back," Craig said. "They need me."

"All right." With a trace of bad temper Damon's voice was loud, and he shook his head.

"I'm sorry, okay? I want to fly. *I want to fly.*"

"It could be fun here. I've taught Gina chess. We could have tournaments, maybe learn mah-jongg, drink and fuck the days away."

"Let's just drink, okay?" Craig walked to the jukebox and dropped coins in. Behind him the slot machines spit out coins with a *chinkachink chinkachink.* He pushed the button for Janis Ian's "Society's Child." "That's us," he told Damon. "Society's children. Fucked-up children."

"You remember the time we couldn't find Jenkins for the afternoon flight?"

Damon shook his head, not sure if he remembered; too many of the stories and myths had run together.

"Sure you do. We looked all over and I finally found him in the latrine and he was eating out the housegirl, the one named Thuyen. His face is buried in her crotch and I'm telling him it's time to fly and he just looks up at me and grins and says, 'I'm almost through anyway.' I almost shit myself, I was laughing so hard."

They laughed together, their voices loud with the booze and comaraderie and the noise around them.

Benny Radcliff, a second-class A-brancher, stood at the table and cleared his throat, coughed, and finally said, "I hate to interrupt."

"Then don't." Craig laughed.

Damon looked up. "Don't tell me, the war's over, right? You left the personnel department to deliver our discharges."

"No." Benny clapped a hand on Craig's right shoulder. "There's good news and bad news. The good news is that no one is hurt. The bad news is you are both booked on the next flight out of Cubi Point for Da Nang."

Craig, suddenly sober, asked why.

"I don't know. Nobody knows. They said the message came an hour ago that all available lingies are to be sent back immediately. They also said there were no attacks, and that no one was hurt. It's like a fucking mystery out at the spaces right now. Hell, even the XO didn't seem to know what was going on. Some order from Richland, though."

Damon waved his hands. "No way, I'm stationed here for the duration. I'm teaching school now."

"They put Roger back in charge for now. They have some lingie coming from the States, Hanratty, I think."

"Hanratty? He's nutso. He's the one who spent thirty fucking days in Da Nang and came back here playing the hero and telling everyone, 'Once you've flirted with death, nothing else matters.' This is bullshit." Damon finished his drink and ordered a double round for each of them.

"I have someone packing your locker up, Craig. Since Thorsen said you had him over to the house and he had met Gina, I sent him to get your things and tell Gina. I figured you might like it better that way, Damon."

"Efficient," Craig said angrily.

"I can't do it. I was never going back." Damon's voice was flat, he cracked his knuckles with exact attention.

"Two hours and the driver will pour you in the truck. I'd suggest you get bombed."

Damon stared at his hands, his drink, and ordered another double round.

One more time, Craig thought, one more time.

U.S. NAVAL STATION PHILIPPINES
DETACHMENT TANGO
BOX 84D
FPO SAN FRANCISCO, CA 96695

FROM: Officer in Charge, Detachment Tango
TO: CT2 Craig J. Nostrum, X32 00 68
Via: Commanding Officer NavComStaPhil

subj: Letter of Commendation

1. You were assigned temporary additional duty at Detachment
    Tango from 11 Nov 67 until present during which time you
    distinguished yourself by your exemplary performance of
    duty. You have indeed become one of the most proficient and
    valuable non-commissioned officers of this unit.

2. You accepted your responsibilities as this unit's most senior
    and experienced linguist in a mature and outstanding
    manner, constantly seeking ways to improve your own
    performance and that of others during your tenure at this
    detachment. Your linguistic ability improved accordingly as
    did your contributions to the accomplishments of this unit's
    mission. Your high personal standards encouraged those
    junior to you to improve their own performances and also
    earned you the great respect of your superiors. Your zealous
    attitude and your persevering devotion to duty, both in
    flight and on the ground, have set you apart as a truly
    exceptional example, worthy of emulation. Your performance
    of duty contributed significantly to the Big Eye effort and to
    the accomplishment of this unit's assigned mission and is
    truly commensurate with the highest traditions of United
    States Naval Service.

                              D.W. Richland, LCDR, USN
                              Officer in Charge
                              Detachment Tango

Chapter 19

The milk run. That's what they called the flight that they took to Da Nang: Cubi Point, Saigon, Chu Lai, change planes for all points north—Da Nang, Phu Bai, wherever. Craig and Damon sat strapped into the webbed slings that hung down from the C-130. Boxes of cargo were tied down in the center aisle of the fuselage so that the men in the opposite seats were lost to their view. The entire cargo bay smelled like oil.

Damon smoked silently, refusing to answer when Craig spoke. He stared at his hands, at the deck, sulking.

"Fine, don't ever talk to me again," Craig said. "Hell if I understand you. *I* didn't do this to you, the fucking navy did. Maybe it was Odin or Buddha, but it sure as shit wasn't me."

Damon stared stonily at the crates.

"Fine. Just fucking fine," Craig muttered angrily.

The pilot's voice squawked over the PA system. "They've been taking some fire off and on in Chu Lai. When we land I suggest you keep low and run for the bunker nearest the terminal. Take your orders and your bags. Someone there will be able to get you to your connecting flights. Thank you for flying MACV, your airway to the war."

"Get low and run?" Craig fumed, and stared at the squawk box on the bulkhead as if it might answer.

Damon crushed his cigarette out in a butt can. "I hate this.

I wasn't coming back. See what happens?" Damon leaned
forward, his elbows on his knees. "It's like flying one too
many flights. You don't know when it's one too many. You
don't know, do you?"

"Shut up." Craig rubbed his fingers on his temples. "We've
been through worse." He said this, but he knew that each time
was the worst. His right leg bounced up and down as steadily
as a metronome. I am losing my patience with you, he
thought. Pout somewhere else. Life is like that, especially
here.

The plane lurched and bucked and finally rolled to a halt in
the center of the runway. The engines shuddered with the sudden backwash of the props. The side door opened and someone yelled for them to grab their things and hit it.

Craig, Damon, and four others hit the runway loaded with
their gear, running awkwardly and panting with the effort.

"We're full up," a soldier at the doorway to the bunker
said.

"Fuck you," Damon said, and pushed past him.

Craig stood outside, hating the claustrophobic closeness he
sensed within. He watched the flares dance along the perimeter, listened to the artillery fire. Guns pounded and recoiled.

"Listen up," the marine said. "Anybody going to Da Nang
better get their asses ready since there's a bird touching down
that is going there. Write your names on this list, just in case,
so we can make sure Mommy and Daddy get their flags and
body bags."

"Fuck," Damon screamed.

Craig shrugged, signed, and recited the poem they had repeated in the bunker during Tet. "Here's your letter, and here's
your flag, and here's your son, in a plastic bag."

Damon stared at the posters on the wall of the Fifteenth
Aerial Port: *Explore enchanting Vietnam, an unfolding vacation spot*. "Nobody's here to pick us up."

Craig shrugged. "So we walk or hitchhike. The navy is not
like Mussolini's trains—nothing runs on time." He grabbed
his seabag and walked out of the terminal.

"Wait up," Damon said.

The barracks were quiet when they arrived, so they unpacked their belongings into practiced disarray. They received

no greetings at all except for the sharp songs of a gecko lizard that skittered across Craig's screen.

"Fuck all of you!" Damon yelled.

"And God bless us every one, and especially Tiny Tim," Craig said. He looked up at the *Playboy* pinups stretched across the ceiling and whispered hello to each month, one by one.

The story unfolded slowly, and each man interrupted the others in their rush to tell it. Craig and Damon were the audience, and Jack Brady stood off to the side keeping silent while the others spoke.

"I was telling the story."

Craig shook his head. "I don't give a rat's ass who tells it as long as *someone* does."

"Tell the goddamned story," Damon said wearily.

Craig glanced at the other men; some of the faces were complete strangers to him. He was not yet twenty-two and he felt old. "Tell it," he said again.

"So Richland and the captain decided to hold an awards ceremony here and hand out the latest air medals. He had someone from the San Magoo base newspaper here. He tried to get *Stars and Stripes*. He issued the order to look strac."

Another man interrupted. "Nobody admitted who might have been behind it, but my money's on Ted Trainer."

"*I'm* telling the fucking story," Terry Denver said.

Craig remembered Denver, he had met him a week before he went to the Philippines. Terry had been training with Mark Mitchell. "Tell it!"

"Anyhow, somebody found this naval regulation that said you could wear shorts in a tropical zone, and so some of the men had their pants cut off and sewn into shorts. They were all strac, pressed uniforms, haircuts, shined shoes, but they were wearing shorts." Terry paused, ran a hand through his blond hair. "So Richland sees these shorts and that vein on his forehead looked like it might sprout a geyser. He called them mutineers. He went nutso. You ever seen him like that?"

"Too often, newie," Craig said.

"Once the brass from the Philippines pulls out, Richland calls them all in and asks them to apologize. They tell him that what they did was okay and to pound salt. Only Brady agreed to apologize. He says fine, and then sends them all off to ship dets and sends out an urgent message for more lingies to man the flights."

"Shit." Damon slumped against the bunk and shrank until he sat down.

Craig could not stop laughing; his breathing came in ragged, giggling breaths. He sipped a scotch and water. "Can you imagine getting thrown *out* of Vietnam? A fucking mutiny of knees, I love it."

Damon glared at Craig and walked down the aisle to his own cubicle.

"Arneault's sure in a rotten mood," Terry Denver said. He blew two smoke rings and shoved his wrists through them like bracelets.

Craig drank a little, looked at Denver warily. "He was planning on staying in the P.I. He's got a right to be pissed off."

"He lose his guts?"

Craig grabbed Terry's shirtfront in his hands, yanked him close until they were nose to nose. "Watch your mouth, new-bie, Damon was flying when you weren't even saying *Cai nay nho* without pissing your pants."

Terry broke loose, eyed Craig. "Want me to genuflect? Maybe just kiss old-guy ass like some of the other guys do? I don't do brown-nose for anyone. I'm as good as any of you."

Craig fixed Terry with his gaze. "Just learn to watch your mouth."

"Hey, just asked a question. You're the touchy one."

"He hasn't lost his guts. He just found out he likes fucking better than bunkers." Craig looked at his short-timer's calendar, the Xs bright red smears on the days. He waited until Terry had left before performing the final rituals: he hung a flight suit on the end rung of his rack, put his shower shoes in the middle of the floor, emptied a case of beer into the refrigerator. He was ready, he thought, ready for the next attack, for whatever.

"Richland's nuts," Damon said angrily.

Craig looked up from the refrigerator, took two of the cold ones out and handed one to Damon. "I think I've said that before. You didn't give a shit then."

"What kind of punishment is getting kicked *out* of a war."

"Great if you're the one getting kicked out."

"You know who's left for tac/air men?" Damon sounded petulant, "Brady, you, me, and the new guy Denver."

Craig sighed. "So we fly doubles again. We've done it before." He wasn't sure what else to say. This place refuses to change, he thought, it demands too much; but he loved it that way. He stared at Damon and knew that his friend had succumbed to the numbers. The weight of this knowledge settled over him. He wanted to shake Damon, to knock him down. Don't do this, he thought, don't bury *me* with your numbers. He found two glasses, wiped them with a T-shirt, and poured scotch, ice, and water into them. He handed one to Damon.

"I was never coming back here, never."

"Things happen."

"Shut the fuck up! You know what happens when you fly too long? Your number gets punched. You crash and burn. You're so fucking gung ho to play spyboy hero that you don't even know what's going on. What makes you so fucking desperate?"

Craig stepped back, stung, sipped his drink, and walked out of the cube.

"Hey, Craig."

He didn't answer and walked outside.

"Fuck with Charlie November and you could end up chipping paint over the side of the fucking *Enterprise*," Barry Youmans said to Terry Denver. He picked at his teeth with a matchstick.

"Why'd he give me so much shit? Everybody knows that he and Damon are like oil and vinegar."

"They're both old guys. I'd have done the same thing myself."

"Then you're as screwed up as the rest of them."

"Maybe it's just that something has to make this all work, all of us hang together."

Craig dangled his legs over the side of the canal bank. He felt like a schoolboy playing hooky, and even the sounds of the artillery and the flares did not bother him. He thought that there he was safe, immune. He flipped through the latest *Spiderman* comic that Ted had left behind when he was ordered to the USS *Coral Sea*.

"Hey!"

Craig focused on the stillness of the water and ignored the interruption.

"I'm sorry, okay?"

"We all are sooner or later. People here, we're the sorriest bastards in the world." Craig tossed his cigarette into the water, folded the comic book and put it in the leg pocket of his flight suit. "I came here for the privacy."

Terry produced a bottle of Scotch and poured some into Craig's glass.

"Thanks," Craig said. "Wait, that's my Scotch."

"I said I was sorry, not generous."

"Asshole." Craig grinned when he said it. "A fucking mutiny of knees. Ted has some ugly knees, too."

Terry nodded. "If you had hit me, I would have knocked you on your ass."

"Maybe. I might have knocked you on your ass."

"I don't think so."

"You feeling froggy, just leap." Craig surveyed the other man, not as a linguist, but as an opponent.

"You're really weird, you know? Everybody knows that you and Damon fight over everything, but you took up for him."

"Comes with the territory. This is Oz, and whether you're from Kansas or Boston, you're still here."

"You don't have to tell, but why's it this way? Why do you and Richland hate each other? Who started all this bullshit?"

"Slow down. Laurence and a couple of other guys started this whole place. Jenkins was one. It just is this way. Richland and I just have different views. I prefer mine rational."

"He got off on me one day when I said I would be better than you. He told me I better be. Like it was a threat."

Craig reached for the bottle, reassured by it. He looked at the fine red silt in the bottom of the glass and poured some more scotch anyway. "There it is."

"I saw this old paper sack that had eyes cut in it and the name *Uncle Gene*, who was that?"

"A relative. I'm his nephew." The continuum, Craig thought, Andy, him, Mark, and now Terry Denver. It just goes on, like the war, like Lucy Ricardo trying to get into Ricky's act. Things happen.

Craig woke in the morning, not sure whether he had dreamed or whether Richland had actually entered his cubicle and woke him. He remembered the OIC standing there grinning at him, saying nothing, just grinning.

He prepared for the flight, straggled to the plane without

attending the briefing. It was the first he had missed intentionally. He climbed the ladder to the plane, his back aching despite the Darvon.

"I've been flying senior on this crew."

Craig looked at Terry Denver. "I know."

Terry grinned, stepped aside, and motioned Craig to the senior position, number seven.

Craig thanked him, and feeling as dull as an ox, sat down and put on the earphones to listen to AFRTS, to the oft-repeated opening, "Gooood morning, Vietnam."

Terry sat down in the junior position, surprised at himself: He wasn't sure what he was going to do until he did it. He wondered if something was catching about the attitude at Det Tango; a contagion of camaradarie.

Brooks Crenshaw, worrying his cowlick and then brushing back his forelock, walked to Craig's side. "I expected a duel or something; guess Denver knows how to play on a team."

"Yeah, he's good, Brooks. When he started flying junior I heard he was sharp from the git-go. Damon says he has the best natural ear he's ever seen."

"Worried?"

"I didn't say he was me, Brooks, just real good."

"Something bothering you?"

"It's weird, but I swear Richland woke me up last night. Just came in, woke me, and grinned at me."

"A dream," Brooks said quickly. He wanted to say more, but would not. Richland had done the same to him a few days before. He shuddered a little and walked down the aisle.

Craig turned the dials slowly, edging to the signal, the static snapping in his ears. "MiGs up."

"How should the report read?"

"Send it out that the MiG blew up, crashed, and burned all on his own. He went into a turn and couldn't get out of it. His engines flamed out."

"You sure there was no hit?"

"I'm sure. He wasn't even close yet."

"Accident by misadventure."

Craig smiled. "As good a name as any. It describes our lives here perfectly."

Craig met Brooks as the lieutenant, wrapped in a towel, walked out of the officer's shower and walked toward the

BOQ. Craig stood before him with his legs spread and his arms crossed over his chest. "What in the hell is this about?"

"What ever happened to 'Hello,' 'Afternoon,' or 'How's your mother?'"

"This report."

"You know taking this out of the spaces is a breach of security."

"Did you read it?"

"I wrote it."

"You wrote this?" Craig slapped the papers against Brooks's chest until the other man took them and scanned it. "Son of a bitch. I told him there wasn't any shootdown."

"Richland's Creative Writing 101 again?" Craig swore softly, took back the report. "Guess we need to have Cookie tell us before any reports go out so we can screen them, huh?"

"Yeah, the bastard's a nut case. He wants his captaincy so badly he'd manufacture the whole war if he had to."

"This is one fucked-up way to run a war."

Commander Richland sat stoically behind his desk. He reread the notes he had just made in the personnel file. *Despite assurances from the linguists that they had insisted that the MiG suffered a flameout, Brooks wrote the report as a shootdown. He seems daily to lose more contact with reality.*

Craig did not knock or salute. "What the fuck is going on here?"

"Yes?" Richland accepted the report, buried his own papers in a drawer. "Must be some sort of clerical error. That was a flameout."

"Funny man. It's real easy to mistake the words *flameout* for *shootdown*."

"Enough of your sarcasm. I'll check into it."

"Don't check into it, just stop doing it."

"I made your reputation with my letter of commendation. I made it and I can break it."

"Sir? I don't care what you or the idiots at the puzzle palace think of me. I do my job, and that's what I protect. Don't ever fuck with one of my reports again." Craig walked out carrying his anger and fatigue on fragile legs.

"Do you hear anything?"

Craig looked at the floor, his wet boots, the muddy tracks. "Like what?"

"Listen!"

Craig cocked his head and glanced up at the ceiling. "Come on, Damon!"

They ran up the stairs to the upper deck and down the squad bay to the closed door that separated the senior enlisted private quarters from the other men. They threw open the door to the Petty Officer First Class Boyle's room.

Phuong, her eyes wide with surprise, was on the bed, the-bodice of her ao dai ripped, her knees folded tight to her belly and pushing Boyle back.

Craig and Damon each grabbed one of his arms and threw his against the wall.

Craig grasped Phuong by shoulders, gently, and took her to the door. *"Co manh khoa, khong?"*

She didn't answer except for a mewing sound with her tears, but nodded. She held her arms across her breasts, keeping the material drawn tightly.

"You go see Mai Linh, okay? Ask her to take care of you."

Phuong walked down the squad bay and disappeared through the door to the stairs.

Craig swung around now and grabbed Boyle's shirtfront. "You ever touch one of them again, even so much as a dirty look, and I'll kill you. Don't mistake this as an idle threat, I wouldn't have a second thought about opening up on you with an M-16 and Damon would back me up that it was accidental."

Damon, his face red, didn't comment, but took a single swing and buried his fist in Boyle's belly.

Boyle, breathing heavily, his face blank and dull, said, "She was trying to steal from me and I caught her."

"You're a fucking liar," Damon said. "You make me sick."

"Wait and see whose word they take. Nobody would listen to you two, or to a gook."

Craig kicked Boyle in the ribs, would have done it again, but Damon grabbed his shoulders and pulled him away.

"You just watch out, Boyle, watch where you walk, watch where you are after dark. I'd be real careful."

"You can't threaten a senior petty officer."

"It's a promise, you beggar asshole, a promise."

"So what happened, Brooks?"

"Richland said that Boyle explained it to his satisfaction. He also said Boyle had confiscated the MAA log since you men were writing antinavy slogans and lies in it. He thinks it might be enough evidence for a general court-martial."

Craig shook his head angrily, "They can piss up a rope. They want to court-martial, I'd love it. Anyone rational ever hears the truth about this place and they're down the benjo, not us."

"Truth is the key word."

"I know. They don't even flirt with it. It's a bitch when even honesty can't help anyone."

Damon, who had stood sullen and silently, spoke. "Her husband is off with the ARVNs fighting in this cluster-fuck of a war and this is what justice she gets? Get real, Brooks."

"I'm sorry. I want the bastard nailed as badly as you do."

"Well, something will happen," Craig said.

Damon agreed. "Something *will* happen."

Lieutenant Commander Richland was forty-three years old and he knew that if there was still a chance for his captaincy, his time was running out. He brooded on the petty rebellions of the men, the disrespect shown, the easy first-name association that Crenshaw had with the enlisted men: each was a nail in his coffin, preventing promotion. He puzzled over those actions, skirmishes in his own private war. He considered *his* war more important than the larger one that engulfed them: this one could ruin him. Now he had a new problem of damage control. If Det Tango were a ship he could order the compartments sealed, hatches closed: Here he had to take action himself. Boyle, who had been Richland's choice, had obviously done something wrong, and even a new fabric of lies, if the affair went to trial, would not hold up. Especially since Craig Nostrum's name was on every set of lips from NSA; they were calling him the new Super Op. Richland smoked his cigar and tried to decide what he should do.

"We can't reason with him. Maybe it's time to really throw in our wings, just stand down until someone comes to investigate this whole thing."

Craig nodded to Damon. "But who watches out for the pilots then? It's a Hobson's choice."

"Maybe it's time we realized that we can't win."

"I won't give up on this yet. I'm going to have Cookie get a message to NSA. I still know some of the people there."

* * *

Richland, his vulnerability apparent even to him, made his decision within an hour and signed transfer orders sending Boyle back to the Philippines. When he saw Nostrum enter the spaces and walk back to the communications room, he immediately walked back as well and made his decision known. He feared Nostrum around the comms room. The teletype machine that Richland considered their lifeline could just as easily become a noose.

"You did this, you little fuck." Boyle pushed Craig back with his hands. "I could knock the shit out of you."

"You might." Craig shoved him back. "But you might not, and if I get you down, I'll kill you."

They both heard a magazine snap into a rifle and turned to the sound. Damon stood there with an M-16 locked and loaded. "You know, I just heard some sniper fire. I might have to try to return fire. Be a shame if someone crossed the line of fire accidentally and died, huh?"

"You couldn't get away with it," Boyle said.

Mark stepped around the corner. "Gosh, there's some heavy incoming sniper rounds. I just witnessed Damon attempt to return fire and clear a zone for us to the bunker. It's sad that despite our warnings someone ran into the line of fire."

Boyle swore, grabbed his seabag.

"Don't lose your way to the Fifteenth Aerial Port. It's a nice walk on a day like this."

"Where's the duty driver?"

"He had to stand watch against snipers."

Boyle swore again and walked down the stairs.

On the twenty-third day of the commemoration of the exile of the linguists, they began to return. The push for more traffic, the increase in the number of bombing missions, the fact some men couldn't make the grade and others got orders had begun to render the unit inoperable, and Richland relented. To show his defiance he did allow Brady a six-day trip to Bangkok for R&R.

"Did you see this?"

Richland accepted the message from Chief Masters and read it. "An urgent request for a second-class petty officer, Vietnamese linguist, for the USS *Jamestown*." He set it down on his desk. "They want volunteers."

"Sometimes a man can volunteer and not even know it."

Richland smiled. "I like that. Can you see that that message is sent without Cooksey being told?"

"I can make a teletype sing, sir."

"Nostrum has always seemed liké a fleetie to me anyhow. He'd like being on a ship and bobbing in the water with no booze and no glory. Be right up his alley."

"That's what I thought, sir, exactly."

To: OIC, NSGA, USS JAMESTOWN
DE: OIC, DET T, RVN

SUBJ: YOUR NEED FOR CT12, VIETNAMESE

YOUR URGENT REQUEST FOR A SECOND CLASS
PETTY OFFICER VIETNAMESE LINGUIST RECEIVED.
WE HAVE A VOLUNTEER AVAILABLE, CT12 CRAIG
JOEL NOSTRUM, SN# x38 00 68.
NOSTRUM IS EXPERIENCED IN ALL PHASES OF THE
LANGUAGE AND HAS SERVED DILIGENTLY AND
WELL AT THIS UNIT. WHILE THIS UNIT WILL BE
SORRY TO LOSE HIM, WE FEEL IT ONLY FAIR TO
HONOR HIS REQUEST FOR TRANSFER IN
ACCORDANCE WITH HIS EXCELLENT PERFORMANCE
AND YOUR DIRE NEED.
HE WILL BE MADE AVAILABLE UPON RECEIPT OF
OFFICIAL ORDERS.

Chapter 20

Cooksey got drunk.

Neutrality had been so carefully maintained, his stand so complete, that he felt guilty without drinking. He caught sight of Craig Nostrum, flushed and excited, wheezing from a volleyball match, and walked over to him on legs that stubbornly refused to move without weaving. He repeated the message that he had dug out of the burn bag. He wondered why anyone would think that a message could be sent, that his equipment could be used, without his knowledge.

"He said I volunteered?"

"Yeah."

"Thanks. I know what it took for you to do this."

"Just make sure it doesn't get out how you heard."

"I'll back you up to the wall."

"So what are you going to do?"

"I need to talk to Benny Radcliff in personnel in the P.I., secure voice, can you do it?"

"Not secure, but I can get some voice. Have to use some air force gear."

"I hate to ask."

"It's just as shitty as everything else I'm asked to do."

* * *

Craig, airborne, scribbled notes on his handlog, transcribed the Vietnamese with ease, and kept yelling for position reports from the R-beats. Even as the MiGs had taken off from Nam Dinh, Craig had sensed theirs was no normal jaunt to check out the clouds.

Brooks, half-asleep, walked down the aisle and stood at Craig's elbow. He rocked back and forth on the balls of his feet. He touched his forehead with eggshell fingers. That was my last drink ever, he promised himself. "Tracking is really limited, they said. Just some new positions on a sporadic basis."

Ted Trainer's voice boomed over the intercom, "Napalm has been shown to be an effective life-preventing artifice that can be of significant value when used in a conscientiously applied program of military regimen and regular immoral use."

The ground controller was An Khe. Craig puzzled for a moment: a new name, or a change in names. He looked at Brooks. "Ask Chris what controller he had running that weather recce out of Phuc Yen."

Brooks was back in a moment. "Burton says it's Dai Nam."

Craig smiled. "That's the same name he used yesterday. Brooks, get a message out, a SPOT report. There are MiGs about to land in Vinh."

"They wouldn't."

"They are."

"You know how close that is to the DMZ?"

"I know, and so do they. I'd say the price of poker has just gone up. Get the message out right away, okay?"

"On my way."

Craig flipped on the intercom to talk to the other lingies: Ted, Gerry, his new junior man, Chris Burton. "There are now two MiG-21s in Vinh. Vinh's call sign is An Khe. Keep an ear out for more planes and for additional SAM sites to be activated."

"Yahoo," Ted screamed. "That's who I have right now. I couldn't place the name or the voice. I even have a nice new set of coordinates to send out. Nice work, hero."

"All part of the free service. Fly Air Willy, for the best in spy news."

* * *

In the officers' club Richland was cheerful, rubicund, expansive. Another Bravo Zulu for the report on the MiGs in Vinh; Det Tango was the first one to report it. Even after the air force analyzed their own data, they added nothing to the report from Det Tango. He bragged without compromising their mission, told stories of how he had found some of the most important targets of the air war. He talked about the use of specialists for minor functions, but that it was the overview, the analysis added by the man in charge, that really made the difference in the intelligence war.

An ensign pilot looked at his lieutenant j.g. friend and said, "That man is a real asshole."

"There it is," his friend answered.

"One of the targets this morning will be the airfield at Vinh. We have to test their defenses and their capabilities and we need some photo recce. Blackbird at ten hundred hours."

Craig, his pain unrelenting, swallowed an extra Darvon. The corpsman had raised his price to three ration coupons now, and Craig had wanted to cut back. He smoked, looked at Chris Burton, and shook his head, "Could have guessed that, huh?"

Chris, tenuous still, small and skinny, grinned nervously and nodded.

Craig liked the new man, thought he would make it, but he kept distant still. Next week he would switch junior men with Terry Denver, each of them to evaluate the man so that decisions could be made on his destiny.

Commander Richland sat at his desk with a half-filled glass of Gilbey's gin. He stared at the glass that distorted the scene behind it like a funhouse mirror. "Did you see that message?"

"Yeah." Masters said and sat down. "He's got some balls getting NSA to intervene."

"How did he do it? Somehow he found out about our message, then got word to that meddler at NSA who recommended that Nostrum be retained at Det Tango, and suddenly Brady's name comes up as a volunteer."

"So is Brady being reassigned?"

"No. I already took care of that, said he was essential and they found someone off the *Sterett* that loves sea duty. How did he do it?"

"Had to be Cooksey."

"I know. We need to send Cooksey back to the P.I., and try
to get a new man, one we can trust. Check with your friends
in the P.I. for a friendly. Get a name and get the whole thing
done. Fast. I don't want someone interfering in this one
again."

"I don't know why the navy and NSA don't see what
they're really like." Masters sounded genuinely perplexed.

"Because we're the stars of the air war, Chief. They're
good at what they do. They don't care about discipline at
NSA; remember, they're *civilians*! What would they know
about the way the navy is supposed to run?"

"I'll take care of it."

"Do that. And do it fast."

Craig had left the orphanage on foot, hitchhiked to the city
and stopped at the Cafe Song Ha and ordered a *cafe sua*. As it
did each time, the sweetness surprised him. He ordered a
small crepe and ate quietly as he watched the people in the
street. Co Mai, who worked at the Hill 327 exchange, had
said she might be here but she was not, and he accepted his
disappointment. He knew it looked bad for a girl of good
character to meet an American, actually any male, without a
chaperon. This was a culture where on the wedding night they
made love on a white sheet and if there was no blood, the
groom could return his new bride to her family and their lives
would be ruined. Many marriages were still arranged by the
families, and nearly all depended on an astrologer to pick the
time and day and place. Even the president, a man of many
Western mannerisms, used an astrologer to determine the best
time to announce his decisions, to introduce changes. Craig
sipped his coffee, finished it, and ordered another cup. Once,
months before, he had flirted with an American girl who
worked at the consulate. They had laughed and he had bought
her coffee. She had left with a reporter from the London
Times.

Craig had to push his way out, past the crowd, past the
beggars, the urchins, a sea of schoolchildren in perfect uniforms who marched like a miniature army from their class. A
trishaw passed with a fat Frenchman and a Vietnamese girl
dressed expensively and laughing with him as he cursed at the
driver, who peddled furiously as if under a whip. Craig had
seen the Frenchman before. He had been told the man had
high connections with the mayor and the province chief and

the government in Saigon. The French had lost the war, but won the concessions. The Frenchman still owned rubber and cinnamon plantations through a series of fronts and names. Craig flipped him the bird.

"You need a ride?"

Craig looked at the marine driving a jeep and nodded. "Back to base?"

"This is all off-limits."

"I broke down outside town and have been trying to get back."

"That's the same one I use. Hop in."

"I'm sorry," Craig said when he walked into Cooksey's cube, unsure of what else to say. He felt stained, dirty, the cause of these new orders, but there was nothing he could do.

"Don't be. I'm glad to be out of here, I think. I asked for a SAR det on the *King*. Looks like I'll get it."

"I appreciate what you did."

"It was nothing. I guess you and your crazy friends got to me at last. I really do believe you belong here. I couldn't let them fuck you out of it. You made me see the pilots."

"You put it on the line for me, I don't even know what to say, what to do."

"Save a pilot. That is thanks enough. Bullshit always runs downhill. I can hack it."

"At least let me buy some drinks."

"Drinks, hell, did you know—"

Craig laughed, yelled, "On this day in history Millard Fillmore found out that jacking off didn't make you blind!"

"A Fillmore party," Terry Denver shouted from down the aisle.

"What's that?" someone asked.

"A sked, a major fucking sked!"

Craig sagged onto the porch step to sit down: he eased himself down like an accordian, wincing with the sharp pangs in his lumbar spine. The flight had been canceled due to weather; it was only the second cancellation he could recall.

"Still having pain?"

"Only when I move, Ger."

They both crowded to the rails to let Chief Masters pass between them. "They say they're going to build a real latrine soon," Craig said.

"Hrrmphhh," the chief answered.

Masters walked across the field toward the three pisstubes pounded in the ground and stood before the one furthest to the right.

Craig began to laugh.

"Okay, come clean."

"Just wait, Ger. The fun is about to start."

They watched the chief wriggle, swear, shrug his shoulders, zip himself up, and begin to jog across the yard toward the road.

"What's the matter, Chief?" Craig yelled.

"Nothing," he yelled back, panting with his efforts.

Craig looked at Gerry. "I believe the chief is going to see the MAAG-11 dispensary because he is peeing blue."

"Peeing blue?"

"A concoction that one of the docs at the dispensary made up for me. He said they used it on first-year med students all the time. He's going to tell him he has some terrible disease."

"You didn't."

"Of course not. The chief did. I only put it in his drink, I didn't make him drink it."

The two of them laughed, and once Craig could stand up, they walked to the slop chute to have a beer.

Mai Linh was Caodaist, which meant she was everything or nothing on the scale of religions. They believed in an all-seeing eye, universal love and salvation, and worshipped a variety of icons and saints that ran from Christ to Gandhi, to Victor Hugo and Mark Twain. Craig, a Universalist, knew that they had something in common in the single sense of universal salvation.

Mai Linh was leaving candles, bits of ribbon, food offerings, all manner of good-luck charms around the barracks and Craig told her that she must stop this, it was making some of the newer men nervous.

"It is for their good."

"It is not what we believe. You understand?"

"Of course." And she left two shiny pieces of paper tucked under Craig's pillow.

Mark, acutely aware of Craig's pain, said, "You need to see the doctor again, this time make him do something."

Craig held the pieces of paper in his hand. "Good fortune will follow, Mai Linh said. I wish I believed it."

"You can't keep taking pills and drinking."

"Don't nag me, huh? I can quit any time I want."

"Fine, fine, I don't give a shit anyhow."

"Good," Craig said, and poured himself a drink.

The doctor shook his head. "I don't know, Chief. It could be a rare urinary tract infection. I'll need another urine sample to analyze. You been with any of the local ladies of the evening?"

"No, sir."

"Then I don't know. We better have you on some light duty."

"What should I do?"

"Just relax and don't get excited. It seems this condition is worsened when you get angry. So try to keep calm."

"Calm."

"That's the idea." The doctor walked down the hall with a corpsman in attendance.

"How could you lie to him like that?"

"I've treated a dozen or more of his men. They get these high fevers and dysentery, one of them had blood poisoning, and he doesn't let up on them at all. One of them asked me for a favor. This might be the only time in my life I'm going to take pleasure in not curing someone."

It was the middle of the night, and as such it was the worst of times to be in Da Nang: attack alley was one to four A.M., the hours when the VC attacked most often. Craig cocked his wrist to catch the light and looked at his watch. Zero one hundred hours. He sat beside Gerry and Ted, all of them perched on the roof of the bunker with cold beers.

"What makes you think it's tonight?"

Ted looked at Gerry and shrugged. "A feeling. I just know they're going to attack."

"Maybe it's gas," Craig interjected.

"It's tonight." Ted was adamant.

"The chief stopped drinking and finally his pee turned yellow again."

Gerry turned to Craig and grinned. "He never caught on, huh?"

"No. Hope he can figure out that toenail polish wasn't a natural phenomenon, but with my luck he likes passion pink."

Under the bleak moonlight, Craig looked at Ted and started

to tell him he was superstitious and silly, and just then he heard the most faint of whistles: a sound so quiet it could have been a parting of the sky by a cloud. "Incoming!" he shouted, and ran to the barracks to yell the same words.

In the morning Mai Linh was sweeping, but Phuong was not there. Mai Linh beat the cement with the broom bristles.

"Her husband has died, and she is mourning," Mai Linh answered when she was asked. She kept sweeping the whole time as if the act could restore the dead. She left more icons than usual: buttons, crackers, rice paper, tiny jade stones.

Though taxes were irrelevant to them, Craig noted that the date was April fifteenth.

Though the passage of time was insignificant to them, oppressive, it was marked by events: May first was when the marine went crazy and shot invisible snakes, the fourth was the day a drunk marine broke Gerry's jaw when he wouldn't give him any ammunition, the sixth was the day that commemorated the shootdown of the drone. They discussed this news the mystical way that word traveled in Vietnam. But now this news traveled from one man to another, and each asked who would be the one to tell Craig Nostrum. Not one of them would accept the role and so each passed it to the next the way the pox passed among children.

"Something's going on, Brooks, I want to know what it is."

Caught, Brooks looked guilty. "I don't know what you mean."

"People are whispering like crazy, they won't tell me anything, but they get quiet when I come by."

Not sure where to begin, Brooks blurted out, "Phuong is gone."

"What do you mean gone? She was in mourning."

"She ran off. Apparently she was too embarrassed to tell you and Damon that she actually had been raped. She left home once the mourning was over." Brooks averted his gaze, watched the shadows dance on the wall. "She probably went back to her village."

"You know better than that," Craig said bitterly. "She's soiled. She went to Saigon, or maybe just Da Nang to work as a whore. She doesn't have anything left to lose."

"I'm sorry."

"The line's old, Brooks. Sorry? We're the sorriest bastards that ever were. I'll kill Boyle if I ever get the chance. I don't even care where it is. I could run him over in Chicago as easily as shoot him here."

"That's the only good news. Boyle's under arrest for being caught in a black-market scheme in the P.I. He's in shit up to his ears."

"I hope he chokes on it."

Brooks stammered for a moment, his tongue clumsy, knowing that this was the hardest part; finally, he rushed the words out. "And Tsu Vien is dead."

Craig, already stunned, said, "No, it's not true," in a small voice that belied denial. Craig felt an opening inside himself, as if he were splitting. His stomach shrank against his diaphragm with a sharp, cruel pain. At last he asked how it happened.

Brooks said, "The ARVN were questioning her and they said she resisted."

It wasn't true, Craig said, knowing this, knowing that it made no difference. He accepted a glass of straight scotch from Brooks and took a swallow. "Bastards," he said at last.

"Are you going to be okay?"

"I'm always okay."

"Is there anything I can do?"

"Leave me alone right now."

With Andy gone, and Damon again returned to the Philippines to teach, the role of senior man fell to Craig, the obligations of the sub-rosa hierarchy: he listened to the homesick, the weary, the abused; he offered encouragement and advice, he scolded and cajoled. But as he sat with his bottle of scotch, he felt totally alone, and his grief for the loss of Tsu Vien and the ruin of Phuong were a vice on his heart.

Damon had been right. He needed Det Tango and he watched as it was being taken from him piece by piece—by orders, by death, by blood—and he wanted to scream for his losses.

Craig slept fitfully, waking with trembles and chills, with dreams, or perhaps the lack of them. He curled under two blankets against the damp cold of the night.

A touch, a finger, damp flesh on his own.

Craig kept his eyes closed, a rabbit convinced that if he did not see the intruder, the intruder did not see him. He tried to

move his arms but they seemed too heavy, the effort too great.
"Who is it?"

"You can't make it."

"Commander?" Craig blinked, his eyes not yet adjusted to
the light.

"You're falling apart."

Craig, no longer immobile, shoved the hand from his
throat with a fast slap of his right hand, struggled to sit up. He
rolled quickly from the mosquito netting, slipped, and fell on
his knees on the cement floor. He stifled a cry, looked around.
He was alone.

He looked both ways down the aisle and saw no one at all.

He poured himself a drink, took a sleeping pill, and
crawled back into his bunk, swimming into drowsiness despite
his pain.

"Craig is drinking too much," Terry Denver said. "He's
acting a little strange, too."

Brooks Crenshaw was sitting on the stoop of the BOQ and
watching the seabees finish off the barracks that Ted had once
tried to destroy. "Sometimes we all act strange. A lot's happened to him lately."

"The new man, Patterson, went to see him about some
problem and Craig told him to see the fucking chaplain."

That was not good, Brooks knew it. Brooks squinted as if
the sun might be in his eyes. "He's just tried," he said without
belief.

"When I got that comms change the other day he didn't
even double-check my tape."

"He trusts you."

"He always has. He trusted Damon and Andy, but he
would have listened to the tape anyway."

"I'll talk to him."

"Gerry and Ted are his best friends, why haven't they come
to tell you?"

"Times are strange."

"Huh?"

"I'll talk to him."

Brooks asked where Craig was and Gerry shrugged in response. "Gone," Gerry said.

"Where?" Brooks asked.

"If I knew, he wouldn't be gone. I mean he'd still be gone,

but he wouldn't be gone gone because I'd know where to find him. I even tried that spot by the canal."

"Shit."

"I'm worried about him, are you going to talk to him?"

"If I find him."

"Bring him back."

"I will, if I find him."

"I don't mean physically. I mean in his head, Brooks."

Brooks wished that he could just go home.

Craig stood in front of the orphanage for a long time before he walked up the driveway. He looked at the playing field that the seabees had carved from the jungle brush. Two marines were erecting a swing set. He said hello to them, stopped by an old man who worked the garden.

"Hello, Grandfather, are you well?"

"Esteemed nephew, I am well, and you?"

"I am well, too, Grandfather. May I help you in the garden?"

"If you work, then there will be half as much to do and what will I do to fill the time?"

"You could go to the cafes."

"And listen to boys with long hair discuss politics? They have forsaken the ways it is meant to be. They stop showing respect, they don't even keep up the altars any more. Their ancestors' graves are in a ruin. What would I have in common with them?"

"You could visit with friends."

"Most of them are dead, or refugees now. No, I have my garden, and this is my life now."

"I wish I had one, Grandfather."

"Sometimes our gardens are inside of us," he said, and began to weed again.

Craig bowed and walked into the orphanage courtyard. He saw a young nun and turned toward her. "I am..." He could not say his name.

"I know, Craig, you were Tsu Vien's young friend. I am Chi Cam Thanh."

"I am pleased to meet you." Craig bowed slightly, averted his eyes, and followed her to the nursery.

A baby cried and Craig looked to Cam Thanh, who nodded, and he raised the baby in his hands and held her to his chest. He rocked back and forth and patted the child's bottom with the steadiness of a metronome.

"We call this one Tsu Vien."

Craig blinked rapidly, not quite catching his tears. He kissed the baby's head. "So tiny."

"She was left for us the day Tsu Vien was taken. It was God's gift to us. He knew we would need someone to fill part of the hole in our hearts. *Deus miseratur.*"

Craig nodded. "God be merciful," he said after her. He handed the baby to her, fell to his knees, and cried for the first time since the news had come of Tsu Vien. He could see the altar with Tsu Vien's picture and fresh rice cakes and red paper money. His shoulders heaved with his sobs and he wept without shame.

Cam Thanh placed a light hand on his shoulder.

Sated at last, Craig rose and took the baby again. "She is very pretty. It is a good name." His voice was hoarse. He reached into his pocket and took out the few American dollars that he had been able to change and handed them to the nun.

She looked at the floor, accepted the money, and buried it within the folds of her white habit.

"Take care of little Tsu Vien, Sister."

"I will. Thank you."

Brooks, Ted, and Gerry were gathered in the field where the seabees had finally laid a cement slab for a new latrine, where the sidewalk was nearly ready to be poured. They drank wine from super-hero glasses that Ted had gotten with the faces of Spiderman and Captain America and Captain Marvel on them.

"This is a hell of a way to live," Brooks had said, and then explained that he could not find Craig anywhere. "I even went to the weed patch he calls Walden Swamp."

"I say if anything happens that we kill Richland." Ted spoke so quietly that the other two had to lean to make out his words, and Brooks shivered when he heard them.

"What can happen here in Paradise East?"

The three of them looked up, surprised.

"Holding a wake for somebody I know?" Craig asked, and took a long swallow of wine from the bottle. "Let me get my own drink and I'll join the party."

When Craig returned with his glass and a bottle of scotch, Brooks asked, *"Where the hell have you been?"*

"Gone. But I'm back now. I'm really back." Craig said this earnestly, softly, looked at each of them and smiled. "I have a flight in the morning, I'm told. Seems I have Chris as a junior man and Horowitz and Gray are the SAM ops. I guess I should celebrate I'm not flying with two guys like you who worry needlessly over their friends." Craig gulped as he spoke, finally stared at the dirt yard. He kicked his toe in the dirt. "I'm sorry, okay?"

"Did you know?" Ted began.

"That on this day in history . . ." Gerry added.

Brooks, bewildered and happy, spoke. "Millard Fillmore got his first piece of ass as president?"

"A Fillmore party!" Craig hollered.

While word passed and bottles were brought out to the yard, Craig sipped his drink in silence, and when Brooks sat down beside him he wanted to say something, but he could not find the right words.

"What's going on?" Brooks asked, breaking the quiet.

"Richland made another late-night visit. Then Tsu Vien and Phuong. It's like it will just keep happening. Everything chips away at my heart."

"But you're okay now?"

"Okay, Brooks? I am the best fucking lingie that ever walked these cruddy ruts we call home."

The Fillmore party was interrupted at its zenith and called off when the VC hit the base with a flurry of mortars and rockets and the fuel dump *whoosh*ed loud and black in the sky, and an F4 exploded in its revetment.

"I'll be go to hell," Youmans said. "Nostrum won the rocket pool!"

"About time," Craig said. "It's about fucking time."

Chapter 21

"They followed me home," Barry Youmans said, and smiled. He balanced a pup across each of his forearms. The two puppies licked at his face with small pink tongues.

"Did you name them yet?" Craig asked, and took one into his arms. He was exhausted and his back hurt, but he held the puppy with the same tenderness he had given little Tsu Vien. He reached out and patted the other one as well.

"The one with the pink nose is Lifer and the one with the black nose is Beggar."

Craig laughed until he coughed. "Beggar and Lifer? I love it." He kissed the pup's nose. "Where'd you get them?"

"Mai Linh. She said she owed them to us because of the money we gave her for Phuong. I don't remember giving her money, though. Guess we Georgia folk don't always have good memories, huh?"

Craig blushed, set the puppy on the ground. "I'll go to the geedunk and get some hamburger for them."

"Thanks."

"You know what, Youmans? I think I love you." He kissed the R-beat's left cheek and ran to the spaces.

Youmans, embarrassed, grinned. "At least you didn't lick my ear like Trainer does."

* * *

The puppies flourished with fifty-three masters to spoil them. They waddled with fat white bellies. "If anything ever happens to them, it will be the result of overloving or over-feeding," Craig said, and dropped some bits of steak on the ground for the dogs.

"Beggar's chewing your boot laces," Gerry said.

"I can buy more," Craig answered.

"Lifer crapped in my cube."

"What'd you do?"

"Cleaned it up, of course."

"Good. Don't want to make Mai Linh's life any harder than it is." Craig lifted Lifer up and kissed his nose, let the puppy lick his chin and nose.

Ted shook his head. "I was never allowed to have a dog."

"Now's your chance. Besides, both of them like the Mothers of Invention. Lifer loves 'Plastic People.'"

Ted grinned, squatted, and let Beggar climb into his lap. The puppy piddled on him and Ted just laughed. "What do I do now?"

"Love him," Craig answered.

Gerry slammed his fist on his fold-down desk and screamed for Brooks.

"What's up?"

"I missed a fucking comms change. There's a new SAM site active south of Haiphong. It's right smack dab on the ingress route."

Brooks nodded, took the handlog, and ran for the teletype machine. He handed his notes to the O-brancher. "Send it out right now."

"Fuck," Gerry said, and nudged Ted in the side. "What's going on?"

"They're getting ready to fire."

Craig flipped on the intercom. "I've got a MiG up after an A4. He's hungry."

The SAM missed, the MiG was shot down.

Brooks sent the messages out.

A year ago he had been a newie, and Craig thought of this when he trudged down from the late flight. He walked into Ted's cube and shook his friend awake. "Get up."

"What time is it?"

"Two."

"I've only been asleep thirty minutes, max."

"What happened?"

Ted sat up, rubbed his eyes; his curly hair looked greasy and dull. "Marshall?"

"Yeah."

"A blanket party."

"I know. I heard. Why?"

"He's the rat here. He's Richland's inside man."

"He got hurt pretty badly. He needed stitches. He didn't even tell how it happened. He said he fell down."

"Don't blame me."

"Why, Ted? We don't beat up people."

"He sold us out."

"I don't think so. I don't think it was him." Craig walked back to his own cube and crawled into his rack. It took three scotch and waters and two Darvons to bring sleep.

Steve Marshall, his right eye swollen shut, a tiny web of stitches over his left eye, showered in silence. As he walked past the others he neither spoke nor was spoken to.

"Why don't you think it's him?" Gerry demanded.

Craig was startled by the question, dropped his letter to Sheryl on the bunk. "He's too far on the outside. He just doesn't need us. He's on his own."

Gerry puzzled for a moment, looked at Ted. "So Craig thinks we beat up the wrong man."

"You did," Craig said.

"I never did like him, he's got a tin ear." Ted was adamant when he spoke. "He's always sucked up to the brass."

"That doesn't mean you're a traitor," Craig said, and mixed himself a drink.

Ted said at last, "It's too late to talk about it anyway. What happened, happened."

"Hey, Beggar!"

Chief Masters whirled around. "What did you say?"

"I was calling the dog."

"You think you're funny, don't you?"

"You're too sensitive, Chief," Craig said, and gathered the puppy in his arms and gave him a piece of hamburger. "If you were real good we might give you a treat, too."

"You . . . you . . ."

"Concentrate, Chief, work at it, and you might get beyond a single syllable."

"Just watch out!"

"I do, these dogs won't use the latrine yet."

Gerry always wore his guilt like a badge. Now, embarrassed, he wasn't sure what to say. Finally, standing next to Craig he said, "Ted thinks you're wrong."

"Ted just wants to think he was right."

"No."

"I think it has to be someone who can be bought. Marshall is too easy. He's a damned analyst because he couldn't make it as a lingie, and he's a good analyst. But he had nothing to gain."

Gerry patted Beggar's sides and fed him a biscuit. "You have any ideas?"

"Not a one," Craig said, and walked off with the puppy waddling behind him.

There was a stranger; he stood in the familiar weedy stubble where Beggar had been buried. Craig winced with memory of the puppy's death. Distemper. He stared for a moment, the stance seeming familiar to him.

"Is he one of yours?" Ba Mai Linh asked anxiously.

"No," Craig replied. He wondered if he was going mad finally. He imagined that a madman must not know he is mad. He must forget it in the same way that men forget their wedding rings. Single, he did not have this option. You always knew you were single. It seemed a failure in other's eyes. "Denny," he said at last.

"Captain Burris, to you."

Denny Burris, Craig's first cousin, grinned and ran to him until they hugged and slapped hands, and spoke so quickly at the same time that neither of them could answer.

"You get these in Crackerjacks?" Craig asked as he touched the army captain's bars on his cousin's shoulders. He thought of the summers they had spent together, the first tenuous double dates they had had with girls more worldly than they were. "Goddamn. Nobody told me you were here."

"I asked Mom not to worry anyone."

"How'd you know where to find me?"

"Your mom. She wrote me and talked about you and I promised that if I ever got the chance I'd look you up."

"I can't believe it. You better take those bars off, we kill for less here."

"Surly group."

"The last I heard you were at Morris Harvey College. Going to be a lawyer or a business magnate."

"That's what I thought. The draft board thought differently. They said, hey, you, asshole, you're it. So I did boot camp and got OCS."

"I thought there was a lottery."

"If somebody wins, somebody has to lose." Denny grinned.

"How long can you stay?" Craig asked.

"Tomorrow morning I go back to the unit. This isn't summer camp anymore, is it?"

"No," Craig answered. Not ever again. He hugged Denny, "God, it's good to see you again."

"You guys live pretty good."

"Pretty *well*, pretty *well*."

"Surly English students are the worst kind of cousins."

"You're really in the shit out there, huh?"

"I wouldn't pick this for spring break. We have about a fifteen-percent casualty rate. It's better than a lot of others. That's a shitty way to look at it, isn't it?"

"It's all numbers here now, huh?"

"We built a school for some village. The VC pulled back for now. They killed the village chief and left his head on a stake. Damn, it's good to see you."

"Come on into the barracks and let me get us some cold drinks. You drink, don't you?"

"Does a wild bear shit in the woods?"

"Welcome to Chez Craig."

They sat down in the cube with cold beers. Craig smiled. "Remember the time we got into Uncle Joe's Dago Red?"

"Ugh, don't remind me. I think I still have the shits from that episode."

Craig laughed.

Denny unpinned his bars from his collars. "You still writing the great American novel?"

"GAN still not being written. I do better at not writing it than writing it. You look so skinny."

"I'm okay."

"Yeah, we're all okay, right?"

"You don't look so good yourself. You have some pain?"

"No way. How're Joey and Sally and Phil?"

"Good. Philly's captain of his football team at Allerdice. Sally's married."

"No shit?"

"No shit, cuz. I like your ladies." Denny looked at the ceiling. "The one lady has her tit cut out."

"Miss Uniboob. Reminds you of Sarah Morris, huh?"

"Not big enough. Sarah had tits to here." Denny held his hands out. "Not nearly big enough."

They laughed, drank, shared their pasts. They heard an explosion, but the sound was so commonplace that neither of them moved.

"You really his cousin?" Ted asked. "We had bets he evolved from an amoeba. You *sure* you're related?"

Denny shook his head. "He's adopted, actually. We try to keep that a family secret. Left on his own he's never been much. I expect you all carry him."

Ted clapped his hands. "He's a heavy load to be sure."

"Adopted, shit! I have Grandpa's eyes. The only thing you have is that you're growing bald like him."

Denny tapped Craig's stomach. "You sure have his gut."

"Asshole," Craig answered. He thought briefly how he resented the others being there. This should be his time. He felt jealous of these moments, each one stolen from the war: it was *his* boyhood.

"Did you know?" Gerry said.

"That on this day . . ." Ted added.

Mark clapped his hands sharply. "Millard Fillmore jacked off in the White House for the first time."

"Fillmore party!" they screamed.

"What the hell?"

"Just go with it, cuz," Craig said. "Just go with it."

Not quite dawn, the sky was dull and flat. Craig stared into space and would not look at Denny Burris. We share blood, he thought, we were closer than brothers. "You have to go, right?"

"Yeah. I don't want to be late. Sets a bad example for the troops."

"I'm glad you came, but . . ."

Denny nodded. "I know. It makes you miss home even

worse. You know, your mom and dad were always my favorite aunt and uncle."

"Yours are mine. Aunt Jane's the worst, right?"

"She kept Jimmy on a choke chain. Wouldn't ever let him go on camping trips with us. Maybe that's better. He's still in school and joined the National Guard."

"Except he won't ever know if he has any balls."

"He doesn't, believe me. He would have told her to stuff it sidewise."

"I'm going to miss you worse than before."

"Hey, we'll get out of this shit and tell our grandkids about it."

"Promise?"

"If I could, cuz, I wish I could."

"I haven't seen you this happy in a month of Sundays."

"Family, Brooks. Denny and I were really close."

"I know. Stay cool."

"He's out in the real shit. He . . ."

"Let it out. Come on. You can't be iron man forever."

"I have to be. I hack it. Right?"

Craig finished a cheese egg-burger at the geedunk at the compound and returned to the spaces to review the day's reports. "How's it going, Jack? How was Bangkok?"

"Fine," Brady said, and riffled through the papers in his hands.

"You like being an analyst better than flying?"

"It's different."

"Yeah," Craig remarked, and took the reports from the desk and fanned through the clipboard. He looked at the kill ratios, the measurement of the war. It was the same with the air war. How many MiGs were shot down, compared to how many U.S. planes. He wondered when the yardstick of death had become familiar to him. "Increasing the raids in Laos and Cambodia, it looks like."

"You aren't supposed to talk about that."

"It's right here."

"You aren't supposed to read anything you don't need to know."

Craig shrugged his shoulders. Brady had begun to concentrate on the latest issue of *Playboy*.

"Four hearts," Craig bid.

"Pass," Ted said, and so did the other three.

Craig shrugged and looked at Mark. "You were supposed to answer, to bid something, asshole."

Mark grinned, slapped his cards down to play dummy. "At least I had some points." He spread out an ace, a king, and four hearts beginning with the jack.

Craig grinned. "You should have jumped me up to slam."

Mark shrugged. "I wanted to listen to the radio. The returns are starting to come in from California."

"Next time think of your cards first," Craig said, and threw down his ace of trumps.

"Bobby's winning. He'll have us home by Easter."

Craig took another trick, and smiled. "Easter, buddy. Home by Easter."

Craig raked in the cards, his bid and two over tricks. He handed the deck to Gerry. "Your deal."

"Thanks."

Craig looked at the cards he had been dealt, at the hand Mark spread on the table. "You said you had a bunch of points. You have shit."

"I wasn't paying attention. Bobby's speech is coming through."

"Pay attention, turkey. *Chu Y Canh Gioi.*"

"Listen to him, he's got it right."

Craig groaned as he lost his third trick to a ruff from Gerry who was playing east.

"You went set," Ted said needlessly.

"I know," Craig said, and dealt the cards.

"Listen up, assholes!" Terry Denver shouted.

Craig and the others were quiet.

The voice on the radio was shocked and unsteady, "Senator Kennedy has been shot. He's been shot. Oh, my God, he's been shot."

Craig looked at his hand and flipped it down face up. He walked to the radio. "No," he said. Craig stood, slumped against the wall, and sat on the floor below the radio. Gerry joined him, then Ted, then Mark, and finally Terry, and then one after another the others all sat down on the floor without speaking.

Craig felt better flying than brooding on the ground. The news was slow with updates, and when they came the news was unconfirmed. He sat in front of his transceivers and spun the dials automatically.

"I've got a MiG-21 up in reaction to an A4."

Brooks nodded. "The ditty boppers have him, too."

"Out of Hanoi Bac Mai."

"Thanks."

Craig listened to the conversation and scribbled it down. He felt as if he were in the cockpit with the pilot, as if they were the same one. Glancing at the English translation that he had scrawled, his native tongue seemed like a foreign language to him.

"He's locking on radar," Craig said. *Bam sat.*

"Senator Kennedy is dead," Brooks said, his voice hushed and remorseful.

"No Easter," Craig mumbled, continuing to copy the traffic.

"Pardon me?"

"Firing missiles," Craig said quickly. "He missed and is breaking off." He wiped his eyes. "He missed!" But he knew that in the hotel kitchen nobody had missed.

"He's dead," Craig said softly. "He's really dead."

He thought of California, of the U.S., and shook his head. This is my home now, he thought, my only home. This place defined by friends and barbed wire, the borders armed and dangerous, but safer than a hotel kitchen. He shuddered and began to search on the radio again.

He repeated the same words, over and over, No Easter.

Never again.

Chapter 22

"*Mau len.*"

"What?"

"Hurry up."

"We're only going to the spaces, not the Indy Five Hundred."

Craig Nostrum smoked a cigarette and watched the scenery pass with familiar contempt. He reached into his pocket, extracted a pill, and swallowed it. Soon. He knew the fatigue would lift soon; the pills always did that. The corpsman had started him on them a month ago. He paid a dollar each, U.S. currency only.

"Why're you going out there, anyhow? You look bushed."

"Review the reports. Flying three days of doubles does that to me. I feel bushed."

"You can't keep this up."

"Don't play Mom, huh? Brooks already has the role down pat." Craig smiled, already beginning to feel a little better; he held his right knee with his hand to stop its bouncing.

"Cut Mark a huss and take his flight, huh?"

Jack Brady shook his head. "I'm senior analyst now, I have a job to do. I'm too busy to take his flight."

"You know something, Jack? Sometimes you're almost as big a pain in the ass as Richland himself."

"We'll get some help soon, just hang in there."

"Spoken by the man who greased the rope."

Brady stood up and brushed past Craig. "I have to hit the head."

Craig stood beside Mark's bunk, concerned and feeling silly. He handed the other man a washcloth with an ice cube in it. "Put it on your eye. Nice shiner."

"I'm okay."

"Greg's bringing a hunk of steak back."

"I'm fine."

"What happened?"

"Sunny Jim Ferris. He told me that it was a good thing that someone took Kennedy out. He said we didn't need a pinko in the White House. I popped him right then."

"What an asshole."

"So I got in two quick shots, he got this lucky roundhouse and blacked my eye, and I coldcocked him."

"Does he look better than you?"

"Worse. Not only does he have a black eye, he also has a split lip. It's cut pretty good, started swelling right on the spot. He told me he's going to see me pounding rocks at Portsmouth."

"I guess I better go visit him."

"He'll want to see you about as much as having hot coals dumped down his skivvies."

"That'll be my second choice for him."

Lieutenant Junior Grade Ferris listened impassively. "You can't get me to drop the charges. You can't intimidate me, Nostrum."

"I'm asking you to just forget it. Both of you got blacked eyes, that can be the end of it."

"He hit a superior."

Craig shrugged. "In rank only. Let's get to the point since you seem hell bent on getting your ass deeper in shit."

"Don't threaten me."

"No threats, promises. How would you like the press to get involved? They'd have a field day with some junior-grade officer who said he was glad that a political candidate got shot to death. Make you look great, right? Even some of those

right-of-Atilla-the-Hun admirals would cringe with that kind
of publicity and you'd be finished. No double bars; you'd be
lucky if they didn't drum you out."

"None of us are even cleared to talk to the press."

"You think I can't get through to them?"

"You wouldn't. You'd compromise your precious missions."

"I wouldn't compromise shit. No talk about what we do,
just talk about a lieutenant who deserves to get nailed for
stupidity, if not incompetence."

"I'll pay you back for this."

"Try."

Mai Linh said many times that the puppy ate better than
many of her people. She said this again now, to the new girl,
Nhu, and she said it without rancor, the way she reported on
the rains, or the drought, or the loss of a crop.

"These men are very strange, and they scare me," Nhu
said.

Ba Mai Linh smiled and said, "It is the secrets. They know
great secrets and the secrets make them crazy."

Brooks worried his hair back, started to speak, and sipped
his beer instead.

"You came here to tell me something, sir, go on."

He looked at Craig. "It'll sound crazy."

"We do crazy here, in fact it's what we do best."

"I woke up last night, and I swear that Richland was just
standing over me, his hands on my throat and just smiling. He
didn't do anything, didn't say a word. He just fucking
grinned. Maybe it was a dream, but it sure seemed real."

Craig, surprised to hear Brooks swear, shook his head. "It
was real. He's done it to me, too. He wants to make us crazy,
to make us quit. He thinks he can win if he screws with our
minds."

"You're sure? That it happened? I didn't make it up, hallu-
cinate it?"

"No way. The man is playing for keeps."

At midnight, with a crash of lockers, Richland called a
surprise drug inspection. He arrived with two SPs. He stood in
the aisle of the squad bay and ordered Ted to open his locker.

Ted smirked, opened his locker, and stood aside. "Help yourselves."

Richland glared at Trainer, finally spoke. "You seem pretty calm."

"The innocent always are." Ted stood in red bikini underwear and leaned against the braces of his bunk. "You expect to find something?"

Richland blinked, walked to the other side of the room to wait for the search to be over.

They found nothing.

At all, at all.

Craig stood at the piss tube, relieved himself, and looked at the framing for their new indoor head. Three seabees were working on it. The flush toilets were lying there, waiting to be installed. He zipped his flight suit up and walked to the stoop and sat back down beside Ted and resumed drinking his beer.

"I know who the turncoat is now," Ted said.

"About time. I figured that little bust last night was your doing. So what about Marshall?"

"I apologized. He said he forgave me. Made me feel like a real shit."

"Christian attitude. Marshall's like that. He still goes to church every Sunday he can. So now you figured out it was Brady."

Startled, Ted was angry. "If you knew already, why didn't you tell me?"

"Didn't want another blanket party. Besides, I wasn't sure until last night. I just had some strong suspicions. He's just been too close to Richland. I think that analyst job was payment for information."

"So what do we do?"

"Just leave him out of things. He'll catch on. No more midnight raids, no fists and kicks and blankets, just the old silent treatment."

"Fine by me. I'm out of my vigilante phase now."

"Good." Craig walked back in the barracks and reached into his locker. These pills would help him sleep. The corpsman had started him on them a week ago. Just another dollar each. The corpsman called them "sleep like a baby" pills.

A whistle, a shout, an explosion: the attack came at noon. Craig huddled with the others, his hands shaking so badly he burrowed them into his pockets. He could feel his heart pounding, a throb at his temples. He wasn't sure which pill would help now. He finally clamped both hands around a beer and drained it in a few swallows. Suddenly aware, he looked around the bunker again, finally asked, "Where's Mark?"

"Not here," Gerry said.

"I'm checking the barracks."

"Be careful, asshole."

"Always," Craig answered. He walked back to the barracks and called Mark's name over and over without getting any response at all.

In the bunker he asked each man if anyone had seen Mark. Finally Greg Devito said, "The last I know he was heading for the spaces to see Richland."

"Why?"

"Richland sent for him. Probably needed someone to hassle."

"You're sure?"

"The last I saw."

Craig hobbled to the bunker entrance again. "I'm going to the spaces."

"Don't be an asshole. There's a fucking attack."

"I've been through them before, Ger."

"What're you doing out here, Nostrum? There's an attack!" The marine guard tossed a badge onto the shelf.

"You seen Mitchell?"

"A couple of hours ago. You're shaking like crazy, you sure you're okay?"

"Tired." He signed the log.

"You're fucked-up CT sailor, man."

"Been said before."

"At least head for a bunker!"

In the spaces, Craig walked down the passageway, his heart pounding so hard he thought it might break through his chest. His hands wouldn't stop shaking. He yelled for Mark.

"Looking for someone?" Richland asked.

"I'm looked for Mark Mitchell, Commander."

Richland smiled. "He was here."

"Where is he now?"

"Maybe he's dead."

"Shut up! Where is he? Tell me!" Craig wobbled, put a

hand out for the wall to steady him. "Tell me," he shouted, but there was no sound. The colors swam around him. He blinked, sucked his breath as if he were drowning. He shook his fist, staggered, and collapsed. His last thought was that he had fallen inside Richland's grin.

"Hey, wake up, man."

Slowly, Craig thought, breaking loose from a river, from water that drowned him, breathe. He opened one eye, then the other, tried to focus. "Mark, Mark?"

"It's me, buddy. Drink this." Mark held the cup of water to Craig's lips and tipped it just a little.

Craig swallowed with effort. "What happened?"

"You were passed out at the spaces. The all-clear sounded and I was walking back inside to do some work and I found you there."

"Richland told me you might be dead." It hurt to talk; he sipped from the glass again, closed his eyes. "He said you might be dead."

"You were drinking, right?"

"A couple a beers."

"The pills. Richland was in a bunker, so was I. Put your head down again and try to sleep." Mark watched Craig's hands jerking spasmodically. "Relax, just let it go."

Craig hummed softly, repeated the same line over and over, the line they sang so often, the line dragged him like a fish on tackle. *We gotta get out of this place* . . .

"The doc said he was probably hallucinating, a combination of all that shit he's been taking." Mark spoke to Gerry and Ted, but knew he was talking to the others who would ask as well. The story would get around. "He hasn't been rational in twelve hours, he kind of drifts in and out of sleep. The doc gave me a pill for him to take, I crushed it in the juice I gave him. He stopped shaking a couple of hours ago."

Mark looked at the others; he was an old guy now, but he felt like an imposter. He drank some coffee.

"You need a break. Go on, grab some rack time and I'll stay with him. Ted'll come by and relieve me," Gerry said, and put a fresh cool washcloth on Craig's forehead. "He's still burning up."

"Flying fever." Ted spoke the words bitterly, remembered how many times they had had this malady, an FUO, fever of unknown origin. A fever that might or might not get better. A fever born in exhaustion. He sat down on the floor.

"Thanks," Marks said, and crawled into the upper rack. "Wake me if you need me."

Brooks was alone with Craig, and he felt awkward. He should have come sooner, but everyone said Craig was just out of it. He remembered when he had first met Craig, Craig had said his name, and Brooks thought he was so young that there could be nothing else to his history. "You're feeling okay, really?"

"Lots better. The nursemaids won't believe me, of course. I needed rest, I guess. They think I'm nuts. Richland was there, Brooks, no matter what they think. He told me Mark might have died and he grinned that shitty grin of his."

"I believe you."

"Don't patronize me."

"I'm not. He thinks he had you on the ropes. He knew about the pills. I went over to the corpsman, planned to bust his ass to seaman, and you know what? He's been transferred out. The new man said nobody was allowed to hand out pills like that. I told him he was selling them, and he just stared at me like I had three heads. He said navy corpsmen didn't do that shit. He's a hardcore medic. He just spent a year on the line with some grunts. He volunteered to return here."

"Maybe Richland's right. Maybe I am nuts, maybe I need to get out of here for everybody else's sake."

"Don't let him win, man. That's what you said before. We can't let him win."

"I know."

"Judi's in trouble now."

"Judi?" Craig thought of Brooks's wife, smiled. "What for?"

"Richland's wife called out to her when she was walking down the beach and asked her if it was true she had been entertaining enlisted men in her home. Judi just smiled and said no, she had been entertaining friends of her husband's and she never thought about asking them their rank. Mrs. Richland went crazy and started lecturing her. She said, 'We don't entertain enlisted men in our homes.' Judi smiled, nodded, and then flipped her the bird. Right there on the sidewalk in front of God and everybody."

Craig laughed and coughed. "I love it! I wish I could have been there."

"So Mrs. Commander Richland told her that she'd be barred from the officers' wives club. Judi just grinned and said, 'Who the fuck cares?'"

"Great. Tell Judi I owe her dinner out, at Papagayo's."

"You're back flying."

Craig looked at Chris Burton. "I'm back, Chris."

"You're okay?"

Craig wondered if the junior man was disappointed. He did not ask, but nodded and took his seat.

"I was worried about you, you know? Don't be crazy anymore, huh?"

Craig, touched, confused, merely nodded and began his preflight ablutions. He touched his white lucky stone and rolled it in the palm of his right hand.

"I love Sunny Jim's new program." It was Ted who spoke while they were getting coffee before things got busy. "I mean incentive and improvement. You look at the test he handed out? It's a fucking *Reader's Digest* word test. If I didn't know these words, I'd suck the tailpipe of an F4."

Craig laughed, giddy, surprised how good he felt with rest, how steady he was. "He wants to improve us. I loved that little speech where he offered days off for the men that scored the best. When he told us we could be better than we are. When he should have been whistling the National Anthem, he was so gung ho."

"So, screw him."

Craig smiled. "*Au contraire*, let's take this test. Just make sure that you get every question wrong. I mean *every* word. Talk to the ditty boppers, too, see if they'll go along. If by any chance someone doesn't know a word, make sure they ask so they don't accidentally get it right."

"All right!" Ted yelled.

"Keep it down to a roar, huh? This is supposed to be a secret."

As the flight was on the way home, Lieutenant Ferris, clucking his tongue, told the men they had scored very badly. "Tomorrow you fly with the new eval, Ensign Willard, but the day after we'll be together again. I'll have a new test. I'll try to make it a little easier."

Craig rolled his eyes, grabbed one end of the huge trash

can, and helped Ted carry it down the ladder. "The man's a weenie, Ted, a true weenie."

It was a game they played on every new evaluator, and Ensign Willard, like the others who preceded him, believed them.

Chris and Barry Youmans were the mainstays this time, sometimes it was others. Chris faked an engagement, Youmans created the plotting courses from memory. Willard, knowing he was in charge of sending the messages, ran the aisles, up and down, back and forth, until he was short of breath. Each time he talked to one man, he was sent back to the other, and so forth, and the exercise was not halfway over when he caught on and just stood in the aisle and grinned at the men.

"Funny," he said at last.

Craig laughed, turned around, and winked at Chris. "This one's going to be okay."

"A keeper," Ted said.

"I've got a MiG," Craig said, on the next day's flight. He listened to the pilot say that he was going to afterburners. "He's off after something."

Ferris nodded. "I caught on to what you're doing."

Craig shrugged. "He's after an F4."

"You think you can fool me, but you can't. You all missed the same question."

"Check tracking, huh?" He continued to copy.

GC: 426, ahead to the right, fifteen degrees, one pirate.
426: Roger.
GC: Ahead to the right, nine kilometers, take heading 310.
426: Roger, 310.

"You're all cheating, you're copying from the same test," Ferris said at last.

Craig laughed. "Just get the fucking coordinates, sir."

Ferris ran back, out of breath. "There a MiG after an F4."

"No shit," Craig said. "He's on his ass right now and about to lock on radar." Incentive and improvement, ignorance and inertia: Craig thought they were the same. "He's firing missiles and has a hit. He sees one parachute, now two. Send it out!"

"You're sure?"

"Move it, Lieutenant. If I wasn't sure I wouldn't say it."

David Richland opened the package and immediately tossed it into the trash can. A box filled with loose navy beans. They rattled like BBs against the tin rim. He stared at the box, the can, and swore. He picked up his pen and opened the file he had been keeping for months.

—Brooks Crenshaw seems to be losing his sense of reality. Today he accused me of standing over him while he slept and grinning. I tried to calm him and he walked off with a threat that he would finish me. His delusions seem to be growing worse.

"You know, don't you?"

Craig nodded, smoked his cigarette, and continued writing his letter to Sheryl. He described the sunset, the incredible colors and sounds of the war. He wrote to her about the orphanage.

"Say something."

"Something, Jack."

"You don't know what it's like. You don't know what I've been through. You and your smug friends are just being assholes. Every time I walk in a room everyone stops talking. Nobody ever says, Hey, Jack, you want to grab a beer."

Craig signed his letter, slipped it in the envelope. "I don't give a fuck, Jack. GAF, remember that?"

"You sanctimonious asshole!" Brady's voice was strident now. "Who the fuck set you up as judge and jury? Where did you get the sudden bout of morality?"

Craig put the letter on the top of the refrigerator and wrote the word *free* where postage was normally attached. "Get out of my face."

"You're so perfect, right? What about that girl you got pregnant in Monterey? She tried to kill herself. She lost your baby. You're a real fucking paragon of virtue."

"Shut up!" Craig thought about Monterey. Sell your body, sell your soul, he thought, and blushed. Sometimes he still dreamed about seaweed-clad fetuses. "You betrayed us," he said at last.

"I was afraid to fly. You know what that's like? I was afraid to fly but I needed the money. Richland gave me a way out. It didn't seem that bad."

"It was."

"You holier-than-thou asshole."

"If you want forgiveness, look to God. *Honi soit qui mal y pense.*"

"Fuck off, Nostrum. You're a psycho and everybody knows it. You're cracking. You're a pussy pretending to be tough."

Craig looked up, stood, took a single swing and buried it in Jack Brady's stomach. "You make me sick."

Brady doubled over, swearing at Craig with short, sharp breaths.

It was dawn and Craig listened to the raucous, mocking cries of lapwings. He hadn't slept and he was tempted to take a pill from the stash he had hidden, but he drank lukewarm coffee instead.

We're all orphans, he thought.

Lost in a desolate land.

"Time to fly," someone yelled to him.

"One more time," he yelled back. "One more fucking time."

Chapter 23

Chief Masters stood at attention, but his hands were buried in his pockets.

Brooks Crenshaw grinned, and offered a salute.

Chief Masters pulled his right hand out of his pocket and offered an awkward, quick salute. His fingernails were bright pink.

"Nice shade, Chief."

Masters scowled. "I tried to buy nail-polish remover at the PX but someone had bought it all up."

Brooks smiled.

"You know it had to be Nostrum and his crowd."

Brooks nodded, but restrained his laughter.

Craig lay in his bunk and felt no particular urge to move. The rains drilled outside the window, and despite two blankets he still shivered. He hugged the blankets tighter around him.

The pills were within reach, but he ignored them. He knew that he had to sleep this time without them. He stared at them curiously, as if they were more of Mai Linh's bright good-luck buttons. "No more," he whispered, "no more."

He rolled to his side fitfully, and turned on his lamp again. He opened his mail and reread the letters: one from his mother, his sister, his high school buddy Bob, three from

Sheryl, and one from Shell Oil Company asking why he hadn't been using his credit card.

"Time for your flight."

Craig opened his eyes, unsure whether he had slept at all. His muscles resisted his insistence to rise. "Yeah," he said at last.

"Pick you up in twenty-five minutes."

"Thanks, Greg." Eat shit and die, Craig thought, and forced himself to roll onto the floor. He grasped the rungs of the metal bunk and eased himself to an upright position.

"Wars shouldn't begin until noon," Craig muttered, and walked naked across the field to the showers. The water was cold, but he welcomed the pinpricks that it brought to his flesh. He scrubbed his skin vigorously. If he hated cold showers, he hated no water much worse. He rinsed off briskly, worried as always that the water could be shut off at any moment.

Nude, his towel around his neck, he shaved. He stuck snippets of toilet paper on the resulting wounds. Tiny red cores filled the white paper scraps. In the mirror, the face he saw shocked him.

Craig staggered back to the barracks, limping with the early morning stiffness and pain that was always with him, and wriggled into his flight suit. He made some instant coffee with a small coil heater, gulped down the first cup, and made another. He wondered when he had come to look like that.

"I've got something strange up," Craig told Brooks, he flipped on his recorder, continued to jot notes. "This is NVN navy traffic, they're talking about a submarine. Shit, I swear they're saying something about a sub in Haiphong Harbor."

"You're sure?"

"They said *tau ngam*. That's the only meaning I know for it."

"Don't say another word about it, okay?" Brooks spoke quickly, finally shrugged.

"You know something about it, don't you?"

"Just do what I ask, okay?"

"That doesn't change what I heard. That's what I do here, Brooks, you can't ask me not to do it the best I can."

"I know."

Craig looked at his recorder, at the pieces of tape that fluttered out like tiny brown insects. He slammed his fists on his desk. "Goddammit. Why can't we get any equipment that works right?"

"Not enough boxtops, yet," Brooks said, and walked off to the aft of the plane.

Craig stood in the central room, the living room of the Pink House near China Beach. He sipped a Coke and glanced at the marines that lounged in the furniture waiting their turns, waiting for friends, just drinking.

"It has been a long time," the mamasan said.

"A long time, *ba*," Craig answered.

"You other place, no place good like this one is. No other place make girls get VD checks."

"I know."

"Other places number ten thou, GI Joe."

Craig laughed, GI Joe: the generic name for the ultimate in generic wars.

"You want number-one clean girl?"

Craig handed over some MPC.

"I no like funny money so much. You no have greenbacks?"

"No."

"Okay, you go to that room."

"Where the hell have you been? Brooks has been looking all over for you."

"The Pink House."

Gerry shook his head. "Great. Off-limits, not to mention a good place to get sliced up by a VC. Shit. Brooks wants your ass out at the spaces."

"What's up?"

"He didn't say."

Mai Linh sat on the porch with Nhu.

Craig nodded to them as he passed, blushed as they giggled, never sure just what they meant with their secrets that seemed foreign more because they were women with secrets than because they were Vietnamese.

He walked to the spaces, surprised at his energy without the pills. He was sure that the sex had something to do with it: it renewed him. He walked into the building and found Brooks in the conference room. "You were looking for me?"

"Richland is ranting and raving that I broke security and told you about the submarines. I told him that you had copied the intercept, and he said where's the tape and you can imagine where it went from there. He thinks we're fucking around with him."

"You didn't tell me anything then, and you haven't now. You're saying there was a sub?"

"Don't ask. Security, need to know, you know the drill."

"So what next?"

"Maybe it'll all blow over. Where were you, anyway?"

"You don't want to know."

"I believe you. You remember when this place used to be so simple? God I miss John Brewster."

"Me, too."

Brooks sat down on the table, looking awkward and young, his legs crossed at the ankles, "I tried to get someone to look into this place. I don't know if they will. I guess lieutenants j.g. don't have many favors to call in."

"I'll back you up."

"If it comes to that."

"Hang tough," Craig said, and walked out.

"I was looking for you."

Gerry was not surprised to find Jack Brady sitting in his cube waiting for him. He stepped past him, stripped out of his flight suit and put on cut-off jeans and a blue striped T-shirt.

"Still giving me the silent treatment? You guys just all follow Craig like sheep."

"Maybe there just isn't anything to say."

"Ted trapped me."

"If you hadn't spied for Richland, there wouldn't have been a way to get caught."

Brady leaned against the locker. "In Monterey we were all buddies. Remember that? Even when we got here."

Gerry stuffed some MPC in his pocket and walked into the aisle again.

"You'll need me someday! What if you want a favor? This could be any of you assholes!" Jack followed behind Gerry, tagging along. "I'm sorry, man, I'm sorry."

Gerry sat down in the spook mess, opened a Coke, and watched *I Love Lucy.*

"You look glum, matey," Ted said. "Lucy's supposed to make you laugh."

"I feel kind of sorry for Brady, you know?"

"Sorry? I'm sorry I ever trusted the bastard. Remember, he's the one that apologized for the shorts incident."

It was for that act, that single betrayal, that Gerry was able to sustain his anger. It was the perfect time for all of them to hang together, just like the earliest days, and Jack had only thought about himself. "You're right," he said at last.

"I know. I'll get us some beers. Innkeeper, rum! Rum for my friends!"

Commander Richland stared across his desk at Craig Nostrum. He was calm, assured, his eyes focused on Craig's eyes. "There is a shared-services security meeting in Saigon and I am sending you as our delegate."

"I don't want to go. I have too much to do here."

"They want a tac/air expert."

"Send Brady, he's the analyst."

Richland, impatient, drummed his fingers on his desktop, but kept calm. "You're always screaming that the intelligence is not coordinated, this is your chance. Your flight is at oh seven hundred, and you'll be gone three days. There will be some free time, so you might pack civvies."

"Consider someone else."

"There is no one else. You've got the reputation. That's what they want."

Craig, despite his suspicion, was flattered. He wondered if Richland sounded so awkward, so calm, because he resented Craig's reputation. Deciding this was it, the trip suddenly pleased him and he stood up and saluted.

Craig walked back to the barracks to pack his suitcase.

The first session ended, and Craig followed a linguist he knew from Phu Bai to a bar on Tu Do Street. The street was clogged with traffic and they walked the distance in the muggy evening. The sky was peach-colored, smog laced it.

There were Americans everywhere that Craig looked: military and civilians. They had come to Vietnam in waves, he thought, on planes and boats, they waded ashore or climbed down off the backs of half-tracks: they came and they came and they came. An endless stream of soldiers, sailors, airmen, and marines: a snaking line of men that swelled by the day.

"Let's try this one," Randy White said.

"Fine by me." Craig followed Randy into Mimi's.

"Too many MPs here," Randy announced, and turned on his heel.

They walked to a bar near Nguyen Hue Street, were seated at a table in the back of the room, and ordered two "33" beers. "So what'd you think?" Randy asked.

"Now you see it, now you don't. They do it with mirrors, right?"

"Lots of bullshit, to be sure. Finding the truth here is like panning for gold with a thimble."

Craig sipped his beer and watched the others in the bar: Vietnamese, American GIs, American reporters, French, some middle Europeans, mostly Czechs and Hungarians. "Did you enjoy Tet as much as we did?"

"More. The whole fucking army of North Vietnam came in. They killed so many, Craig. Thousands. Just killed them."

"Win their hearts and minds, right? Like the general said: grab them by the balls, and their hearts and minds will follow."

"Yeah." Randy finished his beer and ordered a scotch and water. "They found out someone put poison in the chow-hall food."

"As if it wasn't bad enough already."

"There it is." Randy looked at one of the girl's dancing go-go on the stage. "Think those tits are real?"

"No way. Doctored with silicone."

"I guess."

"When we met, you believed in some quasi-predestination —you still into that?"

"I guess. I sure don't seem to have any choice about what happens to my young ass."

"That's the truth."

"Rumor says that you and the OIC get along almost as well as LBJ and Ho Chi Minh."

"Probably worse than that. The man's a nut case in my book, and I'm one in everyone's book."

"Glad you said that and not me." Randy grinned, showing perfect white teeth and deepening a crease in his tanned chin. "Don't get your ass in a crack."

"It already is."

"Let's just get wild and crazy in the streets of Saigon."

Craig laughed and slapped hands with the other man.
"Let's do it!"

"Assholes!"

Craig nodded agreement. "I don't think I've ever been so
happy to go back to Da Nang. Three days of absolute bullshit.
They didn't need us there. All they were doing was rewriting
the war to fit their own scripts."

"Being in the field, as much as I hate it, beats the living
hell out of being around this bunch."

"Save me from Saigon Susies and high-ranking liars."

"Now you know why they call it the five-o'clock follies,"
Randy White said, and lit a cigarette.

Craig nodded and shifted in his webbed sling, uncomfortable and tired. "Did I tell you about the time I saw Oriana
Fallaci?"

Randy smiled. "Three times."

"A flight just like this, I'm so dumb I didn't know it until
she was gone. I stared after the plane and thought of it. She
smelled bad, she was in from the field, she had on fatigues,
she snored when she slept. These little ruffles of noise and her
lips fluttered. I still can't believe it."

"Even after the fourth telling, I can't believe it," Randy
said.

The two of them settled into an aimless conversation about
home, girlfriends, hometowns, their respective units. They
gossiped innocently and intimately about their peers.

The plane circled around the ring of mountains that was Da
Nang. Craig watched the blue of the bay; as always he was
surprised by the depth of the color, by the sampans that skittered under bright sails across the water. The aircraft dropped
and bounced onto the runway.

"Home," Craig said. "It feels good."

"Yeah. Take care, huh?"

"You, too. Write, huh?"

"I will, you, too."

"Promise," Craig said.

One more time.

Craig grabbed his suitcase and walked across the spongy
tarmac to the Fifteenth Aerial Port. He flashed his identifica-
tion and ignored the processing line. He stared at the familiar

yellowing poster from Air Vietnam. UNFOLD ENCHANTING VIETNAM ... VIETNAM THE NEWEST DEVELOPING HOLIDAY SPOT. Someone had written BULLSHIT across it with red Magic Marker.

"Craigers!"

Craig spun around, looked at Gerry Norton. "I hate that fucking nickname." He pumped the other man's hand. "I was going to call for the duty driver."

"We tried to track you down in Saigon, got the old shuffle and two-step."

"What's up?"

"We got trouble, right here in River City."

Craig, suddenly sullen, said, "What's up? Nobody's been hit, have they? The planes all made it back?"

"The shit hit the proverbial fan while you were gone. Richland sent Brooks back to the fucking P.I."

"He's with Judi, huh?"

Gerry looked directly into Craig's eyes, surprised that they looked so brown, but had flecks of hazel. "He's in the hospital."

"What? How is he? What happened?"

"He's fine. He's in for psychiatric evaluation."

"Slow down. I've only been gone three days. Did he lose it, or what?"

Gerry shrugged. "There isn't much to tell. Richland just told us he was in the P.I., it was your friend Bènny Radcliff that told us what was up. Richland had him put in for observation due to chronic lying."

"That's crazy! Brooks wouldn't lie if you promised him a discharge."

"That's all we know. Benny couldn't say much more; he said they were watching traffic because they felt some men were abusing the system to carry on personal conversations."

"Wonderful." Craig slowed his steps, rubbed the small of his back, and winced.

"In pain still, huh? I thought it was getting better."

"It comes and goes. I can't believe this. What's Richland have to say about it?"

"Just says Brooks is in the P.I., and that's that."

"Bastard."

* * *

More news came from Benny, but it took days. Most of the men, especially the newer ones, simply stopped asking about Brooks or discussing him at all. The official story had begun to take root: Brooks had been suffering delusions, had become a pathological liar. That version was repeated so often that it developed an aura of truth. Benny told Craig that it had actually become a private contest of wills: Richland was keeping Brooks hospitalized until the lieutenant agreed to resign his commission.

Craig related this story to Gerry and said, "The bastard has won this round, and he loves it."

"We've only got a couple of months left here, don't blow it now. There's nothing we can do."

"I know. I'm getting a nice buzz. Maybe it will make me calm down, forget it for a while. I do hate that bastard, though."

"Just stay cool."

Craig laughed; the one phrase they had all learned in Korean was a frequent admonishment to North Korean pilots that they loosely translated as "Keep your cool."

Early morning, on the mornings following nights without attacks, the base seemed unnaturally calm and pleasant. Craig limped back from the showers, still wet, his towel tied around his waist. He walked on the new sidewalks that had finally replaced the mud path. He had used the finally completed new flush toilets. He felt sluggish from the drinking the night before, and he had already taken two Darvon capsules. He stood beside his bunk, dried off again, and slipped into jockey shorts, a bright red T-shirt, and his flight suit. He looked at his bare feet, at the patches of pink where wet flesh peeled off, put on clean socks, and laced up his jungle boots. He glanced at the book he had been reading the night before, *Been Down So Long It Looks Like Up to Me*, by Richard Farina, noticed the dried stains of a spilled drink on the page where he had stopped, folded down the corner, and set it on his bunk.

"Morning."

Craig mumbled a greeting to Mark, and smoked silently.

"You're sober."

"Funny man. You want something?"

"I live here."

"Then do it silently."

"Think Brooks will be okay? I'm sure he will."

Craig, exasperated, slammed his locked door closed with a quick kick of his right foot. "Take your damned Pollyanna-everything's-rosy outlook and shove it where the sun doesn't shine, Mark."

Mark blushed, stared at the floor. "Guess I wanted some reassurance."

"Then buy it at the reassurance store. They file it under lies, comma, big." Craig ground out his cigarette. "I'm sorry. That's a broken record here, isn't it? I'm sorry, sorry, sorry. Richland is demented and he's fucking Brooks and there isn't anything I can do. Hell, maybe it's all my fault."

"Drinking help that?" The question was sincere.

Craig looked at Mark and wished that the boy from Indiana had stayed on the farm, out of Det Tango, and had somehow been able to live his life with his naïveté intact. "No, it just dulls things, rounds them out."

"You okay?"

"I am the primo hacker of all times." Craig poured himself a glass of orange juice. "Did I ever tell you about the time I stole the general's jeep?"

"The last time you told it he was a colonel."

"I've promoted him."

Craig settled into his seat on the plane, glad to be flying: it was the place where everything could be forgotten for a few hours; there was only the job. Only he and the North Vietnamese pilots. One on one. *Mano a mano.*

The needless urgency expressed by Lieutenant Ferris standing over his shoulder and wheezing bothered Craig, and finally he lit a cigarette and blew smoke directly in the officer's face twice until Ferris finally moved down the aisle to dawdle behind the SAM operators.

"Stupid bogie at six o'clock," Craig said over the intercom.

"Already spotted, señor," Gerry answered, and rolled his eyes and hooked a thumb toward Lieutenant Ferris.

"I got a bogie," Craig yelled, urgency and adrenaline in his voice, his sudden slap on the recorder when it slowly groaned to life. "Bogie out of Kep, MiG-17, NVN pilot."

Ferris ran back to Craig's side, read over his shoulder.

GC: One pirate, one A4, to the right, fifteen degrees.
360: Roger, fifteen degrees.
GC: Ahead to the right, fifteen degrees, twenty k.
360: Roger, twenty kilometers.
GC: 360, turn right, heading 245.
360: Roger.

While time passed, Craig copied his traffic; he was so intent, it wasn't until the missile firing that he thought he had stopped breathing and suddenly shouted out, "A4 down!"

Ferris double-timed to the communications cubicle to send the message.

"Ferris wasn't so bad today," Craig said.

"Never thought you'd say that."

"He got the message out right away, Ger. We saved the pilot. I got word from the zoomies. We got him out!" Craig wound his arms in circles and jumped into the air. "We got him out!"

Until the next time, Gerry thought. They all had the same thoughts.

The next time is always there.

Chapter 24

The dawn was diluted with the faint glow of landing lights and flares. Craig hoofed his way past the MAAG-11 compound, smoking a cigarette and struggling with the pain in his lower back. Sixty-three days. He had drawn a short-timer's calendar on the bill of his cap, and marked each day off with the faithfulness of a priest at matins.

"You forgot to shave."

Craig looked at the marine guard and then touched his own cheeks and chin. "Shit."

"I have a dop kit you can use."

Craig nodded and accepted the small case gratefully. "Thanks, I'll have it back in a couple of minutes." He walked to the latrine and lathered up. He stroked the blade over his face. Behind the lather was blotched skin, red marks, pimples. He covered two nicks with toilet paper.

"Thanks, man." Craig handed back the case. "I really appreciate it."

"What's my name?"

Craig stunned with the question, startled, shrugged his shoulders. He had passed this marine guard, and so many others, so many times. "I don't know."

"Dave Dehart."

"I'm sorry, huh? Tell you what, Dave Dehart, you come to

the barracks for beers tonight and they're on me."

"I'll be there."

"Do it." Craig walked away, carrying his embarrassment like a cross.

Craig walked into Gerry Norton's cubicle. "Tell me that I didn't see Ted running around the yard with red underpants and a blue towel for a cape."

"Okay, you didn't see Ted."

"I saw him."

"You asked me to tell you you didn't, you didn't ask for the truth."

"I don't want to know this, do I? I think I know why Brooks walked away so often. He's doing this, right?"

"Ted says he won't change, shower, or get dressed until Richland signs a peace treaty."

"That's nuts."

"He's imitating you."

"No way. I would have stuck a flare up Richland's ass."

"You want to do something about it?"

"See how it goes. Hell, it played well in Peoria."

"That near Phu Bai?"

"Closer to Chu Lai," Craig answered. "God, Ted has two ugly legs, huh?"

"Better than yours."

"They are crazy ones, but good men," Ba Mai Linh remarked with the soft voice of authority.

"Even this one?" Ba Dat asked, glancing at Ted from the corners of her eyes.

"Even that one. They have spirits. But they take food and clothes to the orphans."

"They create the orphans," Ba Dat said sourly. "And the widows."

"There are no simple answers." Ba Mai Linh spoke firmly.

"My husband's dead."

"And you are not," Mai Linh replied, and began to sweep the porch.

Within a week of his arrival Junior Lieutenant, Nathan Myers, had already been accepted by the enlisted men. He was from upstate New York, a town not far from Andy Jenkins's hometown, had graduated from Columbia in journalism, and readily admitted that he joined the navy to avoid the army. On his fourth day Commander Richland had told him in front of others that he needed a haircut.

"I guess I need to learn the ropes," Myers said to Craig Nostrum.

"The only thing I know about ropes is either how to hang yourself or how to skip one," Craig answered, and sipped his beer. He sat on the lowest step of the barracks stairs and watched the jets rumble from the runway.

"Richland tells me you are a royal pain in the ass."

"Differing views. I think he's one."

"Oh?"

"I think I'm lovable. Brave, reverent, trustworthy, kind, obedient, and all those good traits."

"Boy Scout?"

"Only until I found girls."

"You're pretty flippant."

"Smart-ass, some say," Craig said with a smile, and stood up. "I can't believe Richland hasn't caved in to Ted's demands yet. The man stinks something awful."

"Richland?"

"Ted. He says he won't shower until they sign a peace treaty."

"Someone should give him an order."

"I did, I wanted eggs up and fries, but he ignored me."

"You ever serious?"

"Only about the job, sir." Craig walked off to book a bet on the exact hour that Richland would sign.

When Craig received a letter from Brooks Crenshaw, it was postmarked Honolulu, Hawaii. Brooks said that he was en route to Treasure Island to get his discharge. It was honorable. He said he felt badly to leave them behind, but that he and Judi were happy to be going home. He said, "Things happen, don't they?" Craig finished the letter and his drink and poured another scotch and water. The Darvon had taken effect and his back felt good. Brooks had also told him that it wasn't his fault, Richland was nuts. He said to be careful.

Lifer, the puppy, grown to waddling obesity, lay down on Craig's feet, and Craig patted him. He had been listless for days after Beggar died of distemper, but now was enjoying the increased attention of the only child.

"Hey, asshole."

"Yo."

Gerry grinned. "At least you know your name." He settled on the ground, squatting the way Craig and the Vietnamese did. He sipped a beer. "Richland extended six months."

"Shit. Sixty and a wake-up, and I thought I'd outlast him."

"Things happen."

"Shit does. Twice sometimes." Craig swore softly, plucked at an invisible guitar. "New song."

"Really?"

"Think Barry Sadler and brave, huh?"

"You got it."

Craig hummed for a moment, then sang.

> *Golden wings upon their breast,*
> *These are men, Det Tango's best,*
> *One hundred men will face the test,*
> *Only three will be so blessed.*
>
> *Trained to live off bargirl's tips,*
> *known to love each bargirl's hips,*
> *these are men, Da Nang will know,*
> *the horny men of Det Tango.*

Gerry laughed, applauded. "Top Ten for sure."

"You know what guilt is, Ger? It's just letting things happen, just adjusting to things. We're masters at adjusting, revising history to suit our moods."

"Huh?"

"I got a letter from Brooks."

"He okay?"

"Read it when you get a chance." Craig handed the letter to his friend.

Mark Mitchell walked up to them. "Hey, how come you're not at the party?"

"Party?" asked Craig.

"Barry Youmans."

"Youmans?"

"He got orders! He's going to fly the milk-run missions from Japan. Off the coast of Korea. He's getting smashed down at the slope chute."

"Movie?" Gerry asked.

"*The Green Berets*, what else?"

Craig laughed. "Let's go. I want to see John Wayne kill the commies again. We win this version, right?"

It began, like many days, with an attack. A mortar left a deep scar in their weedy yard. Craig listened to the all-clear whistle sound and bolted from the bunker. He stood outside and smoked and sipped a Budweiser beer.

Commander Richland, feeling expansive, walked along the fields and stopped in front of Craig. "I got a new picture of my wife, without a moustache."

"She had electrolysis?"

"Things are right now. Crenshaw's gone. You'll be gone soon."

"You need help, sir."

"What I need is some loyal men."

"A psychiatrist."

"You can't bother me now. I've won."

"You need to resign."

"Me? You're the one that needs treatment. You and your hooligan friends."

"We made this unit."

Richland wiped a string of spittle from his lips, swiped at the links of gray pearlike strands. "I signed Ted's truce tonight. But you're not part of it. You'll end up like Crenshaw."

"You fuck me, you better do it right. I might come back and bite you in the ass."

"I'll do it right. You're drinking too much. You're hooked on pills. The men see it. I see it."

"Fuck you," Craig said. "Very much." He walked back to the movie, to John Wayne, to saying good-bye to Barry Youmans.

"Japan," Youmans said.

"*Domo arigato*," Craig said, and bowed. "I'm going to miss you."

"You are always bitching about the heat; I leave you my fan until I come back."

Craig grinned. "Will you buy me some books?"

"Just write down what you want."

"You're not only the best ditty bopper we have, I dub thee an honorary lingie."

"Everybody has to step down in class once in a while."

* * *

"They gave me a hundred dollars American."

Mai Linh touched Ba Dat's hand. "I told you that these are good men."

"They collected it for me. The white hair gave it to me."

"Gerry," Mai Linh said with satisfaction.

"They gave me money to help."

"They wish you well."

"I have no husband now, how can things be well?"

"Benny?" Craig asked. He held the telephone close to his ear.

"Favors? I don't owe you any, Craig."

"I know. I want some anyhow. I'll marry your sister, or better yet I promise I won't."

"That's a deal. She's only seven. What do you need, man? Remember I'm getting short."

"So am I."

"So what is it this time?"

"I want Crenshaw's record cleared, and I want the word out what happened to him."

"That's a tall order, my man. Could get some real tit-wringer trouble."

"Just copy some records and mail them to Japan for me. Send them under classified mail, okay?" Craig relayed his plan quietly.

"Sir Genuine to the end, huh?"

"Atonement for sins."

"I'm not a priest."

"I'm not looking for absolution. I'm looking for a savior."

Terry Denver remarked to Mark, "I think he's going to snap. He's been so edgy lately he can't sit still for a minute." He rolled over on his stomach to get sun on his back, adjusting the towel beneath him. "I hear men just go nuts here sometimes."

"More than once," Mark said. He slopped tanning oil over his legs. "Danny Morseth for one." Craig had told him of others. They just settled into their own insanities. "Time and fate."

"Huh?"

"The time catches us all in the end. Every last mother's son."

*   *   *

"Even your friends think you're going around the bend," Richland said.

Craig supposed this was true. He was unkempt, slept little and then only poorly, and he knew from the way others went quiet when he approached them that they were talking about him. "I've got fifty-one days left here, sir. Fifty-one days, and some odd hours. But then all the hours are odd here, aren't they? Abandoned, lost time. When you fucked over Brooks, I thought, We're finally orphans here. Fucked-up little orphans with grand dreams."

"Crenshaw was crazy, you know the reports. A pathological liar. He needed help. He resigned for the good of the service."

"Gunny was right. I wouldn't piss in your asshole if your guts were on fire."

"I won, Nostrum. You can make this easy time. Ask to go back to the P.I. and teach. End your time there. No disgrace."

"I wouldn't give you the satisfaction."

"Play it out, then. I'm sending Brady and Hawkes and Louis on some R&R, you'll be flying double in the meantime."

"Lex talionis."

Richland looked up. "What?"

"To the victor belong the spoils."

Later on, when Craig tried to relate the conversation to Gerry, he found he could not. Since the truce Richland had become treacly toward the rest of the men. Craig finally shrugged instead of talking.

"What's that mean?"

"Things happen, I guess." He looked at his half-filled glass of scotch, at the two Darvons in his hand, and set them down on the bunk. "I'm going to the chow hall and get some coffee."

"You?"

"I fly soon. Double flights. I love 'em."

"He's scared to fly, he just won't admit it."

Mark looked up from his cards, glared at Terry Denver. "You want to get knocked on your ass?"

"Markie, Markie, Craig's little defender." Terry tossed a pink quarter into the pot. "Raise you."

"He's okay."

"He's jittery and he's back on pills. He can't finish a sentence. You want to close your eyes to it, that's okay. But don't bullshit me. You've seen it, haven't you, Ger?"

Gerry slapped his cards onto the table. "I fold."

"Christ, everybody treats him like he walks on water."

"Shut the fuck up," Mark said, and tossed his cards in as well.

"Ra-ra-ra-rolling Thunder," Craig stammered. He wanted his mouth to work, but he knew that it wouldn't. For two weeks he'd had the stammer; he wondered if he could make it the last thirty-seven days. He jotted a note to Lieutenant Myers that a MiG was after an A6.

Myers nodded and stood at his shoulder. He wondered when he had begun to pity Craig, wished he did not.

"Shoot . . . da-da-da-down. Mi-mi-mi-MiG."

Myers nodded and walked off to send the message.

Craig, the pain intense, threw the pills into the ditch and squatted down to smoke. A cripple. He recalled the doctor's words and watched two flares pop near the base of Tien Sha. Enemy contact. He let himself collapse on the ground. Get it together, he thought. Get it together. He closed his eyes.

Dale Burton read the message, recalled the phrase about killing the messenger, and set it down on Lieutenant Myers' desk.

"This just come in?"

"Yes, sir."

"You want me to deliver it, right?"

"Not me, that's for damn sure."

Myers grinned. "Any chance I can hook someone else into it?"

"Not without a gun."

"Guess I better do it, then." He stood up. "Is the commander at the barracks?"

"Last I heard."

"If I'm not back in an hour, send help."

Craig was at the orphanage and didn't hear the news right away. When he did, he just smiled.

* * *

"What do you know about it?"

"Nothing, sir. Just that Richland was called back to the P.I."

"Rumor has it that Brewster talked to the captain and said that the reports in Brooks's file that were under his signature were false. Nobody can figure out how he even heard about this in Japan."

"I wouldn't know."

Myers laughed. "Really?"

"Hey, I'm just a dumb squid."

"Think it was an act?"

Mark looked at Terry. "No."

"He just stopped the pills, cut back on his drinking, and he's fine."

"He always was. He never fucked up a mission."

"I know. But now he's so quiet it scares me. He doesn't say shit. Ever since Richland left."

"He's okay. The best."

"I'm the best. Maybe he's second."

"Fuck you."

Twenty-six days. Each one a chance for individual doom. Craig turned to the young marine who sat beside him. "Nostrum's the name, spying's the game."

"You ever see any action?"

"No," he answered. Not if you don't count Tet, or snipers or attacks with rockets and mortars. "None."

"I'm going to get me some commie ass."

"Newbie, you are going to wash trucks and drive trucks, and if you're good enough as a ditty bopper you'll fly with the best damned men you ever knew."

"You might think I'm some wuss, but I'm a marine."

"Semper fi, newbie, semper fi."

Fifteen days. Craig stroked another off his calendar. He looked up when Mark came in.

"I've got some bad news. Some grunt just ran over Lifer with his jeep. He's a lieutenant, and Ames is trying to take his head off."

Craig ran around to the front of the barracks. The lieutenant and Ames were squared off; Terry Denver squatted by the roadside with the dog in his lap, rocking on his heels, his eyes closed.

"I'm sorry, man. I didn't see him. He just ran out." The lieutenant was trembling, his voice squeaking.

"Back off, Willy." Craig grabbed Ames by the elbow and moved him back three steps. "What happened?"

"He just ran out. I've never killed an animal in my life, never hit a squirrel even." The lieutenant's voice was raising with more emotion than anyone expected.

Craig walked over, put his arm around the other man's shoulders, and led him to the barracks. He poured them both drinks. "How long have you been in the field?"

"Three months. Fire-fights and attacks and mud. And they kept saying 'We're sending relief soon.' We took over fifty-percent casualties. I didn't mean to kill your dog."

"Drink up." Craig refilled the man's glass.

He listened and kept the man's glass filled until he passed out, and put him to bed in his bunk. He turned to Mark. "Find his unit and find somebody who's a buddy of his, and get him over here, okay?"

"You were good with him, good to him. Willy's still pissed, he thinks you should have let him have him."

"I'll go talk to him. He would have cleaned Ames's clock." Craig walked outside to find Willy. He was easy to locate. He had just finished putting a small wood cross over Lifer's grave.

"I'm sorry." Craig looked at the ground, at the cross. "She was the only thing we had to love here."

Willy nodded. "I know you did the right thing, Craig. I just wanted to hit out. I still do."

"Let's go take Lieutenant Ferris's bunk apart."

"I like it."

"I thought you might. Come on."

"Party time. Tomorrow is the day."

Craig laughed. "It's hard to believe, huh? Tomorrow we head for the real world. I don't want to go. Weird, huh?"

"Don't, man, not now. We're a cunt hair away."

"I know." Craig sat down on his bunk. "I want to go, but I don't. Maybe I'm as fucked up as everyone said."

"Bogie, bogie coming!" Gerry said.

Nathan Myers grinned. "Hey, I'm a friendly. Not on a friendly mission, though."

"I'm declaring this a Millard Fillmore day," Gerry said.

"I need a tac/air man. Mitchell's sick. Brady won't do it. I don't have any right to ask."

Craig laughed, clapped his hands. "I'm not easy, I'm automatic. I'll fly."

"Thanks."

"But I wear my lucky T-shirt."

"You can run naked through Saigon if you want."

"I'll settle for the T-shirt."

Gerry stood up. "No, man, don't do it. This is the last night, don't do it."

"I have to."

"You're being stupid."

"I know."

Myers looked at the two of them. "I hate asking."

Craig grinned. "It's all that I yam, I'm Popeye the sailor man, toot, toot."

They flew in the deep night.

"I've got a MiG up."

"Tracking has him."

"He's out of Gia Lam, Lieutenant." Craig adjusted his earphones, blotted his sweat.

"You're as good as they say."

Craig nodded, flipped on the intercom. "Hey, Randall, you copy this one, huh?"

"Really?"

"Have at it, newbie. A gift."

Nathan put a hand on Craig's shoulder. "Randall's the new you, right?"

"He better be, for all our sakes."

"You're a good man."

"I try," Craig replied.

My God, he's just a baby, Myers thought.

"Shootdown!" Randall screamed.

"Yep," Craig said softly.

"I wish you weren't going. You're a slick article."

Craig looked at Lieutenant Myers. "Sometimes I wish I weren't, either."

The party nearly done, Craig walked to the barrels that held ice and beer, but they were empty. He shrugged his shoulders.

"Sorry," Mark said.

"Things happen."

Ted, his purple cape draped around his shoulders, walked to them, grinned, and reached into his shirt. "Here." He handed a bottle of champagne to Craig. "It's your party."

Craig laughed, hugged Ted and Gerry and Mark and Terry. "God damn," he said.

"He already did."

Craig woke with a rough shake of his shoulders. He pushed the mosquito net out of his way. He sucked in his breath, realized this was not an attack. "Huh?"

"I'm Commander Wieland. Brewster said you might give me a rundown. I feel like hell waking you up."

Craig blinked, rolled from the bunk, and slipped into a pair of jeans and a T-shirt. "I leave in four hours."

"Coffee's made."

"Silver-tongued devil."

"I really am sorry."

"You know Commander Brewster?"

"His wife and mine spend all our flight pay together."

"Good man, Brewster."

"I asked Denver to pack your things for you."

"Thanks."

"Tell me everything you can."

Craig shrugged. "The most important thing to remember about this place is that things happen, sir, they really fucking do."

Chapter 25

The building. NSA. Three months of endings. Craig walked the corridor, his blue badge pinned to his collar. Blue badges into blue doors, don't go into a red or yellow area. Need to know. Secrets.

"You're going to be working on a special project."

Craig nodded. "So?"

"We're designing a course to teach the South Vietnamese to do our jobs. Teach them to fly missions."

"Really?" Craig asked.

"Really. We'll be turning the war over to them someday."

The war. Craig wondered if he thought about anything else. That was his place. He belonged. He shifted back and forth on the balls of his feet. "So what do I do?"

"You head up the project. You translate the tapes, annotate them, make the course worthwhile."

"Okay."

"Jenkins told me you were one of the best. I want you to prove it."

"I'll do it," Craig said. "No kudos, huh? I'll just do it."

"How's it going?"

Craig tossed the pencil across the room. "If you ever showed up, you'd know."

Damon shrugged. "I'm not gung ho like you. Turn me in if you want. Write me up."

"Sorry."

"I'm taking three night courses."

"I sign each of you in like you were here."

"You don't have to do it."

Craig put his earphones on again, rewound the tape. "I do, you know? I do."

"This is all bullshit, Craigers. Absolute bullshit. You don't have to bust your nuts."

"I do. I have to."

"You're nuts."

"I've got work to do," Craig said.

"You're a good friend."

Craig, embarrassed, turned up the volume and began to transcribe the Vietnamese to English.

"We're going out later, Gerry, Ted, and I. Doing the town."

Craig shook his head and kept writing. In the words he thought he might find the memory of who he was. He might be like he was. There.

"The Vietnamese government issued you and the others their own air medals. Vietnamese Air Cross of Gallantry." Bill Travers shrugged. "Command wants to hold a ceremony. I told them that I didn't think you'd want all that. I asked to hand them out in private, and they agreed."

"Thanks. I wouldn't want another awards ceremony in my lifetime." Craig accepted the medal and the letter; they seemed somehow special to him. "Versions in Vietnamese and English. Think they have any idea of what we really did over there?"

"No way. Not enough of them are cleared for anything higher than low-level intelligence."

"Their war, their country, and we can't even tell them what we do in their skies."

"You know how it is. Where're the rest of the men?"

"Off. I wanted to work on some of this alone. They'll double-check it all later, but this tape is the shits. It's also one of the worst handlogs I've ever seen."

"Who did it?"

"It doesn't matter," Craig replied. Jumbo Bravo. Jack Brady. He smiled. "Reports this as TOLs, and it's a bombing practice. They're out of Bac Mai. I know the controller well. He and I are old buddies."

Craig went back to work.

Republic of Vietnam
D   D   D
RVNAF
Ag Division
No 717/TTM/TQT/Qo/PDBT

THE CHIEF OF JOINT GENERAL STAFF, RVNAF,

- Considering the decree 178/SL/CT dated 6-5-64 establishing the Air Gallantry Cross.
- Considering the decree 205/CT/LOQC/SL dated 12-2-65 specifying the organizational system of DOD and RVNAF:
- Considering memo No910/TTM/VP/PCP/3, dated 3-30-66 specifying the conditions, procedures, and authority to award the "Air Gallantry Cross".

DECIDES

Article 1. The Air Gallantry Cross with Bronze Wings is hereby awarded to the U.S. Serviceman named below:

. . . .

Craig J. Nostrum-Communications Technician Second Class, X38 00 68, USN.
"Excellent air crew member, he has recorded many brilliant achievements.
While serving with the 1st Air Reconnaissance Squadron, U.S. 7th Fleet from Jun 3, 1968 to Jan 30, 1969 PO2 NOSTRUM disregarded danger and cooperated with pilots to effectively conduct 150 sorties against the enemy."

. . . .

Article 2. This decision is to be noted and filed in the individual records of the incumbent.

APO 4002   10 MAR 68
General CAO VAN VIEN
Chief of Joint General Staff, RVNAF

. . . .

certified translation by
VU NGOC LUU, Translator/Interpreter
U>S> Naval Advisory Group,   MACV

Bill Travers leaned over Craig's shoulder. "I know all about it."

"I'm busy. The four tapes are done over there."

"They don't even show up and you write their names in."

"Look at the op signs, the whole team is there."

"You're letting them fuck you over."

Craig pushed his earphones off. "You have complaints about the work?"

"No," Travers said. "You shouldn't have to do it alone."

"I'm fine."

In October, a month before they would be discharged, Damon and Gerry and Ted all began coming to the office at night and transcribing tapes.

"It's not for you," Damon said to Craig. "We're just bored."

"Then do some tapes," Craig remarked, and turned on his own recorder. "Thanks, I got a letter from Willy Ames today. They got a new puppy. They named her Spook."

"Everybody else okay?"

"Denver's the new you. Randall's the new me. Gerry and Ted are being played by Rafferty and Holman. Ferris is still playing Ferris, but he's not doing a very good job. Barry says they had a heart-to-heart and he's gotten a lot better. He says Baskins is still on a ship and he thinks they've forgotten that he's there. Youmans is still in Japan. He wrote them that he has a mamasan and house off base."

"I almost miss them all sometimes."

"I know," Craig answered with a grin.

In the middle of the afternoon, on a too-hot day, Craig sat across from Bill Travers and refused to consider a civilian transfer when his enlistment was up.

"You could start as a GS7."

Craig shook his head. "I want out. No more secrets. I've had enough of them."

"You could make a good career here."

"I want to finish college. I want to write. I want to get out of this whole world."

"You could be making a mistake."

"It wouldn't be the first."

"Don't turn it down so fast."

"I don't want it." Now now, not ever, Craig thought. He lit

a cigarette. I want to fly, he thought, I want to fly again.

"Think it over."

Commander Brewster, newly reassigned to NSA, met Craig in the hallway and instead of saluting, hugged him.

"Good to see you, too, sir."

"I got those records. I went to the top with them. Richland had put in bogus entries under my name. The dumb bastard. He won't make captain now. He's been rotated to a ship."

"I'm sorry for him. It's hard to explain. I guess he needed his promotion worse than anything. Once in a while I think we needed each other, he and I. That somehow that's what made it work."

"He was wrong, Craig, he was totally wrong. That's not the way the navy is. That's not my navy."

"I know."

"You want to consider reenlistment? You'd get a bonus. You could get another school. Another language if you wanted."

"No thanks. It's good to see you, though."

"I'm glad, you know? You don't belong in this circus. You get out, get an education, get a wife. And you remember that you have a friend here."

Craig took the cup from the chow hall, reminded how much he missed green tea. This was Lipton's. He carried his tray, a bowl of fresh fruit, the tea, some toast, and sat down at the back table with Gerry. "Travers is ecstatic. We finished the project two months early. He looks like a hero."

"You don't care about it, do you? You busted your ass, made us feel like shit, layed on a guilt trip, and you don't really care."

"I care about getting it done right. I don't give a shit if they're happy or what they do. That's beyond my control. If I was an asshole, I'm sorry."

"You just can't give it up, can you?"

"I wish I could, Ger, I wish I could."

Gerry told Damon at dinner that Craig wanted to start a new project. "He wants to go back, too. I can see it."

"You're nuts, or he is."

"I asked him if he thought this program would work and he said only with the right training. He misses it."

"He's still got back pain, doesn't he?"

"He tries to hide it. We're getting out soon; why does he want to go back?"

Damon rolled his eyes. "Maybe he's nuts."

"At least that," Gerry said.

There were accidental meetings, but this was the first time that Commander Brewster had asked to see him. Craig walked to B section, stood outside the office, and announced himself. Twenty-three days, he thought. "You wanted to see me, sir."

Brewster nodded, stared at the floor, finally nodded. "I don't know how to say this."

Craig said, "What's happened? Da Nang got hit again, right? Tell me."

"Da Nang's fine."

"Then what?"

Brewster, stunned, wanted to shrug off the question. "Remember how we used to talk about the flights out of Atsugi as being milk runs?"

"Yes," Craig said, not sure where the conversation was leading.

"Shit."

"Hey, tell me."

Brewster's eyes filled with tears, "Today, this morning, the North Koreans shot down our bird. PR21. All souls were lost. They're dead, Craig. Potter, Youmans, all of them."

Craig stood there, rooted to the spot, swayed on his feet. "No!"

"God, I hate this," Brewster said. "Thirty-four men."

"No. No way. I gave Youmans's fan to Mark to save for him. It's kind of busted up, but it's the best fan there."

"It doesn't matter."

Craig stared at the floor. "What about the MiGCaP?"

"They didn't have any. Someone in the puzzle palace decided they didn't need it."

"Stupid bastards. Don't they remember the *Pueblo*?"

"They really are bastards," Brewster said, an edge of outrage in his voice. "Stupid fucking bastards."

"I hope the idiots that made that decision rot in hell, sir, I really do. Rot and burn in hell."

"We get out tomorrow and he hasn't been sober in ten days. He called Da Nang four times, Travers said." Gerry, not quite sober himself, hiccoughed and covered his mouth.

"He took things hard. The plane getting shot down, the way they scrapped the project. He took it hard, man." Ted smoked in silence.

"We're going to lose this war. That's why they don't want the secrets given to the Vietnamese. They already know we're going to lose."

"Yeah."

"That's Craig's problem, he can't believe that he went balls out and didn't change a fucking thing. He believed all the hype."

Ted and Gerry both looked at Damon after he spoke.

"It's the truth," Damon said at last.

"I know," Gerry replied.

"I wish it weren't," said Ted.

The doctor looked at Craig. "You get out tomorrow and it's against medical advice. That cyst on your back could be anything."

"I won't spend another minute in the navy, sir. I hope my cyst is nothing, but I don't give a shit. I won't stay around."

"It wouldn't be more than a week, two at most."

"A minute is too long. I get out tomorrow morning at eight A.M., oh eight hundred."

'You're taking a chance."

"I did that when I signed up. You know something, Doc? Everything's a chance, and shit happens no matter what I do."

Craig loaded his belongings—a seabag, two suitcases, two boxes—into his car. It was a Pontiac convertible given to him by his father. He knew the others were asleep. He'd walked past each of them, said a silent good-bye. He'd said good-bye to the others, the ones who would never return, in a prayer at the chapel.

Dawn, pink and promising, leaked over the tree line and Craig smoked a final cigarette in the navy, ground it out with his heel, fieldstripped it, and tossed the litter into the breeze.

He climbed into his car.

He started the engine and was startled with the knock on his window. "Damon?" He rolled the window down.

"I'm all packed. Can you give me a ride as far as 95 North?"

"Jersey's only a couple of hours from here, huh?"

"Yeah. I can catch a ride easy. I just have the one suitcase."

"Two hours isn't so long, is it?" Craig grinned. "Hop in and I'll drop you at the doorstep. I've got nowhere to go in a hurry as long as it's not here."

"Thanks."

"All part of the free service," Craig said, and laughed.

The sun, a yellow balloon on their right, was brighter than a promise, and they drove off together. A team, Craig thought, a crew, friends.

One more time.

About the Author

Wayne Care is a medical-supply salesman who lives in Alexandria, Virginia. During the war in Vietnam, Wayne was a Navy Vietnamese linguist flying out of Da Nang. *Vietnam Spook Show* is his first novel.